Contents

Sell Up, Pack Up & Take Off

Sell Up, Pack Up & Take Off

STEPHEN WYATT and COLLEEN RYAN

ALLEN&UNWIN
SYDNEY·MELBOURNE·AUCKLAND·LONDON

Extracts on pages 112 and 113 from *River of Time* (1997) by Jon Swain, published by William Heinemann, reprinted by permission of The Random House Group Limited.

First published in 2014

Allen & Unwin
83 Alexander Street
Crows Nest NSW 2065
Australia
Phone: (61 2) 8425 0100
Email: info@allenandunwin.com
Web: www.allenandunwin.com

Cataloguing-in-Publication details are available
from the National Library of Australia
trove.nla.gov.au

ISBN 978 1 74331 785 3

Set in 11.75/14.75 pt Minion Pro by Bookhouse, Sydney
Printed and bound in Australia by Griffin Press

10 9 8 7 6 5 4 3

Introduction

It is a time to be free.

There are not many periods in life when you experience freedom. Most of us enjoyed freedom in our late teens, twenties and even our early 30s; pre-marriage and before the kids arrived; before mortgage and debt and work took on a great seriousness.

But once the kids mature and become self-sufficient, and once debts are paid and your working life ends, suddenly you enter another period of immense freedom. It is back to your twenties again.

And you can enjoy it now just as you did when you were young and free.

All you need to do is be clever and brave enough to change your lifestyle and leverage the benefits of freedom.

It doesn't matter if you are 40 or 70. If you have reached a turning point in your life then clean the slate, look at all the options, be brave.

And if you are facing retirement then remember that it is an opportunity, not a death sentence. It is an extraordinary opportunity to grasp afresh at life; to live life to the full. After all, at 60 there really isn't a lot of it left. We need to make the most of it.

This book gives you an alternative. It offers up the chance for another life. A new life in another country for a year, a few years or forever and a cheaper life that will make those dollars go a lot further.

Another time for big decisions

There are a few critical decision-making times in life. One such time was back in your youth when you were deciding on which career to follow, who to marry, where to live, whether to have children.

Now is another critical time when you need to make decisions about how to live a new phase of your life. Do you stay put, and live as you have lived for the past thirty or so years, or do you 'sell up, pack up and take off'?

Whether you are 40 and burnt-out or 60 and facing an entirely new landscape, decision time can be daunting.

If you are a baby boomer the chances are the kids have grown up. The dog is dead. The job has ended or it's just too intolerable to put up with any more. The house where you have lived for decades is now too big. And you've still got maybe twenty good years ahead of you.

What the hell are you going to do?

Stay in that family home? Get another dog to make you feel like you have kids again? Hang about to look after the grandchildren? Count your pennies and scrimp because those retirement savings do not go nearly as far as you thought they would? Go to the same club, pub, restaurant or golf course that you have gone to for the past ten years? Watch your friends die? Watch a lot more TV? Do the lawns a little more than you need to and get those edges really sharp?

Well, you could. But why would you? It sounds pretty mind-numbingly boring. There is a terrible sameness to it.

Sadly, that is the box that most retirees and indeed most people decide to confine themselves to. This is the conventional mindset, but it shouldn't be. There is no need to raise the white flag on life. These days, the old 60 is the new 40. Get positive. Go for it.

There is a lot more living to do.

This book speaks to those who see retirement not as the sunset years, but as the dawn to a new and exciting freedom. However, it also speaks to those, of any age, who want the adventure of living in another country, even if it's only for a few years. It aims to help people climb out of a dreary box and start living again.

> Once the kids mature and become self-sufficient, and once debts are paid and your working life ends, suddenly you enter another period of immense freedom. It is back to your twenties again.

Life has changed—we live longer, healthier lives

Many Australians 'found themselves' by travelling overseas when they were young. And they haven't stopped.

A very popular travel book, first published in 1975, was *South East Asia on a Shoestring*. It was the bible to youth travel in Asia back then. Today, it's more likely to be called something like *Retirement in Asia on a Shoestring*.

Since the baby boomer generation came of age, trips with the kids to Bali and Thailand and Malaysia have been the norm. Many Australians have worked and found partners overseas. And they've embraced medical tourism, whether it is a facelift in Thailand, a new set of choppers in Bangkok or a full medical service in Singapore.

Life for Australians today is much more global than for previous generations—and retirement will be too.

It is no longer a radical step to go and live overseas. Look at the fly-in-fly-out workers in the mines of Western Australia. Many base themselves in Bali today. It is not a big step to retire there.

And for the first time ever, technology allows us to live internationally but also stay close to loved ones. Technology has destroyed the barriers historically confronted by those living in another country. Jet travel allows you to be home in less than half a day from most places in Asia. Email, Skype, smart-phones, iPads and computers allow constant contact from anywhere.

When it comes to keeping in touch, living in Chiang Mai today is not that different from living in Byron Bay and remaining close to friends and family in Sydney.

So here is an alternative. Here is a new approach to life.

Sell up, pack up and take off

Sell that suburban house. Tell the kids and grandkids you love 'em to death. Tell them that you are about to embark on an adventure, but so, too, are they.

You want them to share in your new life and this will offer them excitement and an adventure as well.

Add all or some of the funds from the sale of your house to the superannuation fund. Call a taxi. Go to the airport. Get on a plane. Go and live in splendour. Get a house on the beach in Malaysia, Bali, Thailand, Cambodia or Vietnam.

Get some house help and really enjoy a G&T at sunset. Go for a swim each morning. Forget watching the nightly TV news. Enjoy the exotic life. Have the family over to visit—they'll love it.

And guess what? It can be done at a fraction of the cost of living in Australia. Sure, there are a few financial constraints and visa issues, but these can be easily handled—and you can still receive income from your superannuation or receive your Australian pension.

Radical or sabbatical?

Of course, selling up, packing up and taking off is the radical approach to change. Any move overseas needs a lot more research, and this is what this book is about.

Change can be modest or aggressive.

For example, instead of selling up and taking off forever, some may prefer renting out the family house in Australia rather than selling it, then renting a home for themselves in Thailand or Bali or wherever, rather than buying there.

Also, the move may be just for a few years—a type of sabbatical or extended holiday from your Australian life.

And you needn't have reached those mature years of life, either. You may be 40 or 50 and just burnt out and sick of the life you're leading. You might be feeling like you want to stop the world, get off, run away from that daily grind and try a different life for a while. Or you might just want the adventure. Escape is for all.

The escape spectrum

There is a spectrum of escape: from running away forever, to escaping for just a few months at a time. To put it simply, your options are:

- Sell up, pack up and take off: the plan would be to live somewhere else, perhaps forever.
- Pack up and take off: keep the family home in Australia, rent it out, then go and live for an extended period in a country you have always wanted to live in.
- Take off for the lifestyle change: refresh and recharge. This may mean living for six months in Australia and six months in another country, or three months here and nine months elsewhere, or nine months in Australia and three months overseas, and so on.

The beauty is that no matter who you are, how rich or poor you are, or how old you are, there is an escape route that will suit you.

Often, the need to escape, or the need to embrace change, is triggered by external factors—like a financial crisis, an illness or death in the family, an inheritance or the end of one's working life.

We need to adapt. Many new retirees have dropped a bundle in the latest global financial crisis when the stock market halved in 2009. And who knows what Australian house prices might do over the next decade?

If your nest egg has been crushed or if, in fact, you never had much of a nest egg at all, then life in Australia can become cripplingly expensive. One solution is to move to a cheaper country and make that nest egg go a lot further.

> Add all or some of the funds from the sale of your house to the superannuation fund. Call a taxi. Go to the airport. Get on a plane. Go and live in splendour. Get a house on the beach in Malaysia, Bali, Thailand, Cambodia or Vietnam.
>
> And it's doable. There are few financial constraints and visa issues can be easily handled.

We have 'escaped' several times over our lives. We lived in Papua New Guinea in the mid-1970s, moved to London for two years, then returned to Australia for our child-raising years.

We had two gorgeous kids and waited as long as we could before packing up and taking off again.

Our first move with children was to Washington DC in the mid-1990s where we worked as journalists. Our son Hamish was eleven and our daughter Georgia was fifteen. We stayed for two years. It was politically fascinating but socially stultifying. And we realised that eleven and fifteen were not the right ages to shift children about.

So we came back to Australia and stayed for five years as the kids finished school. But the call to adventure returned and as soon as Hamish completed year 12 and began university, we were off again: this time to Shanghai, both working as journalists for an Australian newspaper.

It was wonderful and enriched our lives and the children's lives.

Hamish had a year or so off university and wrote for the *Shanghai Daily*, the English language newspaper in Shanghai. Georgia also had a year off from university and travelled widely with her brother, and with us when we were on assignment to the backwaters of China. Such trips enabled Georgia to witness terrible poverty and illness and corruption. It had a profound impact on her and brought to her a greater understanding of social injustice.

We were in China for six great years through to 2010, when we returned to Australia. Not only did we witness the economic renaissance of the most populous nation in the world, but we were immersed in a new culture, new language, new politics and a total-itarian system to boot, in a dynamic new city and country.

And it was wonderful for the dynamics of the family. There was space created between our children and us. This, we believe, explains a lot about the great relationship we have with our children today. Eighteen and 21-year-olds are not easy to live with. They want their independence and parents find this transition very difficult. Parents want to keep control. Georgia and Hamish are now 28 and 31, well adjusted, successful and happy.

We are telling you this because our experiences overseas enriched our lives and our children's lives. And also, because we have 'done it', we feel that we have some justification to write about it; to talk about selling up, packing up and taking off, particularly as it becomes such a popular idea for so many people.

A new mega trend: life goes international

The trend of moving offshore for a new life is accelerating. You are not going to be lonely.

Governments in the developed Western world are increasingly unable to look after their aging populations. At the same time, investors are targeting the growing global retirement market. It represents a big new band of consumers.

Today, there are more than 3 million people, or 14 per cent of Australia's total population, over the age of 65.

This will more than double over the next 35 years to hit more than 8 million people, about 23 per cent of the population, according to the Australian Government's Intergenerational Report of 2010.

Australia is on the brink of a retirement savings disaster and the government may not be able to fund the shortfalls. It is the same story in the US and other developed economies. Over the next 40 years in the US, the number of people over the age of 60 will more than double to a staggering 80 million.

The implications are clear. The cost of health care will soar. Medical services in the West will be stretched to the limit and certainly become increasingly expensive. Demands on governments to service an aging population will increase exponentially.

In Australia today about 25 per cent of total government spending goes to health, age related pensions and aged care. The Australian Treasury expects this to increase to 50 per cent of total government spending by 2050.

Governments in the West will struggle to deliver services or financial assistance. Government budgets are already stretched. Debt levels in most developed countries are crippling even now.

Governments in the East, however, see this demographic change as a new trigger of growth and employment creation.

There is going to be a new diaspora—an international diaspora of people aged over 50 moving from the developed world to the cheaper developing world.

Consider the example of Geoffrey and Michael, who we met and interviewed in Ubud, Bali. They moved there mainly for financial reasons. They built and live in a Balinese-style home that flows out onto tropical gardens. Heliconias with their striking orange claw-like flowers, gingers with leaves the size of elephant ears and lush green cordylines surround us as we chat on the verandah that overlooks a pool.

When Geoffrey and Michael retired they realised that they faced a life of poverty in expensive Australia. Now they live a life of plenty in Ubud with staff to cater for their every need. And they have money to spare.

The really great news is that they can do this on an Australian pension.

Geoffrey and Michael are at the forefront of a new wave of emigration. Migration will begin to reverse. Rather than from developing economies to the developed, the trend will be an increasing drift from the developed to the developing.

Life goes international

Once, the end of a working life meant greater freedom to travel around Australia. This gave rise to the 'grey nomads' roaming Australia in campervans.

Or it meant a sea-change or a tree-change from the city to the coast or the country.

That's what Stephen's parents did. They sold their city home and business and bought a little farm near Orange, New South Wales. They found a new life and celebrated the learning that goes with a whole new experience. Their years from 55 to 80 were wonderful.

But the domestic sea- or tree-change does not give you any great cultural diversity. Nor does it allow you to spin those limited funds out for many more years, nor live in a much grander style in a different environment.

Staying within Australia was understandable 30 years ago. That was really the only choice. Moving to another country was extreme and dramatic. You virtually said goodbye to family and friends. That was before the computer, before email and Skype, and before cheap air travel.

These days, those looking for a change of environment are moving from Sydney to Bali, or Melbourne to Bangkok, or Adelaide to Phnom Penh; not from Sydney to Orange.

And the financial motivation is going to be prime.

There is going to be a new diaspora—an international diaspora of people aged over 50 moving from the developed world to the cheaper developing world.

The domestically roaming 'grey nomads' will soon be moving internationally, too. They will become 'international grey nomads'. And it'll be cheaper than roaming expensive Australia.

Governments in Southeast Asia know that a whole new industry is about to expand. They have seen the surge in medical tourism. Now it is going to be the international sea-change—retirement tourism.

This book takes a look at what sort of life you can have in an Asian country, how much it costs to live there, and how you can fund it. It addresses the financial, medical and visa issues of getting a new life.

And it looks at the different places where you can live—the variety of cheap and safe but exotic countries—and the tricks you need to know when it comes to buying or renting a house. It also addresses the problems posed by illness and the financial aspects of managing your superannuation and tax.

We spoke to many Australians who have packed up and taken off, and they share their stories and experiences—the good, the bad, the ugly and the brilliant. They tell us what it's like to actually live the overseas dream.

This book, we hope, will offer up the possibility of a whole new existence for those who are ready for the adventure.

TIPS AND TRAPS

Once you have made the decision to sell up, pack up and take off, just remember that the secret to every good trip is in the planning.

We include plenty of details throughout the book to help you plan your overseas adventure, but just to get you started here's a quick checklist of questions you need to address before you leave Australia:

- **Visas**: How do I get a long-stay visa in my chosen country?
- **Taxation**: Am I better off being a resident or non-resident of Australia for tax purposes (even though I might be living in another country)?
- **Superannuation**: Can I keep Australia's generous tax concessions for my superannuation?
- **My house**: Will my family home in Australia still be capital gains tax-free if I rent it out when I leave these shores?
- **Pension**: Can I still get the age pension when I am living overseas?
- **Health insurance**: Do I need private health insurance in Australia, can I get Medicare benefits when I return to Australia on visits, and do I need health insurance overseas?

CHAPTER 1

Bali

Australians Geoffrey, 62, and Michael, 56, moved to Ubud, an enchanting town in the mountains of Bali, just 90 minutes drive from the island's international airport. They arrived in 2010, have built a new, exciting life in this tropical paradise, and have no intention of leaving.

Geoffrey and Michael spent most of their lives involved in the arts and for thirteen years, in the 1980s and 90s, owned and operated The Tilbury Hotel in Sydney's Woolloomooloo, then known for its sharp-edged political comedy nights and its lively restaurant. Later, Geoffrey went on to become manager of cultural affairs and events at the City of Sydney leading up to and during the 2000 Olympics.

He then moved on to the Australian Film Institute and Chamber Made Opera, where he was chief executive.

Michael, who was the executive chef at the Tilbury Hotel, went on to produce three Australian musicals at the Sydney Opera House.

When their working lives ended, Geoffrey and Michael crunched the numbers on their finances and realised they had to do something dramatic or face a very ordinary future in retirement.

'We were on two good salaries, living in a fabulous apartment in Flinders Lane in Melbourne, having a wonderful time,' Michael said. 'We were renting and had always been renters, so the prospect of retiring meant our lifestyle would have to change dramatically.

'I think we calculated that, on a pension, the only alternative for us would have been a caravan park in a central Victorian town or on the central coast of New South Wales . . . So really, we had to find a place to live that offered a reasonable life . . . and Bali looked like a possibility.'

Geoffrey, however, had his reservations: 'We had only been to Bali once before, to see an old friend of ours. As a traveller, I'd avoided Bali all my life. All I'd ever heard about was Kuta and it sounded hideous.'

But the friend they visited ten years ago in Ubud lived in a beautiful crumbling old villa on the Ayang River where many international five-star hotels are now situated. They look over 900-year-old rice paddies.

Ubud nestles in the foothills of Bali's central mountain range. It is a Balinese cultural hub. The town is dotted with exquisite temples and palaces and with verdant, rich tropical gardens and rainforest.

Ubud since the 1930s has attracted foreign artists and writers and landscape architects. It is laid-back with a bit of an old hippie feel to it.

'We planned to explore Bali but in fact we just didn't leave Ubud at all. We spent most of the two weeks of the holiday on daybeds gazing at the view,' said Geoffrey.

'We saw that life here was possible. We've always been adventurers and always dreamt of going to live in Italy or Spain and learning the language.'

Suddenly, though, Bali was a real contender.

Key to Geoffrey and Michael making the move was their discovery of the Ubud Writers Festival, which had been going for about four years.

'That a village in a foreign country is running a top international writers festival meant there'd be conversation here, an intellectual life, and, you know, people to talk to,' said Geoffrey.

Yet, it was still an adventure—a country with another language and culture. There was something for Geoffrey and Michael to learn. They would have to work at it and be engaged. That's what they wanted.

Then it got exciting. They found a block of land in a quiet lane not far from Ubud's town centre. For A$60 000, they bought a twenty-year lease with a ten-year option on this block and built a classic Javanese *joglo*, an open-plan house that incorporates romantic lush gardens and a beautiful pool. An attractive guest bungalow snuggles into the garden corner as well.

That was in 2010. Prices have risen since but it could still be done at a fraction of the cost of doing the same build anywhere in Australia. Geoffrey and Michael are now in a financially positive position.

And they're not alone.

Already in Bali, 2400 foreigners of all nationalities are living on retirement visas, according to the Bali Department of Immigration. But there are more than 10 000 expatriates living there, many using temporary visas.

'Creating Retirement Tourism in Bali: Retire in Paradise' is a fairly new project undertaken by the government. It aims to provide self-contained communities with attached Western medical facilities, staffed by some foreign doctors, by 2015. The intention is to provide aged care for 100 000 retirees by 2020.

But it isn't just retirees packing up and taking off to Bali—the island appeals to escapees of all ages.

Paul and Kate, who are around 50 years of age, moved to Bali simply because they could live a lot more cheaply and a lot better. Paul is an IT professional who works remotely and Kate is a stay-at-home mum. They are members of the Canggu Club, which is located on the coast up from Kuta Beach, and that's where we met with them.

The Canggu Club is a sprawling white colonial structure that looks over immaculate playing fields. Undercover tennis courts are off to the left, to enable the game to be played through the wet season, and a large pool area sits alongside the clubhouse. Sun lounges, adorned with perfectly rolled blue and red striped towels, surround the pool. Outside, there's also a bar, restaurant and coffee areas. Large French doors, with crisply painted white frames, lead to the club's facilities inside, including the air-conditioned gym, library and cafe.

It is pristine and it is expatriate to the bootstraps.

The club is neo-colonialist in character—testament to a lasting although mythical Raj in Bali. It is a club for 'yummy mummies' swanning from the gym for a post-workout latte; for burnt-out Aussie millionaires wondering what to do with their lives; for couples disillusioned with the mundane nature of life in Australia and wanting more for themselves and their children. And it is a club for retirees looking for a more interesting lifestyle that's both affordable and luxurious.

The staff is predominantly Balinese and the vast majority of members are not—Australians predominate. The children of members are treated like royalty. They have no understanding that their privileged attitudes, particularly towards the staff, edge on the offensive.

Graham Greene's views of Malaya under British rule could equally apply to the Canggu Club in Bali. Greene complained of a society 'of British clubs, of pink gins, and of little scandals waiting for a Maugham to record them'.

At one point during our conversation in the club cafe, Paul suddenly said, 'That's him—that's the porn star.'

And it somehow seemed to fit. A club like the Canggu really needed a porn star as a member to round off its expatriate character and to highlight the social fluidity of life in Bali—or at least the lifestyle of those who live in Seminyak and surrounding coastal areas.

A couple, who were recent arrivals were shocked to discover a rather active expatriate wife-swapping game on the island.

Life is easy here; staff plentiful; there is a lot of free time; perhaps too much. This is one side of a multi-sided expatriate Bali.

But living in Bali is not all about the Canggu Club and the Western comfort and security blanket such clubs provide in the midst of a chaotic Asian country. It suits some people. But, for many more, the sea-change to Bali provides a real alternative to staying in Australia and watching the days pass as they have passed many times before. It is about finding a new, exciting and fulfilling life.

For A$60 000 all up they bought a twenty-year lease with a ten-year option on a block of land and built a classic Javanese *joglo*, an open-plan house, that leads to lush gardens and a beautiful pool. An attractive guest bungalow snuggles into the garden corner as well.

It is a romantic Somerset Maugham-like tropical paradise.

Energised—a new life

John and Sandra could have retired to wherever they liked and they could have lived a resplendent life anywhere they chose in Australia. Quite frankly, they are loaded.

But the couple, who have built their dream home in Seminyak, said that back in Adelaide they were 'just waiting to die'.

'I really felt like I was heading that way,' said John. 'But now my entire attitude to life has changed.'

They bought a twenty-year lease on a property and built their house in 2005. It is Euro-Bali style and made of marble and stone. Not the thatched palm-leaf roof look, but the more conventional two-storeyed, hard-surfaced, Australian open-plan house adapted to the climate. Bedrooms and entertaining areas all open onto an expansive stone deck and infinity pool. The house tinkles with the sound of water and looks out over rice paddies and a creek thick with rainforest trees.

'The most cathartic thing we have ever done is to sell our home and everything else—the lot—back in 2005 and then move to Bali,' John said.

'There is a large expatriate community here, a huge social diaspora,' Sandra said. 'We have a whole set of new friends, some Australian, some French, ranging in age from 35 to 85, and they do all sorts of different things.'

Referring to the vast array of foreign cultures and lifestyles and the different levels of wealth that make up the intriguing character of the country, John said, 'Bali is like a multi-layered cake. I don't miss Adelaide at all. I don't want to go back. Our children and friends all love visiting us here.'

Property

Relative to Australia, buying property in Bali is still reasonably cheap, but the ownership structure is complicated. Always seek legal assistance when purchasing property.

And, before buying, it is wise to rent to ensure you understand the area, legal system, values and, indeed, whether it is worth buying at all. You'll be pleased to know that the cost of renting in Bali is more than 75 per cent lower than in Sydney.

A non-Indonesian citizen cannot own freehold property—land, villas, houses or apartments in Indonesia. (For details, see 'Bali property' in the Appendices.) However, a foreigner can acquire a leasehold title to a property. This is almost the same as a strata title except that the title lasts only for 25 years (or less), with an extension of 30 years for a maximum of 55 years, and then reverts to the original owner (lessor).

Lease periods vary but the leases themselves are tradeable. They can be bought and sold just the same as freehold property.

Some foreigners still insist on freehold ownership and can engineer it in one of two ways: they can use an Indonesian nominee or set up an Indonesian (PMA or *Penanaman Modal Asing*) company. We see this as presenting potentially serious problems. Nevertheless, it is a quite common practice.

Leases are the safest way of holding property in Indonesia because they do not involve an effort to circumvent the law, unlike many freehold ownership arrangements. Leaseholds do not require the participation of Indonesian nominees.

The process of purchasing or renting a property in Bali is simple. There is a sophisticated, and foreign-friendly, real estate industry in Bali. Well-known agencies like Ray White and Century 21 are there to offer advice to foreign buyers.

Geoffrey and Michael are absolutely comfortable with their leasing deal and don't see their lack of freehold ownership as a major problem. Geoffrey compares it to the lease situation in many parts of London.

'To buy a property in most areas of the city of London requires the purchase of a lease, not the freehold title,' he explained. 'You can sell the lease, rent it out, leave it to your family, whatever.'

Before buying, it is wise to rent to ensure you understand the area, legal system, values and, indeed, whether it is worth buying at all.

The increased demand for properties in Bali over the past few years has triggered steep price increases. Bali has had the sharpest rise in land values in Indonesia. According to research conducted by Knight Frank and Elite Havens, average land prices in Bali increased 34 per cent throughout 2011. Luxury real estate prices rose another 20 per cent in 2012.

In some areas in Bali, the price rise was far higher. Land prices near beaches in Seminyak, such as Legian, Petitenget and Batu Belig, experienced the highest jump compared to other areas in Bali; increasing by between 50 and 87.5 per cent in 2011. Knight Frank and Elite Havens said the huge increases were influenced by the high demand among investors to build property on those particular tourism sites.

However, compared to Australia, property in Bali remains cheap. (Or maybe Australia is expensive?) An attractive villa with a pool can be purchased with a twenty-year lease for A$250 000 upwards in the popular coastal areas around Canggu and Seminyak. And the further away from the tourist hotspots you go, the cheaper it becomes. In the Ubud region, prices are significantly less than this and the same sort of property starts at around A$100 000. In Australia, that kind of money doesn't buy anything.

Cost of living

Living is cheap in Bali but just how cheap depends on how you want to live. Still, even if you want to enjoy the high life, it's much more affordable than it is in Australia.

The rather well-off Sandra said, 'The food is exquisite and cheap. We buy export-quality sashimi-grade tuna for A$10 a kilogram. Dinner parties for 30 people are common and affordable.'

'Australia is outrageously expensive,' added John. 'I have one-and-a-half hour massages three times a week that cost A$10 a pop. We have six servants and they each cost about A$100 a month. We don't need to do anything around the house, really.'

He conceded that Bali is becoming more expensive and 'there are issues about good medical services and electricity costs are high'. But John's biggest gripe is the expense of wine. A 300 per cent import

Cost of Living

INDICES
BALI LOWER THAN SYDNEY

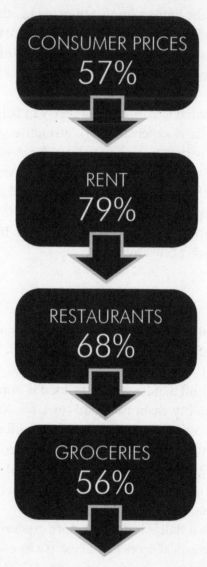

CONSUMER PRICES
57%

RENT
79%

RESTAURANTS
68%

GROCERIES
56%

Source: numbeo.com

Sell Up, Pack Up and Take Off

duty is imposed on wine by the Indonesian government. 'Even so,' said John, 'we drink Beaujolais at A$30 a bottle—that's not too bad.'

> The most cathartic thing we have ever done is to sell our home and everything else—the lot—back in 2005 and then move to Bali.

But not all Australians in Bali are as affluent as John and Sandra. It is a different story for Michael and Geoffrey, who have to be a little more careful with their funds. Even so, they still live a life of relative luxury, with three employees that tend the house, their needs, their gardens and their security—and they do it on an Australian war pension.

Geoffrey, having served in Vietnam, receives a reasonable pension from the Department of Veteran Affairs that easily covers the modest cost of living in Ubud, he said. He receives around $25 000 a year.

'On that amount of money we can live well here,' said Geoffrey. In fact, their lifestyle is superb compared to how they would have to live in Australia.

As Michael and Geoffrey explained, they own their house and the cost of living is low. They even find it cheaper to eat out at local restaurants than to cook at home. Although, of course, they do eat at home and also entertain a lot.

And they can afford three staff. After all, the total cost of the three is just A$200 a month. In the mornings they have a housekeeper who prepares breakfast, makes beds, cleans bathrooms, and does the laundry and dishes, and a gardener who looks after all the outside areas. By getting these employees to come each morning, it gives Michael and Geoffrey privacy in the afternoon. They also have a full-time security guard from dusk to morning.

'It's wise to have security,' said Michael. 'They are local people and in a sense this guarantees security—if you refuse to employ security you tend to get robbed.'

All this is easily done on their pension income. You couldn't live like that if you were a pensioner in Australia.

For Michael and Geoffrey, the hardest part has been getting used to the absence of two salaries coming into the bank account. But this happens to anyone who stops full-time work. They arrived in Bali debt-free but a fair amount of entertaining pushed their credit card debt higher again and they had some early issues with budgeting.

The biggest cost, though, has been the trips home. They return to Australia regularly. 'Sydney is blindingly expensive,' said Michael. 'We can't believe how expensive it is, even compared to Melbourne.'

In Bali, more, and larger, Western supermarkets are appearing; more restaurants are opening and, away from Kuta and the tourist bars, there is not the binge-drinking type culture that exists in Australia. Eating out is very much part of the local life and, like Michael and Geoffrey, many expats revel in the large choice on offer—at minimal cost.

Dining out in an inexpensive restaurant costs 78 per cent less in Bali than in Sydney. At a *warung*—a local restaurant—you can get a meal for less than than A$3. For example, noodles, lemongrass chicken, green beans, chicken satays and a spring roll can be had for about A$2.25. Not only cheap, it's very high quality. If you like going out for breakfast, you can enjoy a healthy egg-white omelette with mushrooms and tomatoes, two slices of wholegrain toast, mango juice, and yogurt with fruit and granola for A$2.75. This beats A$25 (or more) in Sydney.

Almost every *warung*-styled meal is less than A$5. A beer is 70 per cent less in Bali than in Australia. And you can wander out for coffee every day if you like—the local Balinese coffee is excellent and at just 25 cents a cup, it's a steal.

For anyone on a tight budget, these savings make a massive difference to lifestyle. Suddenly, you are free to do things you would simply find prohibitively expensive in Australia.

If you prefer eating at home, the savings are also massive—especially if you shop in the local market and not the supermarket. The local market, or *pasar*, is the best place to buy fresh produce cheaply. But markets require bargaining and a bit of local knowledge and for the Westerner, who is new to Asia, this can be confronting.

Supermarkets in Indonesia are just like supermarkets anywhere in the world, with prices fixed—but much cheaper than Australia.

Bread and rice are more than 55 per cent cheaper in Bali than Sydney; chicken is 60 per cent less; eggs 60 per cent less; and tomatoes 80 per cent less. Overall, groceries are about 50 per cent lower in Bali.

Dining out in an inexpensive restaurant costs 80 per cent less in Bali than in Sydney. A beer is 70 per cent less in Bali.

For a retiree on a tight budget this makes a massive difference to lifestyle. Almost every *warung*-styled meal is less than A$5.

As well as saving on food and entertainment costs, you no longer need to catch buses and trains to get around. Suddenly taxis become affordable. In Bali, taxis are 85 per cent cheaper than in Sydney.

And the cost of utilities, including electricity and gas, even though seen as expensive in Bali, are still almost 40 per cent lower than Sydney.

Critically, rent in Bali is more than 75 per cent lower than in Sydney.

However, it is worth noting that the cost of activities and items of a Western nature aren't much different to Australia. For example, a pair of Levi jeans or a new VW Golf will set you back about the same amount whether you're in Kuta or Melbourne; a cappuccino still costs about A$2.80 (compared to 25 cents for local coffee); dining or drinking in tourist bars and restaurants is expensive, as is the membership to sports clubs.

Elizabeth: Shelter from the storm

For Elizabeth, a 60-year-old, single Australian woman, the lower cost of living has been critical to her staying in Bali.

Bali offered a solution to what was a financial catastrophe in Australia. Elizabeth lost everything, even her house, due to the collapse of Storm Financial, a financial advisory group, in 2009.

Cost of Living

Sydney vs Bali

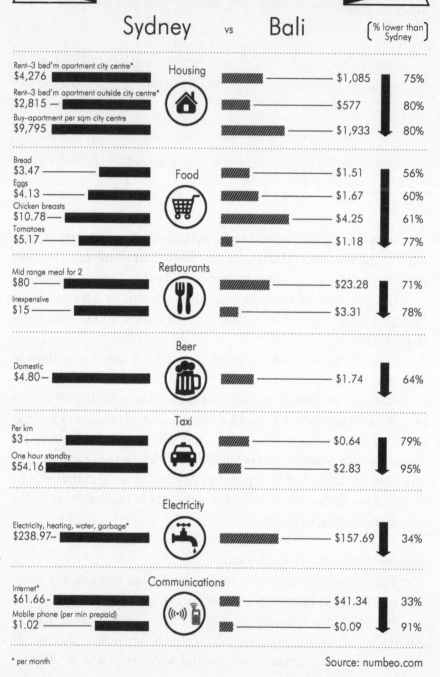

Housing

	Sydney	Bali	% lower
Rent–3 bed'm apartment city centre*	$4,276	$1,085	75%
Rent–3 bed'm apartment outside city centre*	$2,815	$577	80%
Buy–apartment per sqm city centre	$9,795	$1,933	80%

Food

	Sydney	Bali	% lower
Bread	$3.47	$1.51	56%
Eggs	$4.13	$1.67	60%
Chicken breasts	$10.78	$4.25	61%
Tomatoes	$5.17	$1.18	77%

Restaurants

	Sydney	Bali	% lower
Mid range meal for 2	$80	$23.28	71%
Inexpensive	$15	$3.31	78%

Beer

	Sydney	Bali	% lower
Domestic	$4.80	$1.74	64%

Taxi

	Sydney	Bali	% lower
Per km	$3	$0.64	79%
One hour standby	$54.16	$2.83	95%

Electricity

	Sydney	Bali	% lower
Electricity, heating, water, garbage*	$238.97	$157.69	34%

Communications

	Sydney	Bali	% lower
Internet*	$61.66	$41.34	33%
Mobile phone (per min prepaid)	$1.02	$0.09	91%

* per month

Source: numbeo.com

Before the disaster struck, Elizabeth said she had a great life. She'd spent part of her growing-up years in Papua New Guinea back in the 1960s and early 1970s, then moved to Penang, then on to Queensland.

She married, had three children and lived in a wonderful home on the Sunshine Coast.

Although she divorced in 1995, she remained in the family house and it was a trouble-free split.

But the Storm Financial crisis stripped her of everything. Storm Financial was a Townsville-based financial advice and management company that specialised in highly leveraged stock market investments (funded by margin loans). At its peak, Storm Financial had 13 000 clients and $4.5 billion in funds under management. Its business model came under intense pressure during the global financial crisis when bank funding dried up. It was placed in liquidation in March 2009 and many of its clients lost everything, including their family homes.

Elizabeth said she was naive but shocked at what had been done to her. Elizabeth trusted people in an area that wasn't her game. And there were a lot of others who suffered a similar fate.

The outlook is grim for Elizabeth—she does not expect to get anything back, although a class action against Storm Financial is underway.

Fortunately for Elizabeth, the move to Bali was not that traumatic. Elizabeth had always planned to leave Australia at some stage. After a cancer scare a few years earlier, she decided to ease back on her work at the University of Queensland anyway and part of that plan involved a move away from Australia to Ubud.

She had already made contacts in Bali. In late 2007 Elizabeth had moved to Bali, briefly, deciding a change of scene would be interesting. She loved Southeast Asia. 'We had always travelled to Singapore, Sumatra, Java, Lombok and we would stop off in Ubud on the way home. Bali was never a place I had wanted to visit until I came to Ubud. I am very definitely not a fan of the south coast areas.'

After the Storm Financial catastrophe she realised life in a cheaper country would in fact be a lot easier and it would be a challenge as well. She was provided some financial support from her former boyfriend. She had already organised with friends in Bali to help out in a restaurant business and that came with some accommodation. But she could not be paid due to restrictions imposed on working in Bali under the visa she had.

Elizabeth said she can live on around $500 a month and that is because she doesn't pay for her accommodation and she owns her own car. 'But I certainly don't go shopping for anything unnecessary', said Elizabeth.

'My biggest treat is cafe latte a couple of mornings a week and a cocktail or two a couple of nights a week at Bar Luna or Mingle, both places owned by friends that have the two for one offer. Wine is a rare offering.'

Elizabeth has since established a cat refuge centre called Villa Kitty. It does great work. Elizabeth has a new and constructive life. She manages the centre and lives there now.

Suddenly, you are free to do things you would simply find prohibitively expensive in Australia.

Medical services

The lack of good medical services is the most concerning issue when living in Bali, especially for people who are in their 60s and beyond.

This is especially complicated by the fact that after five years living overseas, your Australian Medicare coverage ceases to exist. To acquire re-entitlement to Medicare benefits, you need to return to Australia and prove that you have returned here to live. You need to provide copies of a rental lease or employment contract, for example.

John and Sandra have no health insurance and said their private medical cover lapsed when they left Australia. That's dangerous when you're 65.

'We have to fly to Singapore for treatment. It is expensive,' said Sandra, but she added, 'We are about to buy health insurance.'

The insurance they are considering is very expensive at about A$12 000 a year. However, this covers them for every medical need, including emergency evacuation.

But for many others like Geoffrey, Michael and Elizabeth, the cost of international health insurance is just too high. Yet for them this is not a deal breaker. After all, as they pointed out, there are medical services in Bali and these are not expensive.

Geoffrey, who is uninsured, recently had what he described as a 'heart episode'. It was frightening, but ultimately not too difficult to manage. He went to a local, private hospital in Denpasar, not a hospital for foreigners or tourists. The cost of a specialist, five days in intensive care, an additional five days in a private room, with all medication, was about A$2700 in total.

After that experience, Geoffrey decided that health insurance was too expensive compared to the actual cost of treatment in Bali. And he was more than happy with the standard of service he received. 'I am confident that most illness or injury I get here will be able to be treated at the local hospital,' Geoffrey said, adding that if it were more serious, he'd just have to get on a plane back to Australia. 'And if I can't, well, that's okay. You know, I haven't missed out on much in life.'

For Elizabeth, the decision is simple—she simply cannot afford medical insurance. However, she pointed out that she can go to local hospitals for treatment any time she needed to, and said she has 'great confidence in many Indonesian doctors, although not all are great.'

But most Australians should consider having medical insurance, If you can afford the premiums, get the insurance.

For example, what happens if you have a car or motorcycle accident, or suffer a life-threatening disease? There may be medical treatment in Bali but it may not be adequate. You may need to travel to Singapore or Australia for specialist treatment.

And what if you are too ill to travel on a commercial flight? You will need to be medically evacuated and that is expensive. These evacuations are provided by private companies and, with medical expenses, could set you back A$40 000. Ouch.

The annual premiums for medical insurance plans range from about A$2500 to A$12 000. The more you pay, the better the cover. Some new Bali residents hold travel insurance policies at a cost of about A$700 for a year. This covers baggage losses as well as medical costs including evacuation, but has a limited time span, often of about two years, depending upon the insurance company (see Chapter 10: Health insurance).

It's also worth remembering that Australian private health cover can be placed in suspension for two years. This suspension is renewable for up to six years with many of the big insurance groups. After six years you must resume payment of premiums or lose your cover. Suspension ensures no loss of benefits, and no waiting periods when you return to Australia. (See Chapter 10: Health insurance.)

If you can afford medical insurance, get it.

What happens if you have a car or motorcycle accident or have a life-threatening disease? There may be help in Bali but it may not be adequate. You may need to travel to Singapore or Australia for treatment.

Aged-care services

But there is a very positive flipside to medical services in Bali—and this is particularly relevant to the over-70s who would prefer to be cared for in their own home, rather than move to a sterile aged-care accommodation facility, their only option in Australia.

In Bali, there is the very affordable opportunity to employ wonderful and reliable Balinese staff that act as carers and nurses at a fraction of the cost of similar services in Australia.

Vaile Home, 65, a Melbourne native but a resident of southern Bali in 2012, has been reliant on a walking frame for the past four years after she fell and broke a kneecap. More critically, she suffers from cerebellar degeneration, a disease affecting her motor function and balance.

'I won't leave here. I will be carried out in a box,' she told Deborah Cassrels of *The Australian* newspaper (18 August 2012).

Vaile's husband, Richard, who severely injured his back seven years ago, was treated for tongue cancer five years ago in Singapore, a two-hour flight away, and where the couple regularly undergo check-ups.

The Homes encapsulate a common expat theme, wrote Cassrels. That is, the idea of residing in an antiseptic nursing home or being a burden on their children won't happen. Their children live in Asia so they see no reason to be in Australia.

They, like many other aging Australians, foresee Balinese *pembantus* (housekeepers) assuming increasingly intensive roles as providers of aged-care—unqualified, yet well suited because they are seen as patient, respectful, gentle and affordable.

Vaile is dependent on a rotating roster of four Indonesian *pembantus*. For some time after her accident she was immobile. The *pembantus* bathed and clothed her and tended to her every need. They are now instantly at her side when necessary. Local doctors' mobile numbers are on hand.

The Homes pay about A$100 a month for each *pembantu*. They are also considering hiring a live-in nurse in future, costing between A$300 and A$600 a month, depending on qualifications.

Richard calculates similar home help would cost about A$40 000 a year in Australia. 'We could never afford this in Australia,' he said. 'It just wouldn't happen.'

The Exotic Marigold Hotel factor

In the 2012 film *The Best Exotic Marigold Hotel*, Sonny, the Indian hotel owner, declares: 'I have a dream to outsource old age.'

This is what many are doing in Southeast Asia now.

This film contrasts the excitement, and at times the traumas, of living out old age in India, rather than in a drab British aged-care facility with rails along the wall, a panic button in the corner and the smell of shit and disinfectant in the air.

In India, there are servants, attention and care and the aged suddenly do not feel that they are poor and useless.

Deborah Moggach, the author of the book *These Foolish Things* upon which the film *The Best Exotic Marigold Hotel* is based, said the film touched a nerve with the aging cast.

Dame Judi Dench and Bill Nighy have both recently given interviews deploring Britain's treatment of the elderly.

Dame Judi, 77, said: 'We're not good at dealing with old age in this country. We shove people in a room and leave them sitting round a television.'

Bill Nighy, 62, has bemoaned how the elderly are 'warehoused and medicated, rather than nurtured and listened to'.

He said: 'The fact that they pay taxes all of their lives and then are expected to give all of their savings to maintain themselves is absolutely disgraceful and one of the great scandals of our society.'

Moggach believes that a move to India or other cheaper countries is a real option—partly because living in a retirement home in such countries costs a fraction of what it would in Britain and partly because India has a culture of revering their elderly.

It is the same story for Australians in Bali, where the costs of having live-in care are not prohibitive, and the Balinese people respect age. For those of limited means, services are available in Bali that are just not affordable in Australia—and that means a better lifestyle.

Visa requirements

One of the greatest attractions of moving to Bali is there are no significant visa obstacles. A retirement or renewable-stay visa is available to those over 55 years of age who can prove they have an income of at least US$18 000 a year. Note that this is close to the annual amount of the Australian age pension at the time of writing.

Applicants must also show proof of health insurance in either their own country or Indonesia. They must agree to employ an Indonesian maid, not to work or undertake business activities, and show proof of accommodation that is either rented for at least US$500 a month or purchased for at least US$35 000.

The visas are for one year but can be renewed in-country up to a maximum of five years. After five years, it is possible to apply for a permanent stay visa (See Appendix: Visas for more details.)

BALI TIPS AND TRAPS

1. Rent a property before buying. And with rents almost 80 per cent lower than in Sydney, it may be worthwhile simply renting indefinitely.
2. Housing is cheap in Bali relative to Australia, but the ownership structure is complicated. Foreigners are not allowed to own freehold titles, they can only buy the leases; this applies to apartments, villas, houses or land.
3. Any freehold ownership structure requires some legal engineering. It's fairly common, yes, but it can throw up unexpected and sometimes profound problems.
4. Health and medical services in Indonesia are a concern and a danger, especially for people older than 65.
5. Get health insurance cover and medical evacuation cover, if you can afford it.
6. Beware—you will lose Medicare cover if you live overseas for more than five years.
7. Private medical cover for treatments in Australia can continue if you live overseas, but what is the benefit when you do not live in Australia? You can suspend your private medical insurance cover for two years while overseas, and it can be renewed for up to six years. When and if you return, your policy becomes immediately operative if you resume payment of premiums.
8. Aged care at home is affordable in Bali at a fraction of the cost of home care in Australia.

CHAPTER 2

Thailand

You don't expect to meet a single, highly intelligent, 70-year-old 'English rose' in Chiang Mai, a northern city of Thailand.

That's because blokes, sex and Thailand are almost synonymous in the minds of many people. When they think of foreigners in Thailand, they immediately think 'sexpats' hanging out in girlie bars in Bangkok, Pattaya and Patong . . . And it's true.

There is, however, a Thailand beyond the stereotype. And it has so much more to offer to retirees and escapists alike.

Sure, as Dorothy, our English rose says, Thailand is a 'sexual desert for a *ferang* [foreign] woman'. And there is no doubt that there are a lot more single and often 55-plus foreign men compared to foreign retired women or couples in most of Thailand.

Yes, it's very easy to be judgemental and see this as sex tourism, usury, immorality or whatever. And, without doubt, a lot of it is distasteful and morally questionable.

But there are a number of other sides to this story.

The first is that many Thai women—indeed some of them bar girls and prostitutes—can meet a foreign man and settle down in a relationship that offers them, and potentially their children, a much better, broader, healthier and wealthier life. They are happy with the relationship and so, too, is the foreign male. Nothing sordid about that.

The second is that not all foreign men are in Thailand just for sex—as shown by the ones we met—and not all the blokes who are interested in the women are sexual predators.

Adam, who has lived in Chiang Mai for more than ten years, told us about a 45-year-old Australian male who was holidaying in Thailand in 2011. Adam had a few beers and a chat with this guy and told us his story. 'This guy was very unattractive and overweight. But he was a really pleasant, good guy. He told me he had a Thai girlfriend and he was really enjoying his time in Chiang Mai.'

About six months later, Adam saw the same guy in the same bar so he wandered over to say hello. It turned out the man had returned to Australia and then come back to Chiang Mai. He said to Adam, 'When I left the last time and got on the plane to fly back to Sydney, I cried for about ten minutes. Never before have women accepted me like I was accepted here. Never before have I felt so welcomed, touched and even loved.'

Adam pointed out that this decent man, who was spurned by Western women because he was physically unattractive, clearly cherished his relationship with a Thai woman and Adam figured he would be a very good and loving husband. We don't know what has happened to him since, but his story goes to the good side of many single men visiting Asian countries.

But sex is a fact of life and so is prostitution. And if you decide to live in Thailand, you have to be prepared to face these facts fairly often.

Even so, it isn't a pretty sight seeing a fat, old Aussie bloke straddling a little motorcycle with a pretty young Thai girl riding pillion, as you see constantly in Patong and Pattaya.

Australia's honorary consul-general in Phuket in 2013, Larry Cunningham, said he thinks motorcycles can 'be rented with a young Thai girl attached'.

Our advice—get over it. And just don't live in Pattaya, Patong or the seedy parts of Bangkok. Let's face it, you probably wouldn't choose to live in Kings Cross.

'Do you know what happened to me when I got on the plane to fly back to Sydney when I left last time?

I cried for about ten minutes. Never before have women accepted me like I was accepted in Chiang Mai. Never before have I felt so welcomed, touched and even loved.'

Without a doubt, the advantages of retiring in Thailand far outweigh the disadvantages. It is cheap, the people are friendly and gentle, the climate superb (if you like it hot), the health services excellent, and the choice of places to live is plentiful.

The political system in Thailand, however, is certainly different. And from an outsider's perspective it can, at times, look chaotic. It is uniquely Thai. Thailand has a revered royal family and, most of the time, a working democracy. The issue is that it is interrupted rather regularly by military coups. And coups in Thailand are also uniquely Thai. A Thai coup is very different to an African or South American coup.

There have been 11 successful and 7 unsuccessful coups since 1932. The latest coup was in May 2014. No-one was killed and life continued for most Thais as if nothing much had changed. Many even welcomed the coup as it brought an end to months of political stalemate. The military has promised fresh elections after a period of stabilisation. The military maintains that its actions do not amount to a coup as there is no attempt to take the country in a different direction. The motivation, it claims, is to ensure the prosperity and stability of the Thai economy and society. Democracy will return, probably within two years.

For the expatriate retiree this has made little or no difference. Despite frightening headlines in international newspapers, it is only politically active Thais that have been affected. Foreigners have not been in any danger.

But a move to Thailand does mean that you will confront a rather different political system.

Thailand offers big-city life in its fast-paced and international capital, Bangkok, or a more sedate life on one of its many beautiful islands. Phuket combines an island lifestyle with a touch of city excitement. The islands off Krabi on the west coast are very primitive and laid-back, with monkeys the main source of companionship. There is the Golden Triangle up north and the towns in the northeast that border the mighty Mekong, like Chiang Saen. And there's evocative old Chiang Mai in the mountains, with its tranquil and almost hippie-like vibe.

Thailand is a smorgasbord of lifestyles. You can live in a villa on the beach that would rank with the best in the world or in a traditional Thai timber house nestled deep in a garden of exotic monster-leafed tropical plants. There's high-end condominiums and apartments with every modern convenience you can think of. You can even choose a primitive life in a grass-roofed shack that will cost near to nothing. In Thailand, you really are spoilt for choice.

In Thailand, and indeed Southeast Asia generally, you distinctly sense much greater personal freedom than exists in Australia. This is uplifting. Thailand is no 'nanny state'. If you want to ride a motorbike without a helmet, then that's fine. If you want to J-walk or walk against traffic lights, that's fine. If you want to go to a bar and you are under 18, that's fine. If you don't want to wear a seat belt, then that's fine too.

But don't get caught doing anything wrong. While there may be a sense of far greater personal freedom in Thailand, there are far fewer actual rights.

'Massive personal freedom, but limited legal rights' is a common theme of life in Southeast Asia. And ironically, this is just the opposite to life in Australia, where there are limits on personal freedom but where you have massive legal rights.

For many people, especially retirees, one of the great assets offered by Thailand is excellent yet cheap medical care. Thailand is one of the world's major destinations for medical tourists who flock in from Indonesia, Australia, the Middle East and the US. This has enormously beneficial flow-on effects for those expats who are living there.

And, of course, Thailand does luxury wonderfully well—massages, health and spa treatments, world-class restaurants and, if you want it, party destination after party destination. The beer is good and the people are beautiful.

What a way to go!

Asia calling

For some, the call to Asia is simply irresistible. Unsurprisingly, the ones most often drawn are those ex-servicemen who had fought in Asia, such as in Vietnam or Malaysia.

Many of these men were just kids of nineteen or so when they served in the Australian military. As a result, their formative years were spent in Asia and their personalities and beliefs were forever shaped by this time. For some, it was a harrowing and traumatising experience, as war always is. For others, it was the first time that they felt truly alive. And now, as these men age, they want to grab hold again of that excitement and return to the stomping ground of their youth—Asia beckons.

Barry Petersen was one of those young men who served in the Australian army and as a result he spent most of his early years in Asia. He describes moving to Thailand, when he was in his late 50s, as a homecoming.

We met Barry in his apartment. It was hot. It was central Bangkok. He told us his story as we sat around a table in a small room that was a bit like a mini-boardroom. We sipped water. A fan swirled against the heat but seemed to make little difference. Soon, though, we didn't notice the discomfort; we were riveted by Barry's tale.

Barry, like a number of those who have retired to Asia, had lived and worked there for many years, although his life was perhaps a little more dangerous and exciting than most.

In the late 1950s, Barry lived in Malaya as a young lieutenant with a platoon of 32, chasing Communist terrorists. Then he went to South Vietnam as part of a training team, on loan to the American CIA; his role was to gather intelligence and recruit, train and operate mountain tribesmen in the central highlands, in Darlac Province. The primary aim was to interrupt Vietcong activities along the Ho Chi Minh Trail that ran north–south through the mountains of Vietnam.

Barry then lived with the Montagnard, a Hmong Khmer ethnic group, from 1963 to 1965. It was an extraordinary experience for which he was awarded the Military Cross. He has detailed these times in his book *Tiger Men: A young Australian among the Rhade Montagnard of Vietnam* (Orchid Books 1994).

Living in Asia throughout the 1960s, he fell in love with it.

Barry retired from the Australian army with the rank of colonel in 1979, aged 45. 'I found that life was very boring in Australia,' he said. 'I had a small farm outside Cairns but I was coming back to Southeast Asia every year from the mid-1980s onwards—back to Vietnam from 1987.

'Then one trip I was in Cambodia on the Mekong River. We were going downstream from Kampong Cham to Phnom Penh. I'd stayed on the boat one night, enjoyed a bath at the end of the boat in the river water, and I was having a "Mekong temperature beer", because (the Mekong water) was the only way to keep it cool. I was just watching the sun set and I thought, "A fellow could do a lot worse than going back to Asia to live."

'That's when I decided I would move to Asia permanently.'

These days, Barry lives above the office of his business. It is a modernised (badly modernised in a 1980s sort of way) shophouse. A shophouse is an architectural building style in Southeast Asia. A shop is on the ground floor and a residence is on the next level. Barry's is barred for security. Steel-grilled gates open directly onto the street. There is a tiny courtyard, but it is barren with just a couple of tired, potted plants. Just two steps on, you are at the front door.

Barry's shophouse is in a dead-end lane off a *soi*—a side street that runs off one of the major arterial roads in central Bangkok—in Langsuan. The area roughly compares to Sydney's Woollahra or Melbourne's South Yarra—albeit a bit on the treeless and scrappy side. There's a lot of tar and concrete; it was hot walking down the lane to get to the house. There are no trees in the lane.

This is an ultra-urban environment. It is not the tropical Thailand that many Australians experience in Koh Samui or Phuket. But it suits Barry.

Approaching 80 years of age, he is unwell, but from here he can easily get to local restaurants, coffee houses and to the doctor. And with all his staff working below in the building, Barry has a huge amount of company. He is never lonely.

Moving to Asia was the best decision Barry could have made—Australia was boring him rigid, as he explained: 'Every time I returned to Australia after my regular trips to Asia, I determined that my previously "worldly" neighbours were becoming very parochial. They were interested in what I had been doing in Cambodia and Vietnam and Thailand. So I would tell them. But then the conversation would switch back to potholes in the road and the council rates. I thought, "Oh no, I am going to end up like these people." So it didn't take much persuasion—just that one beer on the Mekong—to make me say, "I'll sell my property in Australia."'

Asia in the 1990s provided Barry a fresh adventure, a new life, just as it did when he was a young man in the 1960s.

After he sold up and packed up, he initially thought he would get a farm somewhere in Thailand. 'Then I got here and thought, you know, it's going to be just as bad down there in the province, in fact worse than it is outside Cairns. All the villagers will only be able to talk about potholes, or their equivalent of potholes.'

So he was loitering, as he puts it, in Bangkok in 1993. And through a rather convoluted process, Barry, then 59, started a new business: a consultancy, Lang Suan House Co Ltd, that focused on foreign companies establishing in Thailand. Taking advantage of Barry's extensive experience in Asia, its services include registering foreign companies for tax and VAT, and assisting them with other business practices like banking, accounting, tax returns, payroll and obtaining work permits and visas.

All of Barry's Thai employees are close to him—they are his family now, his friends, his life. Many of them have already become equity holders in the business, but Barry told us he plans to leave the company to his Thai colleagues.

'I am far better off here than I would ever be in Australia,' he said. 'I wouldn't be able to manage my farm anymore. I would have had to move into Cairns and live in an old men's home and my company would be fellow veterans who could only talk about the same things over and over again. And I wouldn't have a family like this.'

Barry says he can live well in Thailand on his military pension. It was this pension that gave him the income he needed in the early years while he was building up his business. He doesn't think that retirees moving to Thailand will confront many problems; the main issue, he believes, is quite simple: 'You just need to get on with Thais'.

'I was in Cambodia at the time when I decided to move to Asia; on the Mekong River. I was having a "Mekong temperature beer", because that was the only way to keep it cool. We were going downstream from Kampong Cham to Phnom Penh and overnight I just stayed on the boat, had a bath at the end of the boat in the Mekong water, and I was just watching the sun set and I thought, "A fellow could do a lot worse than going back to Asia to live."'

A more interesting and cheaper life

Edward is a friend of Barry's who also now calls Thailand home. An ex-Vietnam veteran and ex-Australian banker, Edward has been living in Bangkok for the past fifteen years. He is married to a Thai woman and has children. They live in a massive five-bedroom apartment in the best part of Bangkok that he bought for a song during the SARS crisis of 2003. He also has a holiday home in Phuket.

Although not retired, he has no plans whatsoever of returning to Australia.

'It's just plain more interesting here,' said Edward. 'You get away from the minutiae of life and you do not live in a social bubble. You mix with a variety of nationalities, live in a different culture.'

Edward pointed out that in Thailand, foreigners can purchase condominiums at less than half the price of those in Australia. 'And security is not a problem,' he said, 'but condos do have 24-hour guards.'

Despite being wealthy, Edward appreciates the significantly lower cost of living in Thailand compared to Australia. 'Food is cheap and dining out is cheap. You can eat at an upmarket Thai restaurant for less than A$20 a head including drinks.'

These savings however, while not so critical to Edward, are terribly important to many others—those less well off, like ordinary

Australian retirees. The vastly lower cost of living in Thailand is a great attraction to these people.

Consumer prices in Thailand are almost 60 per cent lower than in Australia. Rent is around 65 per cent cheaper, restaurant prices 75 per cent lower and groceries 50 per cent less.

One thing about retiring in Thailand is that you are always bumping into Australians. You are not going to feel socially isolated. Bangkok is the busiest consular office in the world for Australia; the second busiest is London. And Bangkok is 50 per cent busier than London.

More than 952 000 Australians visited Thailand in 2012; that's one in 25 Australians. And tourism is growing at 10 per cent a year.

About 40 000 Australians are resident in Thailand, although the figure is rubbery as many do not register with the Australian embassy; but that is the best consensus number.

For Edward, Barry and many other expats, Bangkok ticks all the lifestyle boxes—it is cheaper than Australia, medical services and modern conveniences are superb, and its culture is truly dynamic and fascinating. But for those who are looking for a slower pace than Bangkok, Thailand also has much to offer.

'It's just plain more interesting here,' said Edward.

'You get away from the minutiae of life and you do not live in a social bubble. You mix with a variety of nationalities, live in a different culture.'

Phuket

Phuket contrasts dramatically to Bangkok. The famous holiday destination with its beautiful beaches is more laid-back and much more popular with both Australian tourists and expats.

It's easy to picture yourself living the idyllic beach life in Phuket, but before you get carried away, you need to look very carefully at its many sides—like much of Thailand, there's the good and the ugly.

Let's start with the ugly side

Larry Cunningham was Australia's honorary consul-general in Phuket from 2005 to 2014. When we met him, he'd been in business in Thailand for more than a decade and he was readying himself to return to Australia. He was, in his words, 'Thaied-Out'.

He was also very plain speaking and said that Phuket is, in his opinion, not a good place to retire: 'In 2005, we had 3000 Aussies in Phuket—probably 2500 tourists and 500 expats. Today it is 27 000—2000 expats and 25 000 idiots.

'I looked after 50 deaths a year—50 Australians a year die in Phuket; half are from natural causes and half are misadventure.

'Health insurance [or the lack of it] is a huge problem,' he added.

Larry said that another problem is that Australian expatriates in Phuket tend to live in the cheaper and, therefore less safe, areas. He pointed to the south of Phuket as being one such area.

'A lot of them can only afford to live in the areas of Phuket that are not all that savory. I am talking about the southern part from Chalong down to Rawai—even the Thais don't like living down there. You have the sea gypsies who are renowned house breakers. There have been numerous unsolved rapes—Thais on Europeans. It is a big problem here. Because it is rarely reported, not a great deal is done.

'The safety issue is massive and it comes from not having enough money. You need enough money so that you don't have to live in the south.

'I would say 90 per cent of the people whose passports I renewed here—about 200 a year—were from the south; usually retirees living down there with a Thai girl.'

Extortion is another problem, Larry said, and used the jet-ski mafia racket as an example. He told us that young Thais will intentionally ram a hired jet-ski then demand between A$5000 and A$10 000 dollars to cover the damage.

'Another problem is that a lot of these guys live in Patong. It is sin city with a capital S. The drugs! I had a 55-year-old guy from the Gold Coast come over here and thought he would make some side income by selling cocaine. Selling it in an area where it is alleged that the police sell cocaine. He got five years—he was very lucky.'

Larry claimed that, 'Older people do not feel safe. And they have only got to be shaken down by the police once or twice. It gives older people the heebie-jeebies. And you've got no rights here—absolutely no rights here at all.

'Anyone with brains would not retire in Phuket—maybe to Chiang Mai, that's where the Japanese go, where there are lower levels of crime, limited extortion, and enough money to be above that.'

Yet he believes that more and more Australian retirees will move to Thailand for financial and lifestyle reasons. It's not for Larry, though. 'The day I fly out of Phuket will be the happiest day of my life,' he said.

Massive personal freedom/no rights is a common theme in much of Asia.

This is the opposite to Australia: massive rights/no personal freedom.

And now the good side

Sal and Glen agree with Larry that more retirees from Australia are on their way to Phuket, but they disagree that the south of the island is more dangerous. They've been there for five years, own a cafe and live in a superb house—they love Phuket, and they feel safe there.

The couple, both now 65, retired to Phuket from country New South Wales after half a lifetime in the winery and restaurant business. Sal explained their decision to pack up and take off: 'I really enjoyed the vineyard but we were ready to move on—30 years in the one job. And I got sick of being cold; I hated being cold in Australia.

'We had come here many times on holiday. We just decided we liked it here and our nephew was living here. We thought we could own a little cafe—we had been in the food industry all our lives and had a restaurant on the vineyard.

'Our dream was to live on the beach in Phuket. So we sold everything, packed a container and came. We brought some of our furniture—pieces that mattered to us. We didn't put anything into storage.'

Before they made the move, Sal and Glen were already familiar with Asia and had contacts from a sideline business they operated for a few years importing homewares and high-end textiles from Vietnam.

'We were in love with Asia,' Glen said.

At home they could see the wine industry going down, and down, and it was clearly in a terminal phase for the grape grower and smaller wine producer. 'In the 1980s we used to sell our grapes for A$2500 a tonne. In 2000 we were selling for A$300 a tonne,' Glen said, adding that it never improved.

And, critically for Sal and Glen, their son now lives in Phuket as well, although their married daughter and grandchildren live in Australia.

'The only regret I have in moving to Phuket is the grandchildren,' Sal said. 'They weren't born when we came here. My daughter had been married for more than three years and hadn't decided whether she would have children.'

But, as Sal pointed out, technology these days goes a long way towards overcoming the tyranny of distance. 'I speak to them every day on Skype. When my granddaughter saw me at the airport last time, she kept feeling my face to see if it was a real one rather than a face on a screen.'

Sal also visits Australia three or four times a year, and her daughter takes the children to Phuket once a year. A very practical Sal added, 'A direct flight to Sydney is eight hours—we were four hours away when we lived in country Australia.'

Glen and Sal are downsizing from their large three-bedroom, three-bathroom house in Phuket with in-ground pool and wonderful gardens. They would sell it for around A$250 000.

They enjoy the luxuries that they could not afford in Australia. For example, a live-in maid costs about A$300 a month. 'You can also send out your laundry, have a gardener, have regular massages,' said Sal.

'We only cook at home about once a month—we invite our friends and family over for roast lamb. Lamb here is plentiful and cheaper than Australia.'

And Glen and Sal feel very safe in Phuket.

'Property theft here is not a problem,' said Glen. 'At the coffee shop we can leave all the outdoor tables and chairs outside overnight and nobody touches them. I never lock my house.'

He did warn, though, that there are precautions foreigners should take. 'Certainly, you don't want to put any Thai person seriously offside, especially if you are standing between him and a pile of money,' said Glen. 'But we are hardly going to do that. After all, we are primarily retired.'

When asked about the sex-scene in Thailand and how she copes, Sal said it is easily managed because some towns are worse than others, and she simply avoids those. Being a woman in Phuket is not an issue for her.

'It's no problem here at all,' she said. 'I can go into a bar with the men where they play pool. There are girls there. They are always keen to talk to me. They are lovely. They call me Mama. I don't ever go to Patong—haven't been there for three years.'

And little wonder. The main street of Patong is lined with girlie bars and there is a lot of Thai boxing advertised. Neon signs flicker, cheap market stalls dot the seascape, the tourists are usually middle-aged single men, and the Thai girls in their late teens to early twenties. Patong sits in sharp contrast to the upmarket areas that are also on the western side of the island: Kamala Beach, Surin Beach, Bang Tao Beach and Laguna Beach. There is a touch of Sydney's Palm Beach style in these upmarket parts—but in very limited doses.

In Phuket, though, residential life is a lot quieter and a convenient, relaxing lifestyle is key to Glen and Sal's happiness. Glen plays golf at a public course for about A$40 a round, plus A$7 for the caddie (you are required to have a caddie). Not only is it affordable, there are several great golf courses on Phuket and many retirees choose to live in the middle of the island near the courses. The Phuket Country Club is where the expats go if they want golf-estate living.

As for shopping and Western-style supplies, Sal said these days she is able to get everything that she needs, and mostly at the local supermarket. 'When we first arrived five years ago, there were lots of things that were not available. But now you can get everything you want,' she said. 'We shop at the Villa supermarket—it has things like Jif, Vegemite and mint jelly.'

While Glen and Sal have no plans to return to Australia, they still own property here. 'We think it is in our interest to maintain residency in Australia,' Glen said. When travelling they always tick 'resident departing temporarily' or 'resident returning' on their immigration cards. Glen also added that they have kept their Australian credit cards. 'We would not be able to get a credit card in Thailand,' he explained. (See Chapter 9: Taxation for more information.)

A home for life despite a Tsunami

In more than twenty years of living in Phuket, Susan has seen all the sides of Thailand, including some tragedies, but she has no intention of leaving.

'I will always live here. I regard it as home,' she said. 'I like the feeling of being in Asia—it is more interesting than Australia. Here, every day is different. In Australia, it is always the same. Your friends stay the same. Here, life moves on. It is more vibrant.

'The night life is huge. Thank goodness I don't go out so much now. I tell you, you would be just a wreck if you did everything—you know, expat life . . .'

Susan's main interests are sailing, running and travelling. And Phuket is perfect for all of this. The Phuket yacht club organises four major regattas a year and Susan loves the running club, the Hash House Harriers. 'There is a fantastic social life around that,' said the 60-year-old, who looks closer to 40.

In fact, 40 is how old Susan was when she first arrived in Phuket, in 1993.

Born in Cooma, New South Wales, Susan spent most of her adult life working for building societies in Coffs Harbour and Sydney. She makes no bones about the fact that she ran away from the tedium of her working life—in a rather exciting way, sailing off from Australia in a yacht with her partner. They arrived in Phuket in November.

'We were going on to Italy, but he was killed in a motorbike accident, in June. We had been living on our yacht—anchored out.'

After her partner's death, Susan moved the yacht into the Boat Lagoon Marina and began working for the Cathay Pacific pilots who lived in Phuket and had their boats moored in the marina.

'I would take care of the boats when they were away. It gave me a good lifestyle.'

Susan returned to Australia in 1997 and met Harry, another sailor, before they came back to Phuket in 1999. Harry was about to retire, and said: 'Why don't we sail back [to Phuket] via the Solomons?' And they did.

There was, according to Susan, only one problem with Phuket—no meat pies.

'You couldn't buy a pie in Phuket!' she said. 'I missed meat pies!'

So she asked her sister in Australia to get her an electronic pie-maker. 'Initially, it was just to make pies for myself. Then I thought, "I'll be able to make pies for the Aussie boys at the yacht club." And it went from that. I had never made pastry before, so I had to learn how to do that. I used to stand there with this pie-maker and make two pies every seven minutes.'

Eight and a half years later, it is a significant business—and Susan is known by locals as Lady Pie.

To this day she is still the only Australian pie-maker in Southeast Asia. She even supplies pies to the Hong Kong Sevens rugby competition—not all of the pies, though, just 8000 of them! 'I have been doing it for three years. The pies are like little footballs with laces on.'

But there is always a flipside to being a local and for Susan this was the tsunami that hit Thailand in 2005. She shared a frightening tale:

'We had rented this gorgeous little house in Kamala on the beach. I was in bed and there was an earthquake at eight in the morning. I remember I felt that. Then, at ten, the tsunami struck. And the water came. The whole house got hit by the three waves. The first wave hit and the water came inside. The second wave smashed all of the house. And then the third wave took everything out to sea.

'When it happened Harry was on his hammock, waiting to go snorkelling once the tide came in. We had our yacht in the sea out the front and the dinghy was tied up to the tree. He saw the water coming and he called out to me. I ran around to the front of the house—there was a big glass table there and it exploded with the force of the water hitting it and the wave washed me out the back. I was lucky and was able to run up the hill.

'Harry was fiddling with the dinghy when the wave hit and he got swept out in that. I could see him in the dinghy and watched as he eventually got onto the yacht. He got the motor going and went out to sea.

'The water was really brackish, foamy, brown, with logs and debris all through it—it was horrible. I thought it was the end of the world.

'After the first wave, a local man helped me back down to the house. I was in shock. I remember I saw the laundry hanging on the line and thought, "I better bring that in." I asked the man to turn off the power. All the furniture was floating. Then we heard people screaming, "Water!" I ran up the hill again as the second wave was hitting.

'Then I saw the third wave—it was huge. God, it was big. The road we were standing on was 10 metres up the hill and the wave was curling around the headland and seemed higher than us.

'After that third wave hit, the water kept coming in and going out all afternoon. We were just petrified.

'The worst part was the next day when we went down to the town—all the mud, the bodies, hundreds of people were killed.'

Chiang Mai

For a less touristy and even cheaper Thai environment, try Chiang Mai in the country's north. There's no tsunami threat there—in fact, it couldn't be more earthy. It's also very different to the sleazy parts of Bangkok, Pattaya or Patong—a world away . . .

Chiang Mai feels like real Thailand, not tourist Thailand. It has an old Thai-come-hippie feel to it. It has a tranquillity. It is laid-back—very laid-back.

The town is a former capital of the Kingdom of Lanna (1296–1768) and is close to the highest mountains in the country. These offer a cool climate, stunning scenery, and great trekking and bike riding.

The old quarter of Chiang Mai is surrounded by a wide, tree-bordered, centuries-old moat. Many traditional wooden houses with quiet, leafy gardens have been preserved and there seems to be a Buddhist temple on almost every corner of the old town.

The area that lies outside the old town is dotted with fabulous modern apartments that are cheap to buy and rent. Parts of the city are also known for Western-style cafes, wine bars, restaurants and accommodation. Yet, despite embracing modern conveniences, Chiang Mai has maintained its decorum, a sense of authenticity and history. A walk through the old town makes you feel young. And this is important for a retiree.

It transports you back to the 1970s and 1980s. There is a feeling that the Golden Triangle really is just a short distance to the north; that you can get a joint if you want one; and that it is cool to have a few too many beers or just hang with young European and Aussie backpackers in bars and coffee shops and talk to the women in the bar as well.

For the boomers from the West, who are just entering their retirement years and continue to refuse to get out of jeans and T-shirts and still feel young at heart, Chiang Mai is uplifting. That's why it really is a very popular tourist destination.

In greater Chiang Mai, there are, at the best guess, about 20 000 expats of all different nationalities, but British, American and Japanese predominate.

An English rose in Chiang Mai

Dorothy, our 70-year-old English Rose, loves the place and claims that she is a typical Chiang Mai retiree. Her reasons for being there are common, she said.

'I could afford to live in the UK but I do not want to. My quality of life here is so much better on my UK pension. I never, ever, doubt my decision to retire here. I am only anxious, at times, that the Thai authorities may change the rules concerning expatriates living here.'

Dorothy's story mirrors that of many others in that she already had extensive experience of Asia. Dorothy, and her now ex-husband, were teachers and lived and worked in Singapore for fifteen years. They travelled extensively throughout Asia and their children became international citizens. Her daughter is an academic in the US and her son is a banker in Singapore. She has no grandchildren.

Cost of Living

INDICES

CHIANG MAI LOWER THAN SYDNEY

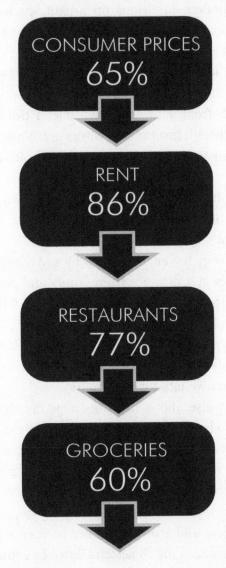

CONSUMER PRICES
65%

RENT
86%

RESTAURANTS
77%

GROCERIES
60%

Source: numbeo.com

Dorothy said her life in Chiang Mai has a rhythm to it and it is a very healthy rhythm. She is up at six each morning to hike up a mountain, Doi Suthep. This is close to her home, so she just rides her motorbike there. Remember, Dorothy is 70.

The apartment she owns cost her the equivalent of A$80 000; to rent a similar apartment would cost around A$500 a month. It is in the Nimmanhemen area, just ten minutes drive from central Chiang Mai. It is a very modern, luxurious, open-plan, spacious, 100-square metre, one-bedroom apartment. There is also a gym and a pool in the condo complex.

Dorothy said, 'It's much better than my apartment was in Brighton and a quarter of the price.'

On the health front, Dorothy is sensible. 'I think it is risky to live here without health insurance. Insurance costs do increase each year, and the company I use will not insure you if you are over 60 when you apply.'

Dorothy's health insurance costs about A$3700 a year. She uses the private clinic of the local public hospital, Sri Pat, which she said she finds excellent.

Again, technology has enabled Dorothy and many other retirees to live comfortably at a distance from family and friends. Without the internet and the computer, Dorothy said that living in Chiang Mai would be too hard.

'I just love Skype,' she said. 'I can talk to my children whenever I like. I regularly talk to my daughter for an hour or so, several times a week—sometimes we talk for four hours!

'The computer also allows me to manage my affairs efficiently and easily. I have a house in France that I manage via the computer, and I do all of my banking on the internet.'

In fact, when we met Dorothy she was trying to sell her house in France. It is interesting that she chose Chiang Mai over France as a place to retire.

'Sure, the cheese and wine is cheaper in France but it's better that I drink less and keep my cholesterol down by eating less cheese!' she joked.

Then she explained: 'In Chiang Mai there is a better sense of community than in France or even the UK. Old people in the UK do not have as good a quality of life. It's an outdoor life here.'

This brings to mind again the film *The Best Exotic Marigold Hotel*.

'Living here, you don't run to the doctor all the time,' said Dorothy. 'The climate allows you to exercise.' And she pointed out that most of the older people she knows in Chiang Mai 'are not taking the massive amount of pills that those in the UK are taking'.

She believes that the problems of the elderly in the UK are financial. But loneliness is also a big issue. She said, 'I do not have to deal with either of these things here. I have good friends. I am never lonely, never isolated. I can walk about town at all hours and feel safe: safer, in fact, than I'd feel if I was walking around Brighton late at night.'

Dorothy says her friends in the UK tell her, 'You are so brave' or 'You are very lucky'. But she maintains that she is neither. It is not hard living here, she stated matter-of-factly. There are some language issues, but most of the time everything is easy.

She is, however, annoyed by the lucky label. 'You make your own life,' she said. 'No luck is involved.'

'I could afford to live in the UK but I do not want to. My quality of life here is so much better on my UK pension. I never ever doubt my decision to retire here. I am only anxious at times that the Thai authorities may change the rules concerning expatriates living here.'

Living is easy
Chiang Mai is cheaper than both Bangkok and Phuket—and dramatically cheaper than Australia. Groceries are half the cost, rent is less than a quarter of Sydney's rent and so are restaurants and power costs.

'Electricity is cheap,' says Dorothy. Bizarrely, it was initially free because she used less than the minimum chargeable amount, but that system has since changed. She uses little air-conditioning, however.

Water costs Dorothy about A$3.50 a month, internet A$20 and the landline about A$3.50. She has house cleaners once a week—two ladies for two hours, which costs A$10. The minimum wage is about A$11–12 per day. Dorothy also adds that food is cheap and she eats out most nights.

Although getting around in taxis and tuk-tuks is inexpensive, cars in Thailand are not. In late 2012 Dorothy bought a new Honda Prio for A$14 500 and spends A$50 a month on petrol. She points out, though, that petrol for her motorbike, prior to going the safer route and buying a car, cost her less than A$20 a month.

Another Chiang Mai resident, Godfree Roberts, writes books on retiring in Thailand and is developing a website called Fun Advisor to help inform retirees about what's happening around the country.

We met Godfree in a very laid-back restaurant on the banks of Mae Ping River which meanders through Chiang Mai. It's about fifteen minutes outside the old town area. People sip coffee under trees on an open timber deck. It's rustic and authentic: cane chairs, old rough wooden tables, the river, the heavy rainforest on the opposite bank. The food is great—local Thai—the coffee is good, and all up it's 20 per cent of the cost of eating in a cafe in Sydney.

Godfree says Chiang Mai is a carefree but quiet place—very few car horns are heard, or ambulance or police sirens. 'When I go home, the girls who live nearby get me over to have a beer and sing some Karaoke,' he said. That's about as wild as it gets.

According to Godfree, the major driver of expatriates coming to Thailand is financial—but most also possess an adventurous spirit. His view is that the Australians who live here are generally odd, independent people. For example, he has an ex-SAS mate and another who is an ex-professional motorcycle racer.

At 73, Godfree looks 63. He walks for two hours each morning and does yoga three times a week. He relishes his laid-back lifestyle on the river, one which he could never afford in Australia. In fact, Godfree told us his monthly living costs are around A$850 a month—which is only a little more than half the current Australian pension.

For this, Godfree gets: a rented flat, including water and electricity, for A$300; food for A$300 (he eats out everyday for breakfast,

Cost of Living

Sydney vs Chiang Mai [% lower than Sydney]

Housing

Rent–3 bed'm apartment city centre*
$4,276

Rent–3 bed'm apartment outside city centre*
$2,815

Buy–apartment per sqm city centre
$9,795

$715.72 — 83%
$432.76 — 85%
$1,285 — 87%

Food

Bread
$3.47

Eggs
$4.13

Chicken breasts
$10.78

Tomatoes
$5.17

$1.14 — 67%
$1.47 — 64%
$3.09 — 71%
$0.92 — 82%

Restaurants

Mid range meal for 2
$80

Inexpensive
$15

$16.64 — 79%
$1.33 — 91%

Beer

Domestic
$4.80

$1.40 — 71%

Taxi

Per km
$3

One hour standby
$54.16

$0.27
$4.99 — 91%

Electricity

Electricity, heating, water, garbage*
$238.97

$78.63 — 67%

Communications

Internet*
$61.66

Mobile phone (per min prepaid)
$1.02

$19.78 — 68%
$0.07 — 93%

* per month

Source: numbeo.com

Thailand

41

lunch, dinner, and has daily iced coffees); a new rented moped for A$120, plus fuel for about A$30; his internet for A$20; and he does yoga three times a week, for A$90.

Clearly, there are very few in Australia who can enjoy anything like Godfree's lifestyle on the old-age pension.

Health and medical services

The sophisticated and very reasonably priced medical services in Thailand make it a particularly attractive place for older Australians to retire to. But it's not just for retirees—medical and dental tourism is now huge in Thailand with thousands of Europeans, Australians and Americans visiting for treatments of all sorts.

'There are three or four Australian dental tours here a week— about 100 people a week,' said Edward, the Australian expatriate living in Bangkok. 'It is phenomenal health care,' he added.

Medical services in a very modern and large hospital, where half the doctors are US-trained, can cost as little as 10 to 20 per cent of what they would cost in the United States. Charges can be as low as A$50 per day for a private room with meals, up to A$150 for a luxurious suite complete with a living room, two bathrooms, a small kitchen and bedroom. The rooms are so well furnished and the service so good that patients say it is more like staying in a hotel than a hospital.

But beware—you should have private health cover.

There are around 100 deaths of Australians in Thailand each year—one every three days. One of the biggest consular problems that the Australian embassy faces in Thailand is dealing with sick people who have not bought health cover.

'They get cancer or whatever and they have real trouble meeting the cost of health care,' said one Australian senior diplomat.

He also warned that a common problem with medical insurance coverage for Australian tourists or residents is that, if they do something illegal—like ride a motorbike without a licence—then insurance will not cover them if they have an accident.

> Medical services in a very modern and large hospital where half the doctors are US-trained can cost as little as 10 per cent of what they would cost in the US.

The good news is that many of the major Australian health insurers are in Thailand, and the premiums are cheaper as well. Edward said he pays about A$2000 a year for health insurance, using a London-based insurance company.

And, as opposed to many other countries in Asia, in Thailand you do not need medical evacuation cover. The medical facilities 'in country' are good enough.

Some expatriates, however, take shortcuts and this is dangerous.

For example, Glen said that he and Sal are insured, but have chosen to use travel insurance rather than a medical insurance policy. He explained: 'We renew our travel insurance every year. It covers 100 per cent of our medical costs in Thailand—the risk is that the insurer can decide to medivac you back to Australia—and then you are on your own.'

This is because Medicare does not cover Australians, like Glen and Sal, who have been out of Australia for five or more years. (See Chapter 10: Health insurance.) Importantly, though, it does not take long to reactivate Medicare once you are back in Australia. All you have to do is prove you are once again a resident of Australia and that you are here to stay.

Susan, aka Lady Pie, tells an instructive tale about health insurance.

'The Medicare people in Australia took my Medicare card off me,' she said. 'I was horrified. I am not entitled to it because I don't live there—but having it just made me feel part of Australia. There was girl serving me at the Medicare office in Sydney and she asked for my driver's licence and I said, "I don't have one but I do have this", and stupidly showed her my Thai driver's licence. She said, "We need to take the Medicare card off you because you are not living in Australia."'

Susan has private health insurance through an Australian company. 'People who don't have it here—it is so irresponsible,' she said. 'Recently a guy we know got bowel cancer and all his friends took the hat around because he didn't have insurance.'

Tom and Sonja have been living in Phuket for thirteen years. They have both worked there but Tom is now retired. They have no interest in moving back to Australia.

'We feel like we are in the middle of things here,' Sonja said. 'We have no regrets after all these years in Phuket. And there are sound financial reasons for living here as well.'

Sonja said they are living the good life. 'We couldn't afford a maid six days a week and a gardener in Australia. We couldn't afford to have a massage at home every Sunday. And we eat out three or four times a week.'

They both have health insurance, which proved to be vital. Tom, who pays around A$3200 a year for his medical insurance, had a very bad motorcycle accident in 2013—his treatment would have cost them more than A$17 000, but it was fully covered by the insurance company. And, because he had insurance cover pre-60 years of age, he was able to continue his policy without penalties.

Aged-care services

> Bill not only had a great second life—a renewal—but as he became increasingly frail, he was able to stay at home. He was well looked after by the Thai carer. He was not put into an antiseptic, nursing home.

One of the great attractions for the older and less agile Western-expatriate in Asia is the old-age care that can be provided.

Moving to Thailand truly gave Sonja's father, Bill, a second life, although the Thai health system itself had little to do with that. Bill moved to Phuket at the age of 77, after his wife's death and a heart triple-bypass in Australia. He was lonely and unwell.

'But he got a new lease of life when he came to Phuket,' said Sonja. 'He was reinvigorated.'

In Phuket, Sonja explained, Bill was looked after by a lovely Thai lady, and was very happy for the last six years of his life, before he passed away in 2013.

He was able to cover the bulk of his living costs from his Australian pension, paying A$400 a month rent for a comfortable apartment. Sonja and Tom supplemented his living costs, paid the Thai carer and bought his medication; but even this was a fraction of what it would cost in Australia.

The point here is that Bill not only had a great second life—a renewal—but as he became increasingly frail, he was able to stay at home. He was well looked after by the Thai carer, and he didn't end up in the antiseptic environment of aged-care accommodation.

Bill did not have medical insurance, and when he fell ill and finally needed hospital care, it ended up costing A$18 000. But, according to Sonja, Bill would say his new life and ongoing independence was worth every cent.

> Sonja says she is living the good life in Phuket. 'You can't afford a maid six days a week and a gardener in Australia. You can't afford to have a massage at your home every Sunday. And we eat out three or four times a week.'

Property

Foreigners can legally, and easily, purchase an apartment anywhere in Thailand, though they cannot own land and houses.

However, foreigners manage this restriction in many ways, including:

1. Buying the land in the name of a Thai person, usually a friend or someone they think they can trust, then leasing it back for 30 years with an option to extend. Some developers already offer house sales using their own 30-year lease option.

2. Starting a Thai company in which the foreigner can own up to 49 per cent of the shares and then buy and own land through the company.

Clearly, there can be problems when you use a scheme to circumvent the intention of the law. So if you want to have a larger private area, perhaps with your own garden and pool, our advice is to rent a house. Alternatively, rent or buy an apartment. Apartment ownership is much more straightforward.

For foreigners to be eligible to purchase a condominium in Thailand, they must present proof to the Land Department that the funds have been remitted from overseas in foreign currency (as demonstrated by a valid Foreign Exchange Transfer Form from a Thai bank). Foreigners can acquire up to, but not exceeding, 49 per cent of the total floor area of the combined condo units.

Adam, a motorcycle enthusiast and an artist, moved to Chiang Mai about ten years ago from Sydney's eastern suburbs. He inherited some money, had a property rented in Sydney, and figured he'd be able to enjoy life in Chiang Mai—a place he had been visiting since the mid 1970s.

Since then, Adam has made some good money from investing in properties in Chiang Mai. He bought a condominium for A$50 000 in central Chiang Mai and has bought, renovated and sold two other condos as well.

'I just love it here,' Adam said. 'I feel relaxed—maybe it's the Buddhism.'

The handsome, lean, congenial 56-year-old has certainly made his life here. He loves riding his bike around the town, joking with the tuk-tuk drivers when he's stuck in traffic, and his favourite pastime is to ride through the mountains outside Chiang Mai. He also has a long-term partner who is Thai and 45 years old; she was Adam's neighbour when they met.

While Adam and his partner have a strong and respectful relationship, he believes that most of the expat men are here for the women. He warned: 'There are dangers of being ripped off by Thai partners—in property and business. Many men are socially vulnerable. It's sad. For example, there are a number of instances where a man will buy a house with a Thai partner and the Thai partner—who may even have a Thai boyfriend on the side—will finally take the house from him. There was one instance where an English guy was beaten to death in Isan [a province in the north-east of Thailand].'

> Foreigners can legally, and easily, purchase an apartment anywhere in Thailand, though they cannot own land and houses.

Adam was smart with his move and his experience provides a good model for many people, especially retirees, who decide to live in a foreign country. He initially rented a shophouse because he did not know what living in Chiang Mai would be like; whether it was dangerous, too corrupt, or just plain boring and not his thing.

'I figured I could leave that shophouse and everything in it if I had to; if anything went wrong,' he said.

It was only after he was sure that he wanted to stay in Chiang Mai, and understood the legal and property ownership structures, that he decided to buy himself an apartment. And only after that did he start to invest in property.

Visas for Thailand

Retirement visas are readily available in Thailand, and applications can be made within Thailand or at a Thai embassy in a foreign country. (See Appendix: Visas for more details.)

There are two financial requirements for retirement visas: either a lump sum of at least 800 000 Thai baht (TB) or A$26 500 in a Thai bank (it can be a foreign bank with a Thai branch, like HSBC) for three months prior to application; or an income test, with the requirement being a minimum of TB65 000 or A$2200 a month or A$26 400 a year (this is a bit more than Australia's age pension for a single person); or a mixture of the two.

One requirement is that visa holders must check in with authorities every 90 days, but Dorothy and other expats we spoke to say that this isn't a problem.

Retirement visas are readily available in Thailand.

Applications for a retirement visa for Thailand can be made within Thailand or at a Thai embassy in a foreign country.

THAILAND TIPS AND TRAPS

1. If you like the lifestyle offered by Australia's Kings Cross, then fine, go and live in Pattaya and Patong. If not, stay away from them and live in quieter areas like Chiang Mai or more upmarket areas in Phuket and Bangkok.

2. Thailand offers a vast choice of lifestyles—city Bangkok; beachy and slightly edgy Phuket and Koh Samui; laid-back and cooler Chiang Mai; hotspots along the Burmese border like Mae Sot; or the traditional towns in the country and north-east, like Chiang Rai.

3. Be aware of, and sensitive to, cultural differences. Thais are polite and deferential. Australians tend to be very direct, which can be seen as confrontational and, at times, simply crude.

4. Thailand and most other Southeast Asian countries offer massive personal freedom—but this is at the cost of limited personal rights. So beware. You should try to live a life according to the laws of the land, but if you get into trouble with the law, then this can mean big trouble.

5. Living in disreputable areas means increased risk of theft, extortion and personal danger.

6. Thai medical and health services are excellent—and cheap. Health insurance for treatments within Thailand is therefore much cheaper.

7. The cost of living in Thailand is low—at least half the cost of living in Australia. And the further you are from tourist areas, the cheaper it gets.

8. Thailand is ideal for the elderly who need constant care but loathe the idea of aged-care facilities. Home care is affordable.

9. Foreigners can buy apartments, but not houses or land. As always, there are ways around this—like buying in a Thai name and leasing the property back—but beware of breaking the law, even the spirit of the law.

10. To obtain a Thai retirement visa for a long-term stay, you need to meet a primary financial criteria of either a lump sum of TB800 000 (A$26 500 in a Thai bank for three months prior to application) or an income of TB65 0000 or A$2200 a month (A$26 400 a year).

CHAPTER 3

Malaysia

Bob is the sort of guy who does a spreadsheet analysis on where the best place is to live in the world. When it was time to retire, Bob's spreadsheet spat out . . . Penang.

Penang, an island of Malaysia, met Bob's carefully considered criteria which included crime, cost of living, health care, climate and culture. It was the place that offered a 60-plus-year-old the good life.

We had a drink with Bob and his partner Marion on the large verandah of their sub-penthouse apartment. The expansive sea views over the Malacca Strait, north-east toward mainland Malaysia, were breathtaking. The apartment was massive, with five bedrooms, five bathrooms, a sauna, spa, maid's room, and a huge entertaining and kitchen area. And the complex had a pool and a gym, too. All this cost about 6500 Malaysian ringgit a month—that works out to A$550 a week.

After a couple of drinks with Bob and Marion, we needed a coffee. So we strolled maybe 100 metres from the apartment to a cafe that served excellent coffee and great chocolate muffins. And we had to agree with Bob's spreadsheet—they are, indeed, living a good life in Penang.

And so, by the way, is their beloved old dog, Billy. In fact, Bob and Marion devote an entire three-square-metre screen in their living room to the dog—it's a sort of doggy-focused room divider, covered with photos of Billy living in various places around the world. There is Billy in the US, Billy leaping through snow in Switzerland, Billy on the beach in Australia, and now Billy retiring in Penang.

Rosemary, a retired 63-year-old from the US, has been living in Penang for almost two years. She moved to Malaysia from coastal Bali.

Rosemary said, 'There is so much to do here. It is a different class of people here. You can have friends. No bald-headed, fat guys in singlets. In fact, you don't see people in singlets. The dress is business-casual. I was very casual in Bali.'

Unlike Bali and Thailand, Malaysia doesn't have a party vibe or the sexpat feel to it. Of course, there are bar areas, like Bukit Bintang in Kuala Lumpur, that walk the wild side with drugs, alcohol and prostitution. But, like many big cities around the world, these areas are the exception rather than the norm.

Malaysia is, in fact, a great destination for Australians to sell up, pack up and take off to. It is often described as 'Asia-easy'—which basically means it's quite Westernised—and very welcoming to retirees, with the Malaysian government offering hassle-free entry and long-term stays. There is a specific long term stay visa called a Malaysia My Second Home (MM2H) visa.

And critically for the retiree, Malaysia provides excellent health care. The importance of good health care cannot be overestimated by anyone who is over 55 years old.

There is a range of destinations within Malaysia that offer vastly different lifestyles. There is the very Western and cosmopolitan city of Kuala Lumpur, commonly known as KL. There is the relatively quiet and sophisticated island of Penang and, just north of it, the more rustic island of Langkawi with its world-class beaches. And there is Ipoh, which provides less of the modern comforts, but offers more old-world character, a quieter lifestyle, wonderful food and cheap living.

Ellen's oasis

Ellen plans to stay in Malaysia. 'Hell, why not?' she said, smiling like a Cheshire cat.

At 67, Ellen is a grandmother and works as a management consultant. She has been very successful in her career, married and divorced once, followed by a long-term second relationship which ultimately ended. She never expected to have another relationship and was content to keep things that way.

But at a conference two years ago, Ellen met a dynamic young Iranian doctor. He had been studying in Kuala Lumpur but decided to remain there and continue his research. He was 33, a handsome 'George Clooney look-alike', charming, perfectly fluent in English, and enjoyed a drink and some good political conversation. And, Ellen added quietly, 'Of course, he is a sex bomb.'

Ellen got lucky. But even if she hadn't she has no doubt that she would have stayed in KL. 'What do I like about living in Malaysia?' Ellen said. And here she made no reference to any nocturnal pleasures. 'The freedom to be who I am.'

She explained, 'If I go home to Sydney, I've got children and grandchildren. I have to be all goodness and kindness and strive to be the perfect mum. Here, I can be the rat-bag I really am!'

Ellen isn't really a rat-bag—she just wants more out of life.

For Ellen, another important aspect of living in Malaysia is the respect they have for older generations. 'The attitude towards older people is much better here than in the Western world. People are so kind and lovely, they will look out for me, make sure I get home safely. In the work place, I am respected for my status at work but also because of my age, and you just don't get that in Australia—it is so nice.'

She said that while many of her friends and associates in Australia are tempted to move overseas, they are too anxious to do so. At the top of their anxiety list is the medical services.

'As you get older you worry about who is going to look after you every time things fall off or don't function 100 per cent,' said Ellen.

She added quickly, however: 'In my view medical services in Malaysia are absolutely fantastic—really, really top notch. The cardiologist I go to studied with my cousin who is now a professor of surgery in Australia. You get better treatment here in lots of ways. Even if I had a life-threatening illness, I would be quite happy to stay and be treated here.' And, she emphasised, it would come at a fraction of the cost of the same treatment in Australia.

> Bob is the sort of guy who does a spreadsheet analysis on where the best place is to live in the world.
>
> When it was time to retire, Bob's spreadsheet spat out Penang.

Ellen really did find a new life at 65 by moving countries. She was happy in Australia but she willingly grasped the move when business offered up opportunities.

She lives in Bangsar, an upmarket suburb of Kuala Lumpur, in a very pleasant and spacious apartment that costs very little to rent. It has three bedrooms, two bathrooms and costs just A$1200 a month. This is about a third of what a similar apartment would cost to rent in an equivalent suburb in Sydney.

Her money goes much further in KL than in Australia and she is meeting a totally new set of people. At the same time, she has remained close to friends and family back in Melbourne.

To Ellen, the move was absolutely the right thing to do.

Meeting Bob's criteria

Bob has a way with words. This is how he explains his decision to live in Malaysia: 'When you sit in the bath and really start thinking about where you are going to go, it turns out there are a number of criteria that you—everybody, really—needs to consider.'

For Bob, these criteria are 'crime, taxation, health care, cost of living, climate, the cultural back-story and animals'.

On crime alone, a whole lot of places are ruled out. Bob's definition of crime is broad. He said it covers: 'The justice system, recourse to law, the legal system, how corrupt the police are, whether or not you are likely to be kidnapped walking down the street—all of those things.'

And he added, 'These immediately eliminate a whole lot of countries—most of South America, for example; you are not going to live in Bogota, you are not going to live in Mexico City.'

Taxation also takes out many countries. According to Bob, 'Taxation becomes a real issue and that counts out a lot of Western Europe, Portugal, Greece and Australia.'

Health care is Bob's next criteria. 'There are two issues,' he said. 'How expensive is it and how good is it? So, for example, the US is incredibly expensive and not very good. Australia is reasonably expensive and reasonably good. The UK is dirt cheap and not bad. Indonesia is terrible, while Thailand and Malaysia are very cheap and of reasonable quality.

'Here, in Malaysia, there is a local health care system which I suspect is pretty awful. Then you have a Western/Chinese system that is moderately priced and of a reasonable Western standard.

'We have Australian private health care cover, but we have to pay for medical services here.'

However, Bob believes the problem with private health cover is that the insurers are in it to make money. 'And by the time you hit 60, anything you can possibly die of is, I can assure you, pre-existing.'

It is a requirement of the MM2H visa that the visa holder has health insurance. However, if you are over 60 and can prove that you can't get health cover, then the Malaysian government waives the requirement to have it. Bob only needed to have one health insurance company knock back his application to receive the Malaysian government waiver.

On the cost of living, Bob pointed out that if you didn't care about money then you could choose to live anywhere: Sydney, London, Tokyo, Manhattan or Paris. But you'd need plenty of it.

Bob himself lived in Switzerland for six months. He didn't pay for accommodation—his brother owns a house outside of Zurich—and he had a car to use for free. But it still cost Bob and Marion and Billy the dog A$90 000 of their savings over six months.

Clearly, Southeast Asia is fundamentally cheap, although Penang and Kuala Lumpur are relatively expensive compared to other countries like Thailand, Indonesia or even Cambodia.

But Malaysia also ranks high on Bob's language criteria—English is widely spoken in Malaysia, a dividend of being a British colony. That gets a big tick.

The cultural back-story of a place is another of Bob's criteria. He explained: 'Because you speak English, you know a lot of the back-story of other English-speaking countries. You know a lot about Canada without thinking you do, a lot about the US, England, New Zealand. But what do you know about Switzerland? Who is the president, how does their voting system work, what are their laws? You have no cultural back-story and you can't speak the language.'

Living in Malaysia has given Ellen freedom. 'If I go home to Sydney I have got children and grandchildren. I have to be all goodness and kindness. Here I can be the rat-bag I really am.'

And while Southeast Asia has little cultural back-story for most Australians, Malaysia may well have more than most.

Shared history

Malaysia has a colonial history that goes back to the fifteenth century when Malacca was conquered by Portugal, then the Dutch took over around 1640, before the British Empire established its reign from 1786.

As a fellow British colony, Australia has been closely involved in defence arrangements with Malaysia for more than 60 years.

Australian defence forces were involved in the so-called Malayan Emergency between 1948 and 1960 and then fought in Malaya in World War Two.

The Malayan Emergency was a guerrilla war fought by the Malayan National Liberation Army, the military arm of the Malayan Communist Party, against Commonwealth armed forces. Back then Malaya was still a British colony.

The Malayan Communist party, rather understandably, believed this to be a fight for liberation against the British colonial domination of Malaya, especially the British corporate domination of the Malayan economy in the critical tin mining and rubber sectors. Britain ended its colonial domination in 1957.

After this handover Australian troops remained based in Malaysia. They are still there today, in Butterworth, an air base close to Penang, though as part of a dramatically reduced Australian force that is now part of the Five Power Defence Arrangements.

These historical ties and a shared back-story—along with the English language being widespread—mean that friendships can be deeper with Malaysian people, not just the expat enclave.

Andy Davison, the publisher and founder of a stable of magazines produced by the Malaysian-based The Expat Group, said that in interviews with MM2H visa holders, one of the questions asked was whether most of the interviewee's friends were locals or expats. 'In just about every case the answer was locals. That is very, very different from most other expat retirement communities elsewhere in the world,' said Andy.

'Language is a factor but so is attitude,' he added. 'The Malaysian locals are happy to be friends with expats. For example, Singaporeans are much less keen to make friends with foreigners and in Japan they have no interest in you whatsoever.'

One of Malaysia's unique characteristics is that it has a complicated yet relatively peaceful mix of religions, cultures and ethnicities.

Yes, it is an Islamic country. Malaysia, however, is tolerant of other religions and cultures and the rule of law is based on English common law. And Islam in Malaysia is moderate, although less so than it was 20 years ago. The constitution of Malaysia, however, provides for a unique dual justice system—the secular laws (criminal and civil common laws) and sharia laws. Sharia law plays a smaller part in the Malaysian legal system and only applies to Muslims.

So Malaysia is undoubtedly a very comfortable place for Australians to live yet, surprisingly, few have so far retired there. Malaysia has been off the Australian tourist radar for the past twenty or more years. Bali and Thailand have dominated, and more recently Cambodia, Vietnam and Laos.

According to Andy, where people have worked in Asia also affects their decision to move there. 'No one worked in Malaysia in the 1970s and 80s,' he said.

Andy explained that there are three broad expatriate groups that have moved to Malaysia: 'First, are the people who like the fact they can spend extended periods here and also enjoy the tax benefits. A lot of Japanese, for example, just come here for extended periods. They don't live here.

'The second group actually relocates here. Of these the largest nationality is the British.

'The third group is doing it because of problems in their own country. Chinese, Indonesians, South Africans and Iranians, for example. Many are not sure they are going to move here. They just want to know that they have the option to do so if it is necessary.

'Also some come here to get their kids educated. Koreans predominate, and often the father is still working in Korea while the mother is on a MM2H visa.'

And the visa story for foreigners wanting to live in Malaysia is very friendly, indeed, with the MM2H primarily targeted at retirees. (See Appendix for more information on visas.)

The most popular locations for expats are Penang and KL. About 40 per cent of the total Malaysian expatriate population live in each. Sabah, one of two Malaysian states on the island once known as Borneo, has about 5 per cent.

'Sabah is a very attractive state but a bit remote,' said Andy.

Sabah has authority for its own immigration, so you have to get your MM2H visa from that state. Likewise, if you are moving to Sarawak, the other Malaysian state on Borneo, you must apply for a visa from the state of Sarawak.

There is no official record of where expats are located. However, Andy said: 'There are around 16 000 expats on the MM2H visa—no one knows how many actually live here, but I would guess 2000.'

He maintains that the major factors that make retirement more attractive in Malaysia are the much lower cost of living and low crime rates, as well as the fact that older people get treated with more respect in Asia than they do in Western countries.

'Also the infrastructure, language, lifestyle and quality of life makes Malaysia a very Western Asian country,' Andy said. 'It is "Asia-light", if you like.'

Malaysia is undoubtedly a very comfortable place for Australians to live.

Yes, it is an Islamic country. Malaysia, however, is tolerant of other religions and cultures and the rule of law is based on English common law. And Islam in Malaysia is moderate, although less so than it was 20 years ago.

All of these western friendly characteristics are clearly evident in the city of Kuala Lumpur, the country's capital and home to about 2 million people. Greater Kuala Lumpur is home to about 7 million.

This city is the economic, political and cultural hub of the nation. It has none of the sleaziness of Bangkok but then neither is it as cutting edge socially and culturally.

Nor is KL as international as Bangkok. It is also not as important as Singapore as a trading and commercial hub. But it is an easy and comfortable place when compared to most other bustling Southeast Asian cities. The road infrastructure in Kuala Lumpur and most of Malaysia is first world. Kuala Lumpur is a picture of calm and western orderliness compared to Jakarta, Saigon and Bangkok.

Kuala Lumpur is also a very easy place to base yourself for travel throughout the region. The discount airline AirAsia is based there and a large new AirAsia terminal opened in 2014.

The political system in Malaysia has been, over the past few decades, more of a pretend democracy than a working democracy. The media is under close government control and opposition parties and leaders are often attacked by a compliant judiciary. In these ways it is very similar to Singapore, although perhaps not quite as undemocratic.

Malaysia, like Australia, being an ex-colony of Britain, is left with the legacies of British values and culture. A tell-tale sign of this is the very English accent of many Malay newsreaders.

The KL suburbs spread out from its hectic centre and many suburbs have a very Australian-bungalow feel to them.

We went for a BBQ one Sunday to a Malaysian family's home in Bangsar. Bangsar is in 'the burbs' and you could have been in the backyard of a house in suburban Brisbane.

The family also reflected the cultural mix and the linkages with Australia. The mother was Australian, father Indian Muslim—a civil engineer who had studied in Melbourne—and the son was a history graduate from the University of Queensland.

Architecturally in Kuala Lumpur there is a broad mix of British colonial, traditional Asian and Islamic styles.

The shopping is good and the bar areas around Bukit Bintang, and other spots, get a real buzz happening, especially on Friday and Saturday evenings. And, of course, as always in Malaysia, the food is superb with an extraordinary choice of restaurants.

Standout destinations—Penang, Ipoh and Kuala Lumpur

As far as we are concerned, there are three standout locations in Malaysia for the Aussie retiree or escapee—Ipoh, Penang and Kuala Lumpur. However, Johor, down the south of Malaysia close to Singapore, is a rapidly developing area. This could be a future region of interest for expats, especially as you can drive into Singapore for a weekend. The same applies to the old Portuguese trading town of Malacca on the south-west coast of the mainland, which is increasing in popularity but still an uncommon location for foreigners, and the island of Langkawi, north of Penang.

Each has its advantages and disadvantages. Ipoh, for example, is much cheaper than the capital or Penang—but you have to be prepared to be a trailblazer if you are going to settle there.

Ipoh

Ipoh is an old tin-mining centre and it nestles between the Cameron Highlands and the coast, less than three hours drive north of Kuala Lumpur. It's an excellent freeway, too.

Leafy poincianas hang across the main road as you enter the town from KL. The median strips are all planted with tropical plants like red cordylines and heliconias. A small river winds through the town, with bars and restaurants on its banks. Above the town are the misty mountains of the Cameron Highlands. Thunderstorms waft through of an afternoon. There are massive rainbows. This truly is an evocative place.

We sat in an apartment in Ipoh one afternoon, looking out towards the Cameron Highlands as grey clouds, lightning and thunder marched towards us. The temperature fell and the tea tasted good.

The apartment was owned by two Australians, Jack and Olga, who visit regularly. Jack, a principal of an Australian engineering group, lived in Ipoh when tin was still mined in the early 1970s and fell in love with it then. He tells of how friends would gather in the evening in his upstairs sitting room, drinking cold beers under the swirling ceiling fans. Often bats would fly into the room so they'd throw open the shutters and crank up the fans to get rid of them.

They bought this three bedroom, three bathroom apartment for A$90 000 about ten years ago and it's not worth much more today. And there is parking and a pleasant pool as well.

They spend a month or two a year here. They are very well-off and can afford several houses. But, our guess is that if they were doing it very tough and those retirement dollars were fast disappearing in Australia, then they'd be living in Ipoh.

And why not? The town has touches of old Malaysia. It is green and leafy, accommodation is cheap and plentiful, and the food is to die for. Ipoh has arguably the best food in Asia and is known for the quality of its coffee. The fruit from the markets—mangoes, pawpaws, pomelos—is extraordinary.

Coffee houses dot the town. But these are not what we know as coffee houses. These are traditional Asian-style eating areas—often open-air, with the seating area surrounded by a wondrous array of food stalls. You wander about choosing whatever you desire—satays, noodles, curries, laksa, fish and any number of local specialties. It is exotic and delicious and cheap—each dish costs a little over A$1.

And you can get a cold beer as well—though at almost A$2, alcohol is 'up there' in price in Malaysia.

There are few Europeans in Ipoh. It is primarily a Chinese town—and some mega-rich Chinese live there. It is where the giant property development group, Ipoh Gardens, developer of Sydney's Queen Victoria Building, began; and an Ipoh family owns the cosmetics group Crabtree and Evelyn.

Ipoh was once very grand and rich. Many of the local families sent their children to English public schools and English universities, such as Oxford and Cambridge. The Chinese families followed the English colonial tradition of doing this. A lot of the descendants of these tin-mining families have two home bases—often one in Australia and one in Ipoh. The inherited wealth is still there, though perhaps a little faded. The decaying grandeur of the 120-year-old sprawling white-walled Ipoh Club, with spacious verandahs and frangipani-filled gardens, tells the story of Ipoh's wealthy, colonial past. The club, which is in the heart of town, looks out over its acres of manicured cricket pitch and sporting grounds.

Ipoh has arguably the best food in Asia and is known for the quality of its coffee. The fruit from the markets— mangoes and pawpaws and pomelos—is extraordinary.

Even today, when sipping on an afternoon gin and tonic on the verandah of the club, you can almost see the English ghosts in their cricket whites, playing out there on the pitch in the tropical heat, clapping a four or cheering the fall of a wicket; the days of the Raj—Malaysia style.

But while the Ipoh Club was once the exclusive bastion of British snobbery, today it is easy to become a member. And the board, once English, is now dominated by Indian Malays. Once the second administrative capital after Kuala Lumpur in colonial days, Ipoh is now a city of contrasts. The grand architecture of the Ipoh Club, railway station, the town hall and law courts contrast to the many shophouses that remain unrestored throughout the city. This rich tapestry of Chinese immigration and English colonialism contrasts with the newly developed areas, like Greentown. Rambling colonial houses with, typically, a large upstairs sitting room surrounded by shuttered windows overhanging the portico where the cars pull up to deliver guests, contrast to the more modern apartment blocks and older, poorer accommodation of some Chinese, Malays and Indians.

And there's a lot to do. The coast and islands are easily accessible for a weekend break and, as mentioned, the city sits below the Cameron Highlands, Malaysia's most famous highland destination. The mountains have a cooler climate and are scattered with vegetable, strawberry and tea farms. It is a very popular location for trekking, being both picturesque and safe.

All of which makes Ipoh a great tree-change alternative. Our tip is that Ipoh will become very popular with Australian retirees in the future—attracted by the elegant but cheap lifestyle and the certainty of the Malaysian MM2H visa system.

Penang

Penang is a large island off the north-west tip of Malaysia and linked to the mainland by two long bridges. It's about two hours drive from Ipoh, and about five hours from the capital.

If we had to choose a location to retire in, Penang is our pick right now.

Penang is like a less-crowded, less-congested and greener Hong Kong. It is filled with British colonial legacies; the power architecture of the Empire. Grand, bright white, ex-British government buildings stretch out behind massive Greek ionic columns. The old High Court building is perhaps a standout testament to colonial power.

But then surrounding these colonial icons is a maze of narrow streets filled with cafes, restaurants, shophouses, galleries and boutique hotels.

These colonial and local ingredients are then thrown into a wok, stir-fried with an exotic mix of Chinese, Indian and Malay cultures and garnished with Buddhism, Hinduism, Islam and Christianity. The result is a surprisingly peaceful but fascinatingly tasteful dish.

Shophouses dot Georgetown, which is the CBD and main town on the island. Timber-louvered upstairs windows, or *jalousies*, often painted white, bright yellow or turquoise blue, give the place a tropical

Euro feel. Unlike the ultra-cleansed Singapore, these shophouses were not demolished to make way for modernity—Penang had the land to expand outwards and development was slower.

And, critically, Georgetown was heritage-listed by UNESCO in July 2008. That was about 220 years after Penang became a 'British possession'. It was initially ceded to the British East India Company in 1786 and remained a British colony until independence and the Federation of Malaya was created in 1957.

Georgetown today still has a lot of rough edges. Most of the small winding streets lack footpaths; many drains are open and you get a good whiff every now and then. There are a lot of rundown properties and cheap boarding houses. But all this gives the place authenticity and romance.

You get a real sense of discovery walking the streets of Penang. And it's safe, too.

Another important point in Penang's favour is its strong Australian links over the past 50 years. The RAAF Air Base at Butterworth is just nearby on the mainland and over the years, until it was handed to the Royal Malaysia Air Force in 1988, it has been home to thousands of Australians. Many of these air force staff based themselves in Penang and commuted to work at the air base—many still do.

In fact, Georgetown suburbs like Tanjung Bungah were developed by the Australian Defence Force. These ex-RAAF areas are very expat-friendly and offer large comfortable homes with gardens, all close to central Georgetown.

Josh and Kendal and their eleven-year-old daughter live in Tanjung Bungah. They are escapees from the Aussie rat-race—having just 'up and left' Australia three years ago.

Kendal said, 'We were nearly 50 and we hadn't really been anywhere. We had been in Australia most of our lives.'

'We were a bit restless, a bit jaded,' Josh added. 'We were thinking, "Is this all there is? There has got to be more to life." We wanted to travel. We wanted to see the world.'

And then, of course, there's always that bottle of red that can be a great life-changer.

'Some friends who were living in Coffs Harbour were having dinner at our place one night,' said Kendal. 'They were about to

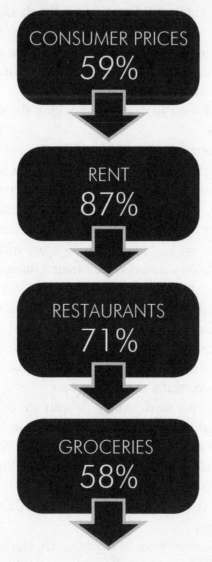

Cost of Living

INDICES

PENANG LOWER THAN SYDNEY

CONSUMER PRICES
59%

RENT
87%

RESTAURANTS
71%

GROCERIES
58%

Source: numbeo.com

Sell Up, Pack Up and Take Off

move to KL to explore options for their own personal development. He was in his 60s and his wife a few years younger. They wanted to expand their horizons. We talked about it over a few bottles of red, they told us of their plans and we told them how stale we felt, and they said, "Why don't you think about doing the same thing?"'

Josh and Kendal's only concern at the time was the education of their daughter, Pip. But they looked into the options—and found that excellent schooling was available. 'We decided our daughter was young enough to move, before she started high school,' Kendal said. 'And so we just thought, "It's now or never—let's give it a go."'

And they did.

The family sold most of their stuff before leaving Australia. They didn't know where they were going to live and had just one visit to Malaysia—'a super-fast reccy'—before choosing Penang.

Now they live in a huge two-storey house with four bedrooms, three bathrooms, a big kitchen and a garden. (And they have a dog and two cats.) All this for A$200 a week in rent. To buy the house would cost about A$600 000, though Josh and Kendal have neither the funds nor the interest to buy.

The MM2H visa, aimed at retirees, doesn't suit Josh and Kendal as they still need to work. So instead they have a visa for guardians, renewable annually, as their daughter is a student at a school in Penang, which according to Josh and Kendal is an excellent private school.

After two years, however, Josh and Kendal are running thin on funds and need to get jobs fast—and it has to be said that this isn't easy for expatriates in a relatively highly skilled, but low paid, environment like Malaysia. Josh and Kendal are hoping to set up a public relations business, and Penang certainly has plenty to promote with jazz festivals, Tropfest, booming tourism, cruise ships constantly in and out of the port, and the annual Georgetown Arts and Entertainment Festival.

UK-born Judith is one of those international citizens who has lived all over the world—in South America, South Africa, Australia and Spain. She stopped working at 38 when she married. Tragically, her first husband died, then she later lost another partner. Having left the UK at the age of 21, Judith has never considered returning there to live.

'I hate it,' she said. 'Can't stand the place, the people, the weather. It is very conservative. I don't know. I just don't get on with the UK, really. I'd rather be in Australia to be honest. I think I should have been born there.'

Judith moved to Malaysia in 2007—but it all happened a bit quicker than she expected. This was because her MM2H visa was surprisingly easy to obtain.

She explained: 'I didn't use an immigration agent. I just emailed the Malaysian government and said that I fancy becoming a resident and joining the MM2H so "What do I have to do?"

'They emailed back and said they needed a copy of my passport, details of my income and proof of medical insurance. These had to be approved [certified] by a notary. And then I sent it all off.

'Not long afterwards I received a letter saying, "Here's your visa. You have six months to activate this." Well, I panicked! I needed to get over to Malaysia, put money in a bank account, attend a medical exam in KL and then the visa was instant. It took me less than seven days to make it all happen.'

But then, Judith was faced with another problem—where to live.

'It had been years since I had-been to Malaysia. I didn't know where to live. I looked in KL, in suburbs, talked to people. It was a bit daunting, really. Norwegian friends, for example, were living on the top floor of a complex in Times Square, in the Golden Triangle, the centre of KL. But it was so busy, and I'm a country girl.'

Penang is like a less crowded, less congested and greener Hong Kong. It is filled with British colonial legacies; the power architecture of the Empire.

So Judith gave up on KL. She hired a car and drove around Malaysia. She was keen on the island of Langkawi, about 120 kilometres north of Penang. She spoke to people there and discovered it was very quiet and she knew it was going to be a solitary and isolated

Cost of Living

Sydney vs Penang [% lower than Sydney]

Housing

Rent–3 bed'm apartment city centre*	$4,276		$608	86%
Rent–3 bed'm apartment outside city centre*	$2,815		$248	91%
Buy–apartment per sqm city centre	$9,795		$2,041	79%

Food

Bread	$3.47		$0.93	73%
Eggs	$4.13		$1.58	62%
Chicken breasts	$10.78		$2.71	75%
Tomatoes	$5.17		$1.43	72%

Restaurants

| Mid range meal for 2 | $80 | | $19.84 | 75% |
| Inexpensive | $15 | | $1.98 | 87% |

Beer

| Domestic | $4.80 | | $4.10 | 15% |

Taxi

| Per km | $3 | | $0.83 | 72% |
| One hour standby | $54.16 | | $6.64 | 88% |

Electricity

| Electricity, heating, water, garbage* | $238.97 | | $59.12 | 75% |

Communications

| Internet* | $61.66 | | $48.80 | 21% |
| Mobile phone (per min prepaid) | $1.02 | | $0.07 | 93% |

* per month

Source: numbeo.com

lifestyle. It would take about three hours to get to Penang by boat, or a couple of hours by car and ferry.

'It is lovely,' Judith said. 'A tourist island with nice beaches. Beaches in Penang are not so good. Langkawi is a great place to visit, but I realised that living there would be very different. If I got sick I'd have to come to Penang.'

And so Judith finished up in Penang, where she has been renting property since 2010; however, despite the suddenness of her arrival, she has wisely taken her time to settle in. 'I initially did not live here. I had my MM2H. I visited, sorted myself out first,' Judith said.

'It is very, very busy in Penang, but it's growing on me. I'm not sure if I'll live here for the rest of my life—the traffic drives me crazy—but I'm liking it more and more because it's so interesting. There are a huge number of cultures and religions here.

'I like the people, the food is good. There's lots to do. I joined the International Women's Association. It's a good way to meet people. I'm not very gregarious and it is not easy for a single person. But they have everything: majong, canaster, mingles, dinners, film nights.'

Judith added, 'Life here in Penang is very transient. It is very levelling being an expat but I don't regret doing it.'

For Australians, adaptation to Malaysia may not be as levelling as Judith found. Bob, our man with the spreadsheet, has, of course, taken a good look at the expat factor.

He said, 'You are living on an island of about 700 000 people, but it's more like living in a village with a smaller population. I have done the math two or three different ways, and I get to around about the same number each time—I reckon 1500 to 2000 is the total Western expat population of Penang. That community is incredibly interconnected.

'There is a downside to it. They all go to the same dry-cleaners, the same bars, the same shopping malls, the same book nights. They're all in the same clubs.'

There is also an upside, Bob said: 'If we really tried hard, tomorrow night we could have a dinner party containing the following demographics: a professional chef, a woman who runs a modelling agency, an orchestra conductor, the commanding officer of Butterworth, some security experts, a chaplain, even a jockey. We are swimming in an incredibly rich social pool—I never mixed with these people in Sydney or Melbourne.'

Bob added frankly, as only he could, 'And for me that is one of the biggest disadvantages of places like Thailand because—now maybe I am being elitist here—I just don't think a sex tourist would be much fun as a dinner companion.'

Australians have also been involved with the recent renewal of Penang. Karl Steinberg and Christopher Ong—well known for their (now sold) Galle Fort hotel in Sri Lanka—have developed a number of restaurants and boutique hotels in Georgetown. Muntri Mews, once an old stable for rickshaws, carriages and carts, is now a 'flashpackers', with a small cafe tucked into a wonderfully tropical garden; as is Noordin Mews, which has a pool as well. Their newest development is the luxurious and romantic Seven Terraces boutique hotel and restaurant: a line of converted shophouses.

Another Australian, Narelle McMurtrie, a resident for more than twenty years, has developed two hotels—Bon Ton and Temple Tree Langkawi on Langkawi Island. In Penang, she has developed China House—a restaurant, coffee shop and gallery. She has also developed a boutique hotel called Straits Collection. These businesses, like Seven Terraces, are located in restored shophouses.

Cost of living—a great attraction

Penang, and indeed most of Malaysia, is relatively more Western than other parts of Southeast Asia. As Grant, a middle-aged Australian who is teaching in Penang said, 'It is easy Asia—99.9 per cent of the people speak English. And it is cheap, laid-back, relaxed.'

However, the flipside is that Penang is not as cheap as many other parts of Asia. Even so, it is still a lot cheaper than Australia.

Rent is more than 80 per cent lower than in Sydney, restaurants almost 70 per cent less and groceries almost 60 per cent cheaper. Your dollar goes a lot further in Penang than in Sydney, that's for sure.

Grant's wife, Fiona, commutes to work in Australia for month-long stints. Recently, though, she took ten months off—long-service leave on half pay—which worked out to be what her pension would be if she retired. She managed to live well.

'Internet is so cheap here,' she said. 'It costs A$20 a month unlimited download. The phone costs A$18.50 a month.' Fiona added that landline calls are 'dirt cheap' and an hour on the phone to her parents in Australia costs about A$1.50; however, she warned, 'Mobile to mobile is expensive'.

For Fiona and Grant, the decision to live in Malaysia was very much about lifestyle as they are both keen divers. They regularly dive off the islands of Langkawi, but also travel to the Perhentian Islands off the east coast, which is a six-hour drive from Penang. 'It is the most glorious place—the water is so blue,' Fiona said. 'It is so cheap. We can say to family in Australia, "Come here and we'll go to the Perhentians, we can have a shack on the beach, hammocks between palm trees."'

At home in Penang, they shop at the wet (food) markets for fresh produce. 'There is no bargaining. It is set price—not a foreigner's price—but very cheap,' said Fiona.

'All fruit and vegies for the week cost us less than A$18 for a family of four,' said Grant. 'You can get pork, chicken and fish there. We can buy chicken fillets to feed the family for less than A$4. A Chinese dinner at a local restaurant for all of us will cost about A$20, with soft drinks.'

One thing that is expensive is cars, especially if you buy an imported car. Local cars, though, are still reasonable. Grant just bought a locally manufactured, seven-seater, manual people-mover, which cost about A$20 000.

Property

It's always wise to initially rent a property in a foreign country before buying. This is especially so if rents are low in relation to purchase prices, as they are in Malaysia.

The rental market
There is very good value for money when you rent in Malaysia.

Look at Bob and Marion's deal. In Penang, they are renting a luxurious, massive, five-bedroom apartment, with a pool and gym in the complex, for A$550 a week. This apartment would cost more than A$1 million to buy, so the gross return on it, as an investment, is very poor at just 2.85 per cent.

For a retiree, of course, A$550 a week is a large amount, especially if the plan is to leave Australia to spend less but live better. Bob and Marion's place is, however, on the five-star end of the scale—for those with more modest needs, there's even better news.

Rent in Kuala Lumpur for a comfortable, furnished two-bedroom, two-bathroom apartment, with parking, starts from A$100 a week. It goes up from there, and a luxury apartment costs about A$450 a week.

A very comfortable and large three-bedroom, two-bathroom furnished apartment in an upmarket area of Penang, such as Gurney Park, virtually on the water and close to Georgetown, rents for less than A$200 a week. For the same amount you can get a four-bedroom family house with a garden in one of the ex-RAAF suburbs. Or you can get a three-bedroom, two-bathroom apartment near the beach at Batu Ferringhi in Penang for A$125 a week.

Ipoh is even cheaper. You can rent a spacious apartment with three bedrooms, two bathrooms plus ensuite, parking and views over the Cameron Highlands, for A$100 a week. You could buy this apartment for less than A$90 000.

> Penang, and indeed most of Malaysia, is relatively more western. Compared to Cambodia or Vietnam or even parts of Thailand it is 'Asia-easy.'

Purchasing property in Malaysia

Non-residents are allowed to purchase residential and commercial property in Malaysia, although with some restrictions.

All purchasers are subject to restrictions on Malay Reserve Lands and properties allocated for Bumiputras (ethnic Malays). There is a minimum investment value of A$170 000 (RM500 000) for property purchases but this can vary by state.

In Penang, for example, the state government has raised the floor price of property for foreign buyers from A$170 000 (RM500 000) to A$340 000 (RM1 million). This applies to all types of property in the state. In addition, foreigners who wish to own landed property on the island will have to meet a A$700 000 (RM2 million) minimum purchase price.

Craig and Fiona have done well out of Penang property. They bought a ten-year-old penthouse that has eight bedrooms, six bathrooms and overlooks the water. The living area is massive with 20-foot windows. They paid A$200 000 in 2010, just before a property boom. The condominium next door is now selling for A$510 000.

For around A$300 000 you can buy a very pleasant three-bedroom, two-bathroom apartment in KL and Penang. For that price in Ipoh, you can purchase a luxury apartment or a house.

Malaysia land law is based on the Australian Torrens System. The rights of foreign investors to own and possess property and to seek legal redress in the courts are rights guaranteed under these laws.

From 1 January 2010, the effective tax rate on disposal of property is 5 per cent subject to the provisions of the *Real Property Tax Gains Act 1976*. No tax is imposed on profits if the property is disposed of after five or more years of ownership. Or at least, that was the case at the time of writing this book. Laws are forever changing, especially tax laws.

Bank Negara Malaysia, the national bank, does not impose any restrictions on the repatriation of profits, rental or proceeds from divestment of investments in Malaysia by a non-resident. There is no withholding tax on property disposal and no inheritance tax. However, investors may have to pay tax on earnings depending on their place of residence and income tax band. (For more information, see Chapter 9: Taxation.)

> Non-residents are allowed to purchase residential and commercial property in Malaysia, although with some restrictions.

Medical services

One of the great attractions of Malaysia for those over 55 years of age is the country's excellent medical services and facilities.

Like Thailand, Malaysia is a destination for medical tourism. There are more than 70 flights a week from Medan in Indonesia to Penang alone, and much of this is driven by the Indonesian need for good medical services.

> One of the great attractions of Malaysia for those over 55 years of age is the country's excellent medical services and facilities.
>
> Like Thailand, Malaysia is a destination for medical tourism.

In Penang, Kendal and her family have no medical insurance. She explained: 'We cancelled our health insurance. Most expats don't worry about health insurance unless their company pays for it.

'The medical care is very good. Most medical staff are internationally qualified. The dentists are excellent and cheap.

'You can just walk into a GP, no appointment. For us, appointment plus antibiotics costs about A$25. At pharmacists here, you can get everything you need over the counter.

'We have not heard of any medical horror stories here. There are apparently nine hospitals on the island. It is now the medical tourism hotspot. Cosmetic surgery is big.'

Kendal and the family are under 55 years of age and so that explains some of their reluctance to pay up for private health cover. But Ellen, in Kuala Lumpur, is 67 and she also said she doesn't bother with medical insurance.

Ellen explained that people over 65 can't get insurance cover in Malaysia (see Chapter 10: Health insurance). But, according to Ellen, the standard of medical service is excellent and the costs are reasonable so 'I am quite prepared to wear that'.

She pointed out that medical treatment may cost hundreds of thousands in Australia without health cover, but in Malaysia it would cost tens of thousands. 'I take that into account. I know that I need to have enough money to cover high medical bills if I get really ill,' she said.

However, this is the high-risk approach. What if you have an accident or a serious illness? One option is to go to Singapore, only about four hours drive from KL, or return to Australia—both of which will cost you plenty when you get there. Our advice is to always have private health cover if you can afford it, at least until you're settled into your new country and know what medical services are available.

MALAYSIA TIPS AND TRAPS

1. Health care in Malaysia, like Thailand, is cheap and excellent. You could confidently use the local medical facilities and services, and Singapore is nearby as well. But remember, it always pays to have health insurance.

2. Malaysia is marketing itself to foreigners and that includes international retirees. It offers a specific visa type—Malaysia My Second Home (MM2H). You need proof of liquid assets (cash on deposit) of at least RM350 000 (A$120 000) and an income of at least RM10 000 (A$3400) a month if you are over 50. It is slightly higher for the under-50s. Don't forget that visa applications must be made separately to the Sabah and Sarawak state governments.

3. Malaysians are very Eurocentric. This partly results from the country's long colonial history and because its independence from Britain was only gained in 1957.

4. Malaysia is 'Asia-easy'. But there are still traps for the naive if you are in the wrong place at the wrong time. Simply be sensible.

5. Malaysia, like Indonesia, is a Muslim country. But, like Indonesia, it is moderate Islam and there is no need for Western women to wear a head scarf.

6. There are numerous good places for retirees to live—Ipoh, Penang, KL, Johor, Malacca, and the more exotic Sabah and Sarawak—and the excellent road system in Malaysia makes it easy to drive about the country. All of these destinations

have their advantages and disadvantages so it pays to visit a few to get an idea of what best suits you.

7. Rents are significantly cheaper—around 80 per cent less—in Malaysia than in Sydney. And this makes the 'always safer' option of renting in a foreign country very attractive.

8. Apartments, houses, villas and land can be purchased by foreigners in Malaysia. There are few restrictions and title is relatively clean. But be careful. You are spending a lot of money in a country you do not know that well. Ensure you have excellent legal representation.

CHAPTER 4

Vietnam

Vietnam has a special place in the hearts of many Australians and none more so than the baby boomer generation—the generation that is now moving into retirement.

Many boomers were conscripted to fight in the war that raged during the 1960s and up until 1972 when Gough Whitlam pulled out the last remaining Australian troops. Others were regular soldiers who served in Vietnam as part of their military duties.

And then, there were those who refused to register for conscription and there were conscientious objectors as well. And there were hundreds of thousands who had marched the streets of cities and towns in protest against that war. For many, it was their first ever protest. It was also the first time that some had even questioned the actions of government.

Vietnam, or at least the war in Vietnam, politicised and shaped a generation. It radicalised many and dramatically altered the lives of those who were dragged into that war as soldiers. For some of these men, it was their first exposure to a world beyond the borders of the Australian continent.

Ian, who served as a regular soldier in the Vietnam War said, 'We were nineteen-year-old kids. Everything was new and different. We had eyes as big as dinner plates. Before the war, if someone put a map in front of me, I doubt if I could have said where Vietnam was. But those turned out to be the most formative years of my life.'

'In Australia I was just existing, existing. And getting old. Getting old very quickly...I was existing in Australia but when I got over here the last piece of the jigsaw puzzle, that I didn't know was missing, fell into place—it was just Vietnam.'

And therein lies the magnetism of Vietnam, most especially for veterans of the war.

Howard returned to live in Vietnam about a decade ago. He could never really readjust to life in Australia after the war where he fought as a member of the regular Australian infantry.

Like many young soldiers in the 1960s, Howard had a pretty tough upbringing. He joined the army because, he said, 'My mother was a bit mad.' They were just kids, seventeen or eighteen years old, the army was their education.

After the war, some soldiers, like Howard, felt let down by the Australian government and senior army officers because, as he said, the troops were told it was a war against an aggressive Communist north and it was a cause that needed to be fought.

But Howard soon realised, 'There was this huge disconnect between what we were told about the downward thrust of Communist expansion and what really happened. And a big disconnect between what our leadership in the army told us and what was actually going on.'

Also back at home, there were many residual traumas for the war veterans to confront, most often alone, as they struggled to fit back into Australian society.

'I really didn't appreciate it but I'd been pretty badly affected by my Vietnam War experience all my life,' Howard said.

He told us about the night before he was wounded, when he was drinking in a bar at the Australian base of Nui Dat, north of Vung Tau. This is how he recalled what happened:

'The bar normally closed about eight o'clock. We were all drinking and I was getting my shout. I was standing at the bar, waiting to be served and then this orderly corporal walked in and said, "Right, the bar's closed."

I said, "Hang on, Corporal, I've been standing here for ten minutes and I just want to get one shout."

'And he says, "I said the fuckin' bar's closed and that's it."

'So I said, "Well, you can get fucked, you bastard." And those were the last words I said to him.

'One morning we get up, get ready, get in the "tracks" [troop carriers] and we go all the way down to an area . . . (south of Nui Dat where we begin an operation). We walk into this lovely grove of trees and then—*bang*—the corporal's dead. He was one of three people killed in the (landmine) explosion.' Howard was wounded by shrapnel from that same landmine.

The corporal had six children and was on his second tour of Vietnam. He had survived his first tour but, according to Howard, went back to Vietnam so that he could earn money for his family. His death shocked Howard to the core.

'I thought, "Jesus, you can have all the plans in the world but it is so easy just to step over that line. And then your plans mean nothing." I mean, you can hold back from doing something now, thinking you can do it in the future, and then you can be dead tomorrow.'

It was these sort of traumas that continued to haunt Howard back in Australia after the war. 'So I sort of went on this crazy lifestyle . . . You know, I lived a pretty edgy sort of life. The 80s in Sydney were bad enough as it was. Drugs and alcohol, broken relationships and all that shit. I jumped out of aircraft and did all this sort of stuff for kicks. And I was working shifts at the ABC, getting up at four, five o'clock in the morning, going to work, then going out at night . . . it was just terrible.

'I was pretty dysfunctional. I didn't make friends. I didn't play with people well. I never got very close to anyone. I had no social skills because I had all these sort of weird things I'd learned in the army. Oh, you know, it was awful . . .'

Howard paused to chuckle, shake his head and look down at the table before continuing his story.

'I was breaking down a bit physically. It took me a while to get the TPI [totally and permanently incapacitated] pension. I really didn't want to retire . . . but I did anyway. And, well, it's been the best thing that's ever happened.'

Howard came back to Vietnam, married a Vietnamese woman and now has a young son—his only child—although he was previously married in Australia in the 1980s. He lives in a town of about 50 000 people north of Ho Chi Minh City (previously called Saigon), where he is the only foreigner. When he was in the army, he learnt to speak Vietnamese so he is not isolated by language.

'It's a country town. No condos. No foreigners. We built a house. It cost me about A\$25 000. It's basic but very convenient. It is 26 metres long and 5.5 metres wide. There are three bedrooms. It has a lounge room, a kitchen area and a utility area at the back. It's surrounded by a fence and there are no security issues. I bought the land off my wife's brother. She has eight siblings.'

'And I thought, "Jesus, you can have all the plans in the world but it is so easy just to step over that line. And your plans mean nothing, they mean nothing." I mean you can hold back from doing stuff to do something for the future and you can be dead.

Howard often takes visitors of all types, including veterans, on motor scooter tours through Saigon, or on longer tours through the countryside and the old areas of Australian involvement in the Vietnam War, especially around Nui Dat and Vung Tau. He speaks Vietnamese fluently and has a deep knowledge of the political history of the war and Vietnam post-war; it is with real passion that he talks about the country where he lives.

And why not? For many Australians, and not just war veterans, Vietnam offers a very attractive and cheap alternative to life in Australia. And it offers the chance to enjoy a new life, whether it's for a year or forever.

Ho Chi Minh City (Saigon)

There are stories around every corner of Ho Chi Minh. The city is rich with the history of the struggle of the Vietnamese against the French, American, Australian, New Zealand, Korean and other foreign armies.

At one intersection sits a massive statue of Thich Quang Duc. This is the place where in 1963 the Buddhist monk set himself ablaze in protest against the persecution of Buddhists by the South Vietnamese Government. That was the first of many tragic self-immolations.

Ho Chi Minh City has just so many hidden intrigues. There is the street where there was a riot in March 1950 when two US war ships came into port. The Vietnamese story is that 500 000 people rioted for three hours. The important issue is the political back-story. It meant American intervention in the French war in Indo-China. And indeed, in May 1950, Truman started to commit materiel to the French in Vietnam. By the end of the French war in 1954 the US was underwriting it by 75 to 80 per cent.

The French colonial legacy is clearly evident. There is the old Cercle Sportif—the former French Club, downtown. In Lam Son Square, previously called Place Garnier, in the centre of town is the former Opera House, built by the French in the late nineteenth century. This is now the Municipal Theatre. But between 1955 and 1975 it housed the Lower House of the State of Vietnam.

Lam Son Square is where a bomb was exploded—as written about by Graham Greene in the *Quiet American*—by a Vietnamese right winger, aimed to increase US involvement.

The Rex Hotel, Caravelle Hotel and the Hotel Continental are also on this square. It is easy to picture French planters back in the early 1900s drinking wine and smoking Gauloise in the sidewalk cafes of these hotels as the cyclos carry about beautiful Vietnamese girls in their tight, silk, long dresses (ao dia).

Also on the Square was the building (now demolished) where, during the Vietnam War, the 'Five O'Clock Follies' were held. This was the derogatory name given by journalists to the press briefings held by the US military.

Ubud, Indonesia. The laneway leading to the home of former Sydneysiders, Geoffrey and Michael.

Ubud, Indonesia.
Geoffrey and
Michael's home,
surrounded by water,
verdant gardens and a
pool—not bad for
A$60 000.

Phuket, Thailand. White sandy beaches dot this large island off the western coast of Thailand.

Phuket, Thailand. Glen and Sal's three-bedroom, three-bathroom house with a pool was on the market for A$200 000 in 2013. It is a short walk from the beach. A similar place in Australia would cost many millions of dollars.

(Top) Chiang Mai, Thailand. The old quarter of Chiang Mai is surrounded by this wide, centuries-old moat, bordered with trees. (Bottom) Penang, Malaysia. These shophouses have been converted into the Seven Terraces boutique hotel and restaurant.

(Top) Ho Chi Minh, Vietnam. The Hotel Continental and surrounding area was the hub of the US forces and the South Vietnamese government during the war throughout the 1960s and early 1970s. (Bottom) Vung Tau, Vietnam. This peninsula, lined with a beach on both sides, has a laid-back feel, though still has something of the old wild R&R Vietnam War about it.

(Top) Phnom Penh, Cambodia. Bars look out over the grand Mekong River, the scene of terrible hardship—yet the tropical warmth and Cambodia's attractions remain an intoxicating mix. (Bottom) Vejer de la Frontera, Spain. This hilltop village, in Andalucia, southern Spain, looks out over the ocean. Orange groves and vineyards dot the landscape and the beach is just 10 minutes' drive away.

(Top) Provence, France. Gordon and Penny's terrace is in a wine-producing region. The renovation was an absolute adventure and now they live the dream. (Bottom) French Alps. Chris and Suzanne's twelfth-century tower, called La Tour du Treuil ('The Tower of the Trellis'), dates back to 1170. They are converting the top two levels into a boutique hotel.

Cost of Living

Sydney vs Ho Chi Minh [% lower than Sydney]

Housing

Sydney		Ho Chi Minh	%
Rent–3 bed'm apartment city centre*	$4,276	$1,173	73%
Rent–3 bed'm apartment outside city centre*	$2,815	$532	81%
Buy–apartment per sqm city centre	$9,795	$1,660	83%

Food

	Sydney	Ho Chi Minh	%
Bread	$3.47	$1.05	70%
Eggs	$4.13	$1.44	65%
Chicken breasts	$10.78	$4.07	62%
Tomatoes	$5.17	$0.65	87%

Restaurants

	Sydney	Ho Chi Minh	%
Mid range meal for 2	$80	$15.39	81%
Inexpensive	$15	$3.08	79%

Beer

	Sydney	Ho Chi Minh	%
Domestic	$4.80	$0.67	86%

Taxi

	Sydney	Ho Chi Minh	%
Per km	$3	$0.72	76%
One hour standby	$54.16	$0.91	98%

Electricity

	Sydney	Ho Chi Minh	%
Electricity, heating, water, garbage*	$238.97	$56.19	76%

Communications

	Sydney	Ho Chi Minh	%
Internet*	$61.66	$15.88	74%
Mobile phone (per min prepaid)	$1.02	$0.11	89%

* per month

Source: numbeo.com

After the Follies, journalists and US military officers would adjourn to the rooftop bar of the nearby Rex Hotel—still a magnificent place for a drink, with sweeping views over the city and beyond. Howard said that battles could often be seen raging in the far distance from the rooftop of the Rex.

From the Caravelle, if you look across the Opera House and up Dong Khoi Street, you can see the twin towers of the Notre Dame Cathedral. It was along Dong Khoi Street—once called Rue Catinat—in 1975 that a North Vietnamese tank rolled down to Lam Son Square. It stopped outside the Caravelle and its turret was turned towards the Caravelle Hotel's façade. It never fired a shell.

That's the type of story that hides behind buildings and around many corners of Ho Chi Minh City.

Another infamous rooftop—of the apartment block from which US officials clambered onto a helicopter in the frantic withdrawal in 1975—is still there. The War Remnants Museum is a horrifying reminder of what foreign troops, especially the Americans and earlier the French, have done to this country.

The city resonates with its textured past, but these days it's a big and noisy place, throbbing with activity. Which is what attracts people like John, who aren't Vietnam veterans and have no previous ties with the country—instead he came in search of a more exciting life.

At the age of 62 and a barrister in Sydney, John was outwardly a successful man—but he didn't really like himself or his life much at all.

'I'd had a dysfunctional marriage that ended 25 years ago and have two adult sons who also endured the pain of family dissolution from which they have still not recovered,' John said.

And even though he always had a girlfriend, good mates, and was, as he put it, 'enjoying a reasonably successful career, making good money and living comfortably in a nice middle-class home on the northern beaches', he wasn't happy.

'I was bored. I was just representing the same type of criminals all the time, drug traffickers and the like, and it was getting to the point that I was looking for new challenges in life.'

John was also overweight. 'I was very concerned about my health,' he added.

Vietnam, or at least the war in Vietnam, politicised a generation. It was a radicalising force for many and it dramatically shaped the lives of others who were dragged into that war as soldiers.

It was the first time that many even questioned the actions of government.

Then along came what John described as 'a life-changing case'.

It was 2011 and he was representing seven airline attendants who worked for Vietnam Airlines. They had been arrested by the Australian Federal Police as they were passing through customs on their way to board their flight from Sydney to Ho Chi Minh City. They each had many iPads, iPhones and a considerable amount of cash in Australian dollars in their carry-on luggage. The police suspected these were the proceeds of crime.

John won the case, which was satisfying, but he never expected that it would change the direction of his life: 'This case resulted in me meeting many ordinary Vietnamese people and Aussie expats living in Vietnam. The airline pilots were ex-Ansett and I was invited to visit Saigon and stay for an extended holiday.'

Stale, unhappy and overweight back home in Sydney, John started to give the idea of a sabbatical a lot of thought, and decided he'd like to try it.

'My major concern was that I would become a full-time tourist, which I didn't want. So when the opportunity arose to actually undertake some work here in the profession I was trained in, albeit somewhat limited work, I grabbed it with both hands.'

Even though it wasn't the lower cost of living that inspired John to pack up and take off, it did factor into his decision. 'I'm going to try and run a little business here, but I never thought I'd make the same income as in Australia. They are two vastly different economies and Australia is far more expensive than Vietnam.

'For example, I live in a two-bedroom fully serviced and fully furnished apartment close to the centre of the city. I pay US$900 a month. And the cost of food here is so low that you can eat out every night. You live well but you don't need much income here.

'So I figured I could rent out my house in Sydney, and with income from the business, I can live on that. And if worst comes to worst, let's say I make no money at all here, I'm still in front.'

John's approach to his move was admirably planned and executed—his preparedness is a lesson to us all—but little did he know that his exciting new life was about to take another unexpected and life-changing turn.

One day he was having coffee with a business associate in Saigon and he started chatting to a Vietnamese lady at the next table. Her name was Thanh and she wanted to practise her English and saw this casual conversation as a good opportunity. Initially they didn't think much of each other. He thought she was 'a dark-skinned little Vietnamese village girl who was a bit of a fatty'. While to her, John was just old and fat.

But, Thanh said, after they'd met a few times, 'He stole my heart.'

Thanh is nearly 25, John nearly 65. Despite the age gap, they are extremely happy together. Thanh may come from a village north of Saigon, but she is no rural hick. She is in her final year of university, and the only member of her family ever to get a tertiary education—her entire extended family contributed money so she could go to university. She's also a great help to John as he tries to establish his legal practice in Ho Chi Minh City and cope with the culture and the bureaucracy. And they've both lost large amounts of weight and can no longer accuse each other of being fat!

We met John and Thanh on the rooftop of the Majestic Hotel on the Saigon River. It was built in 1925, a classic white French colonial building. It was sunset and the air was at body temperature. There were panoramic views from the rooftop bar over the city and across the river to less developed areas that, in the 1960s, were active with Vietcong soldiers.

John said that primary to his decision to move was simply the fact that he could. 'I thought, I can do anything I like. I am now at an age where I have done my job as a barrister. I am reasonably successful. I have no debt. I want to enjoy the rest of my life—what there is left of it—and I am not enjoying it in Australia.

'I admit I miss the beaches in Australia, but there's so much to do here. And I often have people just coming up to me and wanting to chat, even if it's just to practise their English.

'I walk in the park each morning. I see the same people there because I always go at the same time. Eventually, a few came over and joined me and now we walk together. Yesterday there were five of us walking and I was the only one who could speak English. Still, we were able to exchange names and have a basic conversation and, you know, it was really pleasant.'

John likes the friendliness of the local people but a characteristic he really admires is their attitude towards older generations. 'The aged have respect. Our society used to be like that. My father died at age 94 and he had always expressed the strong desire to stay at home. And he did. He died at home.' John believes that in Australian society today, respect for the elderly is fading.

Unlike other Australians who've been drawn to Vietnam by association or by cost, John said he moved both because he could and because he needed to. He needed a change and a new life.

Clearly, John now has a very new life and he is enjoying it.

Another Australian who came to Vietnam purely for the adventure was Rose, who moved to Saigon in 2012 with her partner Sam. In fact, Rose made it happen after she fell in love with 'the smell of the place'.

Rose explained: 'I had been on two holidays in Vietnam and I was struck by the place. And I had seen [the film] *The Quiet American*. There was something about Saigon (Ho Chi Minh City). It was something I wanted to experience in a deeper way. Living there was the next exciting thing I felt I could do in my life.'

In Sydney, Rose had sold a business and the children were mature and independent, so she and Sam had few ties. But at first they couldn't get past the usual hurdles: Where in Vietnam would they live? Should they buy a house or rent? What would they live on?

'A host of places would have been good to live in, like Hanoi or Hoi An, but Sam was interested in working and Saigon suited him the best. There was more going on in Saigon for him, more business, more opportunities.'

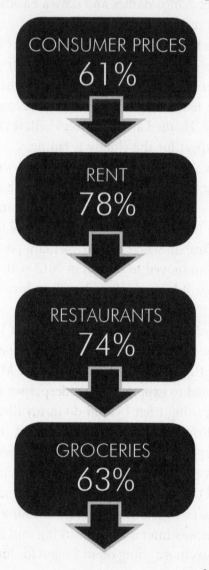

Cost of *Living*

INDICES

HO CHI MINH LOWER THAN SYDNEY

CONSUMER PRICES
61%

RENT
78%

RESTAURANTS
74%

GROCERIES
63%

Source: numbeo.com

Sell Up, Pack Up and Take Off

The couple prepared themselves extremely well. Before they moved to Vietnam they studied the Teaching English as a Second Language (TESOL) course at Sydney's Institute of Technology. It cost about A$3000 and took Rose three months part-time to complete, though it can be done intensively over one month on a full-time basis. Rose said the course was tough, and, even though she did it part-time it felt like full-time.

Her hard work and preparation paid off. Even though they were both over 60, they had little trouble finding employment in Ho Chi Minh City. Both of them immediately got jobs teaching English.

When they first moved to Vietnam, Rose and Sam stayed in a few hotels while they looked for apartments. 'We didn't know where we were going to live, what schools there were. It paid to do this as some schools and areas are pretty crumby,' Rose said.

'The choice boiled down to living in the expat area out in An Phu or living in the centre of the town in District One.

'We decided to live in an upmarket and furnished apartment in District One. It cost $A5000 a month. That is expensive in Saigon, but we had three bedrooms and three bathrooms and the apartment was very well appointed and spacious. And it was fully serviced, the reception was manned 24 hours a day, it had full concierge services, the complex had a pool, the gardens were tended, and everything we needed was close by.

'We had so much help already, but then one day a lady knocked on our door and said, "I would like to cook and clean for you." I explained that we didn't need any more help but then she told me it would only cost $150 a month, so we agreed and she was just delightful.'

Tennis courts were opposite their apartment and Rose and Sam love tennis, so they played three mornings a week with their own tennis coach. After that they would have a swim at the apartment pool.

Not that tough huh?

The markets were nearby and they loved wandering down to buy food and flowers and to practise the Vietnamese they were trying to learn. And, Rose said, there were very interesting people that lived in Saigon (Ho Chi Minh) as well.

And it was cheap, apart from their expensive accommodation.

'One day I had an armful of orchids, masses of them, and Sam said, "We have to stop this spending," and I said, "Look, this cost us just $5." You lose track of how relatively cheap the place really is.'

'You can live well, buy clothes and flowers, eat in the street stalls or in more formal restaurants—they are all cheap.

'And the food in Vietnam is just delicious! We ate out constantly. Often at street stalls, just sitting on stools, and if it started pouring with rain you rushed to get under some tarpaulin and ended up chatting with everyone else clustered there.'

Most importantly, they felt young and free again. 'We used to jump on the back of taxi motorbikes for transport around Saigon,' Rose said. 'This was efficient—and cool. At our apartment block, the same man was always waiting for me at 8.30 and he'd pillion me to work. He just seemed to know my timetable, almost better than I did. If we had friends staying, I'd sometimes ask my bike driver to bring a few other bike taxis and we'd do a tour of the city. It was so much fun.'

Rose and Sam went to Vietnam for an adventure—they felt they needed to enrich their lives, and they did. 'I am a shy and nervous person,' Rose said, 'so the experience was initially a bit stressful but ultimately very rewarding.'

A business commitment required that they return to Australia. But Rose said, 'I could have easily lived in Saigon (Ho Chi Minh City) for the rest of my life.'

Vung Tau

Ho Chi Minh City is a big interesting city, but we decided we needed to get closer to a few of the Vietnam veterans. Many have been attracted back to their old stomping grounds during the war, which meant a trip to Vung Tau.

It's a two-and-a-half hour drive from Ho Chi Minh City. The highway is excellent, although the traffic is a bit congested near the city. Or, you can do what we did, and jump on a hydrofoil in Ho Chi Minh City and take off down the Saigon River to Vung Tau. It takes less than one-and-a-half hours. It's a pleasant journey—even if the ferry is very utilitarian. The diesel motor is throbbingly loud and the smell of diesel strong.

The ferry travels through a vast expanse of mangrove trees. These mangroves were all killed during the war by the defoliant Agent Orange; in the 1970s this was a wasteland. Now the mangroves have rejuvenated although the dioxins in the mud and soil must be horrendous. About 45 million litres of Agent Orange were sprayed over Southeast Asia during the US involvement in the war.

Vung Tau, a critical Australian base during the Vietnam War and a rest and care (R&C) centre for troops, is on a peninsula south-east of Ho Chi Minh City. It's easy to see what the attraction is—the peninsula is edged with long golden beaches encircled by the South China Sea and the bay formed by the delta of the Saigon River.

Vung Tau, like the mangroves, has changed and grown, but just as the dioxins sit in the soils around the mangroves, so too does Vung Tau remain a place that tells the story of once being an R&C base. There is still an active nightlife, dominated by a string of girlie bars. Plenty of restaurants offer great seafood and accommodation and living is cheap.

Vung Tau is a magnet for old Aussie Vietnam Vets.

Many of these men are rediscovering their youth. It was in Vung Tau that, as 19 or 20-year-old soldiers, they first experienced a world beyond the borders of Australia. It was here that they experienced profound mateship, got drunk and probably had their first sexual experiences.

Many are getting away from a past full of shadows and difficulties in Australia and revisiting a place that they feel may help them understand just why life became so hard after the war; revisiting trauma and facing up to demons.

And for others still, the very low cost of living and yes, the girls and the associated attention and company, even if paid for, are the great attractions.

But all of those who have returned are having a second chance at life. Ian is one of these.

'In Australia I was just existing. Existing, getting old, and getting old very quickly,' said Ian. 'When I first came over here again, well, the only way I can explain it is—I was existing in Australia but I didn't even know that something was missing. There was a bit of a hole in my soul—I don't know what you'd call it. But when I got over here, the last piece of the jigsaw puzzle just fell into place—it was Vietnam.'

Ian had been 'existing and getting old' in Wagga Wagga, in country New South Wales. He was in his mid-50s, retired and, until then, had never really thought about returning to Vietnam. There had been no great pull.

'Then a really good friend of mine—a bloke called Garbo—asked me, "Why don't you go back?" And I replied, "Well, I've never had the inclination." And he said, "I'd like to visit Vietnam and I don't want to go by myself. Will you come with me?" I didn't really think too much about it at the time, I just said: "Right, let's go."

'That was in 2001. I came back for two weeks to Vung Tau where I was posted during the war. So it was relevant to me. And I fell in love with the place all over again.

'After that I came back for a month. Then I came back for three months. And then I thought: "Why am I donating all this money to the airlines when I haven't got the money to donate?" So I decided, after three or four years travelling backwards and forwards, to just give everything up in Australia and move over here.'

The return to Vietnam made Ian realise that the life he was leading in Australia was all a bit pointless. He needed to break out and find himself again at the age of 58.

'I was living in Wagga, on the Murrumbidgee River. It's a nice place. But . . . life becomes very predictable. They knew what I drank at the bar of the Wagga RSL. I knew what everyone else drank. I knew which topics you could talk about and which topics you couldn't. I just sat there, getting older and older and older and doing nothing.'

Ian said that the country town seemed increasingly dull after his trips to Vietnam and people appeared to have no interest in anything but their own lives.

'I'd come back after being in Vietnam for six months and I'd say, "Hi, how are ya fellas?" And they'd say, "Have you been crook?" And I'd say, "Nah, I've been in Vietnam for six months." And they'd say, "Aw, well you wouldn't have heard the latest footy scores, would ya?" Not, "Hey, what's living in Vietnam like?"

'Mind numbing. Just mind numbing. There's no other horizon,' said Ian, who has only been back to Wagga Wagga twice in nine years, both times for medical reasons.

'If I'd stayed in Wagga I'd already have one foot, if not both feet, in the grave. There was no stimulation for me. Nothing different happened. I knew where I was going to sit at the bar. I knew who was going to sit next to me. I knew what was going to be talked about. I knew . . . my whole day was boring, just boring.'

Ian rediscovered his youth. It is very apparent when you chat with Ian that he is a happy and motivated man. His new life keeps him busy, challenged and fulfilled.

Along with a group of veterans, Ian runs Long Tan and Nui Dat Tours. But, critically for him, all the income from this venture goes to a charity very close to his heart—the Vung Tau Veteran and Friends Children Fund. This fund builds, equips and assists in maintaining schools in Vietnam.

Ian, like many Australian men living in Vietnam, is on a war pension. And because of injuries incurred during the war, he has a TPI (totally and permanently incapacitated) pension of A$1000 a week. 'I live very well on my pension here,' Ian said. 'And I even save.'

But before you start thinking that A$1000 per week sounds generous, remember what these men have been through. As Howard said: 'We also get a Gold Card [free medical and dental care in Australia], so it's a good deal for us. They don't short-change us. Mind you, we had to fight and risk dying to get it . . . And, you know, they didn't pay us much to kill people at the time. But seriously, it's not a terrible deal. By comparison, Americans and New Zealanders get little.'

The cheap cost of living is one of the reasons more Australians are moving to Vietnam, according to Ian, and not just war veterans and retirees. 'In the last four years there has been an increase. A lot more Aussies have come over here,' he said. 'It's the lifestyle and there are big financial advantages.'

The lifestyle in Vung Tau is unique, and to be honest it probably hasn't changed much since it was filled with foreign men during the war. We met Ian for a drink at Offshore 1, a girlie bar in the town.

Thatched cabanas were scattered through a tropical garden. We sat in one to chat. The acidic smoke from mosquito coils wafts up from underneath the table and slightly stings the nose. Two tiger beers and two gins and tonic cost $A6 all up.

The music was pumping (though it was more Neil Young than techno). English rugby union was playing on big screens behind the bar. There were ten or so young Vietnamese girls hanging about the bar, all very pretty and very friendly.

You almost felt like the war might still be going on—all that was missing was a uniform or two and 45 years age difference between the diggers that would have been in the bar then and the old ex-diggers in it now.

We were staying over the road in Offshore 2. Which was, of course, also a girlie bar, but with accommodation.

There's a reason for the 'offshore' theme. Today, Vung Tau is the hub of Vietnam's oil industry. This industry was developed in the 1980s with the assistance of Azerbaijan—then part of the Soviet Union. In fact, a key road running through Vung Tau is called Baku Street, after the capital of Azerbaijan. Many Azerbaijanis and Russians stayed in Vietnam after the fall of the Soviet Union. They claimed political asylum. They maintained that it was imperative to their wellbeing that they not return to a nation that had gone capitalist. The communist Vietnamese Government was accommodating.

This adds another layer of interest and culture to the town. A Russian compound still exists in Vung Tau and the occasional babushka can be seen walking with bags in hand from the markets back to the compound.

During the war Ian said he 'had a reputation of liking the Vietnamese.'

'There was an awful lot of racism; there was racism everywhere, especially between black and white Americans,' noted Ian.

With Australian troops Ian said, 'There was a lot of ignorance about the Vietnamese. The only thing I knew, and my friends knew, about Vietnam was that there was a war over there.

'I was just an average 18 to 19-year-old and saw it as a big adventure. I suppose being young and open, I couldn't see anything wrong with being Vietnamese. It was their country. I didn't want to make them European. Like anywhere, if you try to learn the language then many doors open for you and I tried to learn the language back then. Failed miserably, but I made the attempt.'

Vung Tau has more to offer than cheap booze and girlie bars. The beaches are great, although the sea is polluted. There are excellent restaurants that are extremely cheap, the seafood is of extraordinary quality, and there are many Western facilities, like a great air-conditioned gymnasium that costs A$10 a month to join, tennis courts that can be rented for A$3 an hour and a handful of upmarket hotels. The Rex, for example, has a pleasant pool area, and visitors can pay A$3 to enjoy the facilities for a day.

Dan, a conscript, spent six months at Nui Dat during the Vietnam War.

At 55, after the sudden death of his long-time business partner in a menswear business in small town South Australia, Dan had another look at his life.

'We had a good business,' Dan said. 'It was going well, actually, but my business partner and I were getting a little bit older—it's a young man's game—so we got out of that, around 2008. Within six months, he died.

'That was a shock. He was everything I wasn't. I was a bit crazy. He was a lot more conservative, happily married, a God-fearing man. He didn't drink, didn't smoke. He went for a check-up for prostate cancer, as it was in his family, and then he was gone.

'And there was me. Drinking and doing everything else wrong, and I was still going. So I thought, "I better live my life now."'

Dan thought there should be a lot more to life than what he was doing. He felt like he was wasting away whatever was left.

'My wife was a good woman, don't get me wrong,' Dan explained. 'She had a fair bit to put up with, with me. But she was one of those people who would stay at home all the time, sitting in the armchair watching TV. Occasionally we might go along to see the local singing group—all these geriatrics, like, our age, up there on stage, singing and clapping and whatever. And I thought, "I don't want this shit. I might be old but I'm not old up here,"' he said, pointing to his head.

Dan already had his doubts about the direction of his life but a visit to Vietnam made up his mind.

'After that, I just walked out. I said to my wife, "You can have everything, the lot, I don't want it." And she said, "What's the catch?" "There's no catch," I said. "You can have it all. I have my war service pension, and that's enough for me. I just want to get out, do my own thing."'

Dan pays A$250 a month plus A$50 for electricity. He has two floors of the terrace house. He has two bedrooms, two bathrooms and two verandahs, both with a leafy outlook.

These days Dan is living with a 40-year-old Vietnamese lady in Vung Tau. 'I met her the second time I came here. But irrespective of that, I would have come to live here anyway. The cost of living is just so cheap. I can easily live on A$500 a week and that's going over the top.'

Dan rents a classic Vietnamese terrace house, much like what you'd find in Surry Hills in Sydney, which costs A$250 a month, plus A$50 for electricity. He has two floors of the terrace house, with two bedrooms, two bathrooms and two verandahs, both with a leafy outlook. Bikes and cars zip along the street. The area is busy and noisy but full of life. Bars, restaurants and shops are just 50 metres away and the beach 250 metres.

Dan and his partner travelled for a holiday around parts of Vietnam for about ten days: 'That was 20 million dong [A$1000] for the two of us. You can have a great holiday on a wing and a prayer.

'We've hopped over to Hong Kong for the races. I'm going to Thailand next Anzac Day. You can afford to do those sorts of things from here. Everything is so close.'

But Dan cautioned: 'It is very easy to get bored here. Very easy to fall into the trap, like a lot of veterans do—a lot of them get on the grog mid-morning then drink all day.'

To avoid this, he tries to keep to a healthy routine: 'Normally I'll go for about a two-hour walk. I'll walk for a while, then sit down and have a coffee, then continue my walk. I'll also go to the beach and have a swim, and there's a good pool close by as well.

'The lifestyle here is great. I can walk everywhere. There are the two beaches. I can walk along one then across the peninsula and back along the other. That's seven kilometres and a lot of that is on sand.'

The move to Vietnam has been rejuvenating, Dan said. It made him feel young again.

'Coming back here, you just don't feel old. If you look around here most of the Westerners are around my age and they've got girlfriends who are 30 to 40 years old. From the Vietnamese perspective, you're an old girl if you're over 30. These women have no chance of marrying a Vietnamese man who'd do the right thing by them. We treat them with respect.'

Dan does not, however, spend his entire life in Vietnam. He flies back to Australia two or three times a year, and stays with his children, his brother or friends. 'I generally spend a few months here, then back there a month. Then a few more months here, then another month in Australia. Over the year I have about eight months in Vietnam and four in Australia.' He pointed out that the money he saves living in Vietnam allows his regular return to Australia.

Hoi An

It would be wrong to think that all Australians living in Vietnam are single or divorced men. There are a lot of couples, too, like Kevin and Jean. They live near Hoi An, an old port town and World Heritage site on the coast near Danang, about halfway between Saigon and Hanoi. The pair moved north to Hoi An about a year ago, after living for four years in Vung Tau.

It was the sale of their business five years ago that prompted action. Kevin and Jean had two primary reasons for moving to Vietnam: adventure and cost.

'Our move to Vietnam is pretty selfish, really,' Jean said without apology. 'Basically it's a lifestyle choice.'

After they sold the business, Kevin and Jean had some time to think about the rest of their lives. They had a friend living in Vung Tau who suggested they go over there and see what it was like.

'That's when we came over for the first five months,' said Kevin. 'Now we spend nine months near Hoi An and three months back in Australia, each year. We don't know anyone else who does this. A lot of people see our lifestyle and say they'd like to do it, but they don't.

'We enjoy our life here. People say, "What do you do each day?" But every day is different. There's always something different happening.'

Jean explained: 'The thing is, if we lived in Australia we'd still need to work maybe twenty hours a week each, while here we can live on our investments and have a far better life than we possibly could in Australia.

'We go back around the end of October through to mid February, to see the family and spend Christmas there. While we're there, we probably do about nine weeks work. We used to own a post office, so we do relief work there. We run it while the new owners have a bit of a holiday. And there's another post office in Southport that we manage in January to give the owners there a break.

'We still have property in Australia: a house in Tassie and a unit on the Gold Coast. We rent out the Gold Coast apartment and eventually we'll sell it, and probably move back to Tassie.'

Kevin and Jean left Vung Tau because it felt like they lived in a Western enclave. Now near Hoi An, they are the only Westerners in the fishing village.

'That's what Jean and I like,' said Kevin.

'Having said that, there is plenty of Western contact around if you want it because Hoi An is a pretty big tourist destination. We also do a bit of work with a friend of ours who heads up an English school that is run out of a hotel here.'

Kevin and Jean's living conditions are comfortable, but rather unusual. They rent the bottom floor of a four-storey house—the remainder of the house is occupied by swallows.

'We share our house with about 200 swallows!' Jean said.

The Vietnamese landlord, who lives next door, built the house with the intention of renting out the bottom level and breeding swallows on the top three floors. Kevin explained that swallows live on a nearby island, but the landlord brought some of them over here and after three years he'll be able to harvest the birds' nests—a delicacy in the local cuisine.

'The house is only seven months old,' Kevin said. 'It has many Western conveniences that a lot of other places don't have. It has two bedrooms with two ensuites, an external toilet, a good living area, a good kitchen.'

Kevin and Jean have a three-year lease on the house. They pay A$275 a month in rent and that includes electricity and wi-fi. And they get on very well with their landlord.

'He's great. Last night we had a light tea and next minute, little Bing, their son, comes racing in and says, "Kevin, Kevin, come, come." They invite us over for a Vietnamese feed at least three times a week.

'We get invited out a lot. The Vietnamese people are very generous and very giving and sometimes it can even get embarrassing. If you go out for dinner, they won't let you pay, and you know you're in a much better financial position than they are to foot the bill. But, nah, they won't let you.'

There are cultural differences, though, and that requires a period of adjustment. 'Vietnam is different. You know, the Vietnamese are lovely people but they work and live at their own pace a lot of the time. And a lot of people get very exasperated. Like you might organise people to come for dinner at six and then they rock up at 7.30, you know, that sort of thing.'

However, it is the local people and the friendships they have developed with them which makes Hoi An a better choice for Australian couples than Vung Tau, according to Kevin.

'Vung Tau is a girlie bar, party town,' said Kevin, who is in his late 50s. 'Jean got on okay, there were a few partners of expats who were not from the girlie bars and she was friends with them. But she also got on well with a few of the local girls who had worked in the bars previously. They were lovely people and you can't judge the girls because that is what they had to do to support their families.

'When we were living in Vung Tau, Jean and I would have gone to the bars four times in total and that was generally after a night out at a restaurant with some friends. On those nights we might end up in a bar, say, like the Rainbow Bar, which is not a full-on girlie bar. And if you're with other women, the girls who work there don't bother you.'

But Kevin and Jean prefer Hoi An, where the pace of life is much slower and the cost of living is cheap.

Kevin said: 'The nine months that we live here cost us A$30 000 and that includes a holiday to a different Southeast Asian country every year as well as an annual visit to Cambodia. This year we went to Laos. Last year we went to Thailand. Every year we visit Cambodia for a couple of weeks. And believe me, when we live here, we live extremely well and we don't miss out on anything.

'Our move to Vietnam is pretty selfish really. The thing is, if we lived in Australia we'd still need to work maybe 20 hours a week each, while here we can live on our investments and have a far better life than we possibly could in Australia.'

'Most mornings Jean and I walk down to the beach, about two kilometres, and I swim about two kilometres, then walk back. Sometimes we have breakfast on the way back. Sometimes we have it at home.

'The beaches here are good. The sea is fairly placid. There are also resorts about and we can use facilities there.

'In Vung Tau, Jean and I used to swim each morning as well. I got used to swimming into plastic bags, jellyfish and turds. One day I had a clump of grease on my foot that was like a cow pad. But here in Hoi An the water is clean.

'I like to exercise and do something everyday—at least an hour. I can then enjoy the life here. When we go out to a seafood restaurant, eat lots of seafood and drink lots of beer, it costs the two of us about A$20. You tend to live a bit excessively. It's a good life, that's for sure. Hopefully it'll extend our life, too.'

Other expat-friendly towns in Vietnam

Vietnam offers the expatriate a wide variety of places to move to, other than Saigon, Vung Tau and Hoi An.

Hanoi, the nation's capital in the north, is a beautiful and refined city that sits on the banks of the Red River. It was largely undamaged by the war and offers an exotic mix of imperial Vietnamese history and French colonial history.

It is Vietnam's second most populated city. A building boom is underway in Hanoi. The city has an energy to it.

It hasn't the glitz of Ho Chi Minh City but it still offers many comforts to the Western expatriate. The shopping is good, the restaurants excellent, and it is the political and intellectual epicentre of the nation.

Modern apartments are available for rent from as little as A$500 a month, with more upmarket apartments situated near the West Lake in central Hanoi costing between A$1500–3500 a month.

Hanoi is relatively close to the very beautiful Halong Bay. With its 2000 or more islands, Halong Bay was designated a World Heritage site in 1994. Massive limestone cones jut out of the waters of the Gulf of Tonkin.

In central Vietnam sits the historic city of Hue, on the banks of the Perfume River and just a few miles inland from the South China Sea. Hue originally rose to prominence as the capital of the Nguyen feudal dynasty, which dominated much of southern Vietnam from the seventeenth to the nineteenth century. The citadel, which occupies a large, walled area on the north side of the river, was the seat of power of the dynasty. It was a 'forbidden city' where only emperors, concubines and their close associates were granted access.

A city of palaces, tombs, pagodas and temples, many fringing the Perfume River, Hue is also a UNESCO World Heritage site. It was the national capital until 1945, and a window into the Vietnam War, being just 70 kilometres from the old demilitarised zone (DMZ).

Hue is north of Danang, and Danang itself is just a little north of Hoi An.

During the Vietnam War, Danang was home to a major US air base that was used by both the South Vietnamese and US air forces. The base was considered one of the world's busiest airports during the war, reaching an average of 2595 air traffic operations daily.

Danang also hosts China Beach. This was the name given to My Khe beach by American and Australian soldiers during the Vietnam War. The 30-kilometre stretch of beach on the South China Sea is extremely popular with tourists, especially Americans, and is developing fast to become one of Asia's luxury hotspots with high-end resorts. The area has celebrity-designed golf courses, a new airport terminal and lies about 100 kilometres from three UNESCO World Heritage sites—Halong Bay, Hue and Hoi An.

Cost of living

Vietnam is cheap, really cheap. Rent is 80 per cent cheaper in Ho Chi Minh City (Saigon) than in Sydney. It costs 75 per cent less to go to a restaurant. You can eat in a local restaurant for A$3. A beer will cost you about A$1. And these are the prices in Ho Chi Minh. It is even cheaper in the countryside.

John, the barrister, agreed: 'It's just so much cheaper here. Sydney is just off the planet when it comes to costs, especially restaurants. That's why I think a lot of Australians come here; they realise they can live a lot better, then they make arrangements to stay.'

Ian warned us in Vung Tau that the cheap cost of living in Vietnam, especially for single men, can be dangerous. Easy access to alcohol and the bar-focused lifestyle pose great health risks.

When Ian first came back to Vietnam he stayed in hotels in Vung Tau. 'In the hotel I had a serviced small suite with a kitchen for A$600 a month. Then I found some friends, and worked out the best area to live in. The trouble with living in a hotel is that you end up in the bar each and every night. You have to have a lot of self-discipline here,' said Ian.

After all, beer costs just A$1 a bottle. As Ian pointed out, 'That in itself can be a trap. I have a rule that I don't drink before six o'clock because you see so many blokes start drinking at three in the afternoon, then it gets earlier, twelve noon, then eleven in the morning, and before long it's wake up and have a beer, and their life is over.'

'Most mornings Jean and I walk down to the beach, about two kilometres and I swim about two kilometres, then walk back. Sometimes we have breakfast on the way back. Sometimes we have it at home.

'The beaches here are good. The sea is fairly placid. There are also resorts about and we can use facilities there.'

Visas

Visas are a constant concern in Vietnam because there is no twelve-month multiple entry visa available, and therefore most expatriates are on tourist visas of three or six months. The tourist visas can be easily renewed but there is always uncertainty. (See visa section in Appendix.)

Howard's situation is different to most expats. 'I am married to a Vietnamese so I am on a "no visa". I just have to go over to the provincial capital every three months and get an extension. I could get permanent residency here. And I have to report to the police. But everyone has to report to the police. Everyone in Vietnam is registered.

'My dealings with the Vietnamese authorities have been very good. When I go to the capital, the officials all know me, they are very friendly, they don't ask for a bribe and they do the thing for A\$10, the right price.'

Ian, who is not married, said he has no visa issues. 'I just get a three- or six-month tourist visa and simply renew it here (in Vung Tau). After nine years I recently had to leave the country to renew, but that was the first time in nine years.'

Sam and Rose who lived in Vietnam for a year also had no issues with their three-month visas, which they renewed as required, and they also used an agent. Rose advised, though, that it is important not to use photocopies, always original documents.

Medical services

For Vietnam veterans a Gold Card gives them free medical and dental care in Australia. But that means nothing in Vietnam, where medical services are not free and are generally of a poor standard.

Most expats seem prepared to risk this, but as Ian, who has a Gold Card, pointed out, medical services are an issue in Vietnam unless you have expensive health insurance.

'I couldn't afford to go to the international clinic (SOS, which is an international medical group operating clinics in 70 countries),' he said. 'I go to a local hospital. Vietnamese doctors are very cheap. I go to Medicoast (a Vietnamese Hospital) down the back beach here, and I get full blood work done for A$40.'

Dan said he really needs to give health insurance more attention. 'I have travel insurance through my credit card, and I am fully covered back in Australia with a Gold Card, but I do need to look at my international insurance cover.'

However, he added, 'It doesn't cost a lot of money to go to the doctor here.'

Ross is another Vietnam veteran we met in Vung Tau. He said, 'Health is probably one of my biggest concerns. When I first started coming here, I had health insurance and now the price is through the roof because I have pre-existing conditions, including atrial fibrillation.

'A couple of times I have been concerned about treatment and thought of flying home. I go to the hospital and the doctor can't explain his findings to me. My wife's English isn't that good—she can't explain what I want to say.

'But, on the other hand, the doctors are pretty good here. One female Vietnamese doctor I go to was trained in Melbourne—she is based in Ho Chi Minh but comes to Vung Tau occasionally.

'And services are cheap. I can go to a heart specialist here with all the tests for A$70.'

Rose and Sam, who were only covered by travel insurance, also found that medical services of good quality were available—and the cost affordable. The only time they needed a hospital, after Sam had a fall and required stitching, they used the international SOS clinic. 'We found it perfectly fine,' Rose said. 'He was treated by an American doctor.'

She added that she went to a dentist in Saigon, whose sister was a dentist in Brisbane, and the quality of work was as good as any in Australia. 'But it was like one-eighth the price of dentistry in Australia—I was shocked.'

However, if you are living in a country like Vietnam and have no evacuation or medical insurance and you are over 50, you are flirting with danger. What happens if the local medical service cannot cope with your injuries or illness? You will have to be evacuated by plane to another country. This evacuation costs tens of thousands and then there are the medical costs that will be incurred in Singapore, Bangkok, Australia, or wherever else you may be evacuated to.

Even if you are still a resident of Australia, like Kevin and Jean of Hoi An, and are covered when you arrive in Australia, the cost of evacuation is still an issue. As well, Australian medical cover does not cover you for treatment in Vietnam.

Importantly, if you have been a non-resident of Australia for more than five years, your Medicare cover ceases to exist.

All of this points to the need to look into some form of international private health insurance cover (see Chapter 10: Health insurance).

Property

Fancy a luxury apartment on the beach in Danang? Well, you can buy a one-bedroom pad for about A$200 000, or go up to A$1 million for a four-bedroom penthouse. Or how about an oceanfront villa with massive open-plan living area and infinity pool? Take your pick, for an asking price between A$700 000 and A$2 million.

It sounds great, doesn't it? But before you start real estate shopping, beware—there are strict restrictions on foreigners buying property in Vietnam.

For a start, foreigners can only purchase apartments with a maximum lease period of 50 years and cannot buy land. And the current law only allows for five specific categories of foreign individuals and organisations to own apartments. They are:

1. people who invest directly in Vietnam or who are employed in management positions by domestic or foreign-invested companies in the country
2. people who receive certificates of merit or medals from the president or government for their contributions to the country
3. people who work in socioeconomic fields, hold a bachelor's degree or higher, and possess specialist knowledge and skills
4. foreigners who are married to Vietnamese nationals
5. foreign-invested companies operating in Vietnam that need to buy homes for their employees.

Vietnamese lawmakers have been debating draft laws that would allow foreigners to buy more than one apartment, secure apartment leasehold rights for longer than the current limit of 50 years, and buy land. But don't count on any of these things happening soon.

In the meantime, it is probably safest to rent in Vietnam. And the options are cheap—and many.

For example, that luxury beachside apartment in Danang can be rented for A$500 a month or upwards.

In upmarket District One in the centre of Ho Chi Minh City, Sam and Rose's fully serviced and furnished apartment was top of the range, at A$5000 a month. However, you can get a high quality, furnished and serviced apartment for A$1000 a month.

In Vung Tau, Ian and a mate share a house with three bedrooms, each with ensuite. The house is partially furnished and costs A$400 a month, of which they each pay A$200. While Dan's two-bedroom townhouse is merely A$250 per month.

VIETNAM TIPS AND TRAPS

1. Vietnam offers a vast array of different lifestyles. From city life in Ho Chi Minh or Hanoi, to the more cultured laid-back existence in Hoi An or the beachside wilder lifestyle of Vung Tau or Danang. It's ideal for those who want to get out of a rut, even if only for a year or two. Vietnam is full of

foreigners who have done this, especially Vietnam veterans.

2. The food is sensational. Don't be shy to eat at street stalls.

3. But beware—because food and beer is cheap and good in Vietnam, you need to exercise, too.

4. Try to learn the language. It is very difficult but it will help you to understand the culture. And it is great for your brain.

5. Cultural differences can be confusing. Vietnamese are laid-back and time can flow freely. They can be late for dinner and think nothing of it. And they are generous and may insist on paying, even if they can't afford it. Protest politely, but let them pay and ensure that you return the generosity later.

6. And, importantly, the Vietnamese accept foreigners with open arms. Amazingly, there is little or no residual animosity about the war and the associated suffering of the local people.

7. Ho Chi Minh City is fascinating but never carry your wallet or purse—only as much cash as you need at the time and perhaps a credit card in your front pocket.

8. District One in the centre of Ho Chi Minh offers a lot. It is an upmarket area with restaurants, bars, great history, the Museum is there and it is the embassy area. You can get a great furnished and serviced apartment for $A1000 a month.

9. If you plan to visit Vung Tau—and it is a very pretty beachside town—be aware that some girlie bars have hotels attached to them. It can be a little crazy, and confronting, staying in one of these.

10. Visas for those planning to stay long-term are a concern, although not an insurmountable problem. Normally, a visa needs to be renewed each and every three months. This, as opposed to a long-term visa which is not available, creates some anxiety for those living there.

11. Medical and health services in Vietnam are rather third-world. Expatriates are advised to have private health cover and medical evacuation cover. A sudden trip to Singapore, Malaysia, Thailand or back to Australia may be required if you become seriously ill.

CHAPTER 5

Cambodia

Cambodia has a wild, untamed intrigue to it. It is a land of contra-dictions. For those susceptible to its magic, it transfixes; it burrows into the soul. Watch out, you might get hooked. Some Aussie retirees and adventurers already have, though it is not an expat hotspot yet.

Many visitors find that they simply have to return—some frequently, some forever—often they have no idea why.

Perhaps it's the intoxicating heat, or the Mekong River—the country's heartbeat. This wide, muddy river flowing through time has seen so much joy, pleasure, disaster, war and cruelty. And all so recently.

Cambodia, today, is the tragic centre of Indo-Chine. This term refers to French Indo-China which, from the late 1800s until the 1950s, included Vietnam, Laos and Cambodia.

The Vietnamese and the Laotians all suffered terribly under the French and then the Americans. But the Cambodians were especially harshly treated. They were pawns in a power game and it was a game that they had little real interest in. Back in the early 1970s, theirs was no fight for independence and sovereignty, unlike the Vietnamese.

Twice as many bombs were dropped on Cambodia during the Vietnam War through to 1975 as were dropped on Japan during all of World War Two. Tens of thousands of Cambodians were killed. Innocent villages totally wiped out. And all this was the 'illegal' secret war promoted by former US Secretary of State, Henry Kissinger, in the late 1960s and early 1970s.

But it got worse after that—because then came the Khmer Rouge. This was the name given to the followers of the Communist Party of Kampuchea in Cambodia. It was formed in 1968 as an offshoot of the Vietnam People's Army from North Vietnam and was the ruling party of Cambodia from 1975 to 1979. The Khmer Rouge began its reign by storming into Phnom Penh in 1975 and set about liquidating—through torture, slaughter, starvation and disease—nearly 2 million of its own people.

The hallmarks were the Killing Fields, the torture and genocide in the extermination camp in Phnom Penh known as Tuol Sleng (S-21)—only one of more than 100 extermination centres across the country—and the forced march of hundreds of thousands out of the city to the countryside where so many starved to death.

It was an unbelievable, ideologically driven and cruel form of madness.

Fighting and severe political instability continued to dog Cambodia through to 1997. That was when Hun Sen, who is still the leader of Cambodia, wrested control from his co-premier Prince Norodom Ranariddh to become sole Prime Minister. Arguably, this marked the beginning of Cambodia's recovery.

Cambodia is also notorious for human trafficking, child prostitution and prostitution in general. Human rights abuses did not end with the Khmer Rouge. But importantly, the visceral cruelty is now part of history.

There is no doubt that today Cambodia has a raw, edgy, Indo-Chine authenticity about it. Today, the peaceful smiling Cambodians make it near impossible to understand how such horrors could have been perpetrated. It feels like the country had a schizophrenic episode. It is impossible to reconcile where the madness could well up from. The people are so charming and gentle. Today's Cambodians are desperate to move on.

Cambodia resonates with its French colonial past almost as much as it does its legacy of war. It is the closest you can get to how 1970s Asia would have felt. Cyclos still exist, albeit in far fewer numbers. Many have been replaced by the motorised version: tuk-tuks. You can buy a 'happy' (marijuana-laced) pizza on the main drag by the river, if you like getting really happy.

You can just ooze into the totally laid-back environment; drink some cheap beer and wine, swim and luxuriate in the tropical heat.

And then, of course, there is the majestic Mekong, cutting through the middle of all of this with a wild nonchalance.

All these things together trigger a love affair with the country. It is different to the attraction that many other Asian countries offer. It is less explicable.

And this confusing deep attraction to Cambodia hit Australians Janet and Rick like a sledgehammer. They visited Phnom Penh more than a decade ago and it's kept a hold on them since.

> For those susceptible to its magic, Cambodia transfixes; it burrows into the soul. The Mekong River is its heartbeat.
>
> Watch out, you might get hooked. Some Aussie retirees and adventurers already have. But it is not a retiree hotspot yet.

Janet said, 'We didn't choose to live in Cambodia; it chose us. But I found it intoxicating every time I returned.'

Rick added, 'I don't recall ever making a decision—it just happened. We got the house because Janet was coming here for a month or two every year for work.'

'I like the unpredictability of it,' Janet said. 'In Australia, you get on a bus every Monday morning in the rain or whatever and know exactly what is going to happen. Here, you wake up in the morning and you don't know what is going to happen. You want to leave the house but you can't because there is a buffalo walking down the street. There is electricity or there isn't—which I find very frustrating yet exhilarating.'

Rick joked that he just loves the heat, then added, 'but there is so, so, much more.'

Of course Khmer culture is rich. You only have to visit Ankor Wat to understand that. But equally, from a Western perspective, Cambodia is no cultural wasteland either, said Janet.

'There are films, concerts, plays. There are art openings, performances. There are two websites—one on music, what is on this week, and one on the art scene. And it is incredible; you cannot actually keep up with it all. There are book clubs, choirs, a lot of music. And the restaurants, my god.'

Janet and Rick live in a traditional-style Khmer house that sits on poles and nestles by the Mekong river. The house is less than 30 minutes drive from the centre of the city. Wide verandahs watch over the expanse of the fast-flowing yellow-brown Mekong. Chickens and ducks scratch and quack about the garden. There's even a goat.

The Mekong, this time of year, laps over their lawn. At times it floods back under their house as well—but that's what the poles are for. And hey, why worry? This is Cambodia.

When we visited it was the end of the wet season in Southeast Asia. The Mekong is swollen both by tropical rains and by the snow that has melted way up in the Himalayas in China—the source of the river. Water from China, Burma, Laos, Thailand and Cambodia floods into the river.

It is here, in this house that they built by the river, that Janet and Rick spend leisurely days and warm, dreamy nights. The fans turn, the staff brings tea and coffee and the odd drink. They have a driver, gardeners and cleaners.

It is as close as you get to the old days when the French were 'colons' in Indo-Chine. Not that Janet and Rick are exploitative. In fact, they continue to employ a number of staff because of concern for their well-being rather than the need for help. But, relative to the poverty about them, they are undoubtedly privileged. They know this only too well.

Janet and Rick not only have a great lifestyle, it's also meaningful. They are both semi-retired. Janet is a part-time university lecturer and Rick is in the IT game. And they are both deeply involved with the Cambodian people and their lot.

'But will we stay forever?' said Janet. 'Yes and no. Nothing is forever.'

> It is here in their house on the Mekong that Janet and
> Rick spend leisurely days and warm, dreamy nights.
> The fans turn, the staff brings tea and coffee and the
> odd drink. They have a driver, gardeners and cleaners.

Janet and Rick built their house in 1999 when Janet was travelling regularly to Cambodia for work. Janet said: 'We are deeply interested, enmeshed in Cambodian relationships and people and institutions . . . We are pretty enmeshed in our village.

'But at first we didn't say we were coming to Cambodia to stay. We built the house with friends because we were coming frequently and because they were here and it sounded like a good thing to do. And it was fun to do—building it—and we thought we couldn't lose on it.

'Then my mother came here in 2000 and stayed for a month or two—she was quite elderly at the time, 83—and she said to me one day, "Now I understand you will never come back."

'I was really taken aback when she said that. Then we began talking about whether she could possibly come and stay, too.

'Several friends of our age have brought their elderly mothers—in the three cases we know—to Phnom Penh, and they have had a really wonderful end to their days here. Living with their children in a different situation with lots of support and lots of care. It is a million times better than the opposite which is what they'd have had in Australia. So we were talking about that with my mother, but then she got sick in Australia and died very quickly.'

Janet's mother's death in 2001 was another factor behind the permanent shift to Cambodia.

The country is not yet a common destination for Australian expats. There are several reasons for this: Cambodia is 'Asia-tough' compared to, say, Malaysia, which is 'Asia-easy'. Australians are not as knowledgeable about Cambodia, unlike perhaps Bali or Thailand, and there may well be reservations because of the terrible war and cruelty endured by the country late last century. The name given to the area just outside of Phnom Penh where thousands were executed—The Killing Fields—still resonates.

This annoys Janet. 'It is taking so long for the country to shed this image. They want to go beyond that. They don't want Cambodia to be the Killing Fields anymore.'

'Apart from the genocide itself, which of course was appalling, every foreign press article about Cambodia has the obligatory paragraph: "Hun Sen former Khmer Rouge strong man, authoritarian, da da da." That is the boilerplate that just gets dumped in. You just can't get a view of what is going on without this prism to look through.

'To describe Hun Sen as former Khmer Rouge—he risked his life to get rid of them and without him they would not be gone today. It is just the wrong cast. Yes, there are elements of it—but it is so judgmental,' said Janet.

Rick added, 'So much of the population now was born after all that time anyway.'

War, though, has deeply marked Cambodia. This is hard to scrub away. And the Mekong is there always, holding that history.

Jon Swain, a journalist who lived in Cambodia in the early 1970s and was lucky to be trucked out by the Khmer Rouge in 1975, rather than executed, can't let go of Cambodia; and understandably. In his wonderful book, *River of Time* (William Heinemann Ltd, 1995), he talks of how the Mekong itself holds so much of this meaning: 'There is something about the Mekong which, even years later, makes me want to sit down and watch my whole life go by.'

Even though the river brings so much joy and feeds the lands of Indo-China, Swain says, 'For myself, there are certain things I shall never forget: the bodies I saw being tossed about in its violent eddies near a ferry town 32 miles south of Phnom Penh in the early morning mist when the Mekong is at its most majestic and mysterious; or the dawn tragedy of the B52 bomber of the US airforce which prematurely unleashed its cargo of high explosives on the same little town, turning its centre into a flattened mass of rubble under which many people lay dead . . . (Four hundred were killed. Colonel Opfner, the American air attaché, told a press conference that it was "no great disaster".) Nor shall I forget the day when a Cambodian general marched his soldiers behind a protective screen of Vietnamese civilians into the waiting guns of the Viet Cong.

'"It's a new form of psychological warfare," the general said as the bodies dropped in front of him.'

Yes, it's impossible for these sorts of horrid events to quickly fade away.

But Swain still loves Cambodia. 'What carries me back to the Cambodia of my dreams is those first days (when I arrived) . . .'

He came from a bleak grey Paris winter and burst into the tropical heat of Phnom Penh. 'On my first day I felt I had entered a beautiful garden. As I stepped off the Air France Boeing 707 onto the hot tarmac of Phnom Penh's Pochentong airport to begin a new life, I forgot about Paris and began an adventure and a love affair with Indo China to which I have been faithful ever since.'

There he confronted war, death, opium, intriguing women, love, sorrow, heartbreak and joy.

Swain's friend and longer term Indo-China resident, AFP correspondent Bernard Ullman said, 'Indo-China is like a beautiful woman; she overwhelms you and you never quite understand why . . . Sometimes a man can lose his heart to a place, one that lures him back again and again.'

The times got bleaker as the terror of the Khmer Rouge came closer. A popular hotel for expatriates and journalists back then, as now, was *Le Royal*, now called the *Raffles Hotel Le Royal*.

As tensions built, the behaviour became more risqué; war does that to people. Swain tells of 'eerie occasions of forced jollity and horseplay in the pool. Its unfiltered water was badly in need of change but that did not stop one girl photographer making love to two men on the same night, one in the deep end, one in the shallow, to general applause.'

Phnom Penh has changed a lot. *Le Royal* has regained its grandeur and the pool is now sparkling.

But all this history is still there. It's floating just below the new reality of life in Cambodia.

Phnom Penh

The capital of Cambodia, Phnom Penh, is located on the banks of the Mekong, Tonlé Sap and Bassac rivers. It still echoes with its history and 'old Asia', but it also has a new and exciting aspect to it. Phnom Penh is changing rapidly and for the spoilt Westerner the comforts of life are fast appearing.

'Indo-China is like a beautiful woman; she overwhelms you and you never quite understand why...Sometimes a man can lose his heart to a place, one that lures him back again and again.'

Ted and Helen, who are in their late 50s, came to Cambodia thirteen years ago and run a restaurant and bar in the upmarket area of Boeung Keng Kang 1 (commonly referred to as BKK1). Helen said: 'We were lucky in terms of the period we were here—2000 to now. It is a long time and we have seen a lot of changes, particularly in the last five years. Big corporations coming in, more wealth. Between 2000 and 2004 it didn't change that much. The heart of the city didn't change.'

But Helen added that, sadly, a lot of the 'soul of the city and the edginess has gone'.

Safety was an issue back then, although Helen is very nonchalant about this. 'It was still safe then because you didn't go where the problems were—you would get a text message that there had been a hand grenade thrown here or a shooting there and you would not go to that area. But all of that has gone now except for the army commanders shooting in karaoke bars.

'What has changed is that it is a lot more modern, cleaner, more accessible, safer. There is a lot of investment in the city. The landscape has changed dramatically. The division of the rich and the poor is getting bigger. But the middle class is growing.'

As always there is a dark side to development. 'When we first came here the French architecture was extraordinary but rundown—now a lot of the major buildings have been destroyed.'

Helen added that there is a drift to the city with people looking for work, and many have lost their land as corrupt government

Cost *of* Living

INDICES
PHNOM PENH LOWER THAN SYDNEY

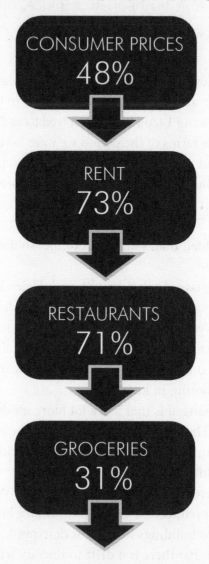

CONSUMER PRICES
48%

RENT
73%

RESTAURANTS
71%

GROCERIES
31%

Source: numbeo.com

bodies sell it off. A land grab has been underway. Logging has also contributed to dispossession, as well as environmental degradation.

'You get really angry about it. You get angry about sex-trafficking and the amount of rape in this country. We don't have any rights, no one has any rights,' said Helen of the dark side that continues to underlie exotic Cambodia.

The contrast between good and evil is still very apparent.

Just like the Tonlé Sap River can flow backwards and, yes, uphill, when the Mekong River floods, so too can time flow backwards in Cambodia; backwards to the darkness of the 1970s and 1980s.

The streets in Phnom Penh are grubby. This makes it a tough place for the unadventurous, especially a retired couple who are used to suburbia in north Melbourne or western Sydney.

'It is dirty here,' said Ted. 'There is a lot of garbage because of the massive influx of population. It is no one's place and there is no education.'

There are other challenges as well and sex tourism is way up the top of the list. It's a big industry in Cambodia and in the bars along the river where the tourists drink and eat and party, it's obvious.

Alan Parkhurst, editor of the *Phnom Penh Post*, said there are a lot of retirees here from Australia, but they are mostly single men of 50-plus.

'A lot of them are in Sihanoukville [a seaside town in the south of Cambodia on the Gulf of Thailand]. They rent their house out, back at home, and live quite comfortably here on that income.

'In Phnom Penh you see a lot of them at the Walkabout Hotel—a sports bar and pick-up joint with a lot of bar girls. It is quite sad. They are in the bar from lunchtime. But, on the other hand, a lot of guys have set themselves up well here, and have ended up in a long-term relationship.'

Alan added that, 'Just about all my expat friends in Thailand are married to local girls and 99 per cent of them are happy. There is this misconception in the West that the Asian wives are subservient. It is not true. If I tried to tell my wife what to do, well . . .'

As visitors to a country, we all have to be careful not to moralise or judge the culture, and that includes sex tourism. But when you've lived somewhere like Cambodia as long as Helen, your daily experiences colour your opinion—and Helen does not think the country is suitable for couples.

In her frank and open manner, she explained: 'Ninety per cent of the time the male will get "rice fever". Guaranteed. Six of my girlfriends have left this year—all turned 40, single. They left for two reasons—their careers and no blokes. It is a really lonely place for foreign females.

'And Cambodia can be difficult to adjust to. It is not like moving to Chiang Mai or Bangkok. There is too much going out to bars and getting drunk is so easy. Alcohol consumption is way too high.

'It amazes me how stupid white men are—you see it so much here. A friend of ours here is 56 and recently got married to an eighteen-year-old woman.

'After thirteen years I still find it incredible that single males come here—and a lot of the reason they are attracted to a place like Cambodia is that they can't have a relationship in their own country and they can't handle the stress and the restrictions of their own country. So they come here and they go with taxi girls, don't use condoms, the girl gets pregnant and the bloke says, "Oh woe is me."

'They don't think about HIV, let alone any other sexually trans-mitted diseases, and then they get a girl pregnant and go "woe is me"? I have no time for those people any more. They end up doing it two or three times. And remember the whole Asian package—you don't marry the girl, you marry the family and the village, too.'

Even so, Helen sees a change in trend with more couples appearing recently. 'We have met a lot of couples in the last year, mostly Americans, who often work from home, travelling through Southeast Asia to find a place to live. They want a new lifestyle.'

Ted added, however, that a lot of them end up choosing Thailand or Malaysia over Cambodia. 'You have to be a certain character to get on in Cambodia,' he said. 'It is edgy for people who haven't been in Asia before.'

Still, it is an increasingly popular location for expats, both singles and couples. Helen said: 'Almost everybody who comes here wants to stay and they come back. All the time we meet people who say, "I was here five years ago. I always wanted to come back." Or people here for the first time saying, "Oh, I had no idea it would be so nice."'

The great advantage of Cambodia, even over Thailand, is that English is very widely spoken and most hotel staff, taxi drivers and shopkeepers speak English. Even in five-star hotels in Thailand, many of the staff do not speak English well. But in Cambodia, you can step off the plane—in Phnom Penh, in Siem Reap, down at the beach—and English is all you need.

One couple living happily in Phnom Penh is Garry and Rita.

Their shift to Cambodia—or indeed the shift out of Sydney—was driven by factors other than retirement or need for a change. It was a move of necessity, driven by the need for work. And it is a story that fits with many people working in the West who are over 50 years old.

As Rita explained, 'Garry is in marketing and he got to around 50—it is extremely difficult in that field once you are past your 40s. The company bosses told him that, looking forward, they really didn't have anything for Garry in Sydney but they wanted to expand in Asia. We got here on a twelve-month contract and we loved it so much we have stayed for nearly five years.'

Garry was given the choice to work for the company anywhere in Asia. They chose Phnom Penh and they are now sure they made the right decision. Garry believes that many other Asian cities, like Hanoi, Ho Chi Minh, Kuala Lumpur, Singapore, Bangkok and Jakarta, are just big and relatively expensive cities, especially if Australians are looking for a cheap, laid-back lifestyle.

'When you boil it all down, it gets to just a few places,' he said. 'Cambodia is one. Vientiane (in Laos) is another—but there are problems with Vientiane and Laos. Thailand is fine, if you get out of Bangkok. A lot of friends have retired to Krabi in Thailand. Penang is another one.

'But Cambodia is old Asia—still intact, the way it used to be. It is exotic. It is French. It has got French colonial architecture. It is the way Hanoi used to be.

'Cambodia is not going to get ambitious because the Cambodian people are not ambitious like the Vietnamese or the Thais. Cambodians are very laid-back, not lazy, but laid-back in their style. They are more like the Laotians.'

The Laotians, according to Garry, were voted the happiest people in the world recently. He cited the example of a cab driver who might take three fares one day and then decide that's enough, he's happy with what he has earnt that day, so he will take the afternoon off and have a drink with his mates.

Rita is aware that corruption and human rights violations in Cambodia remain real problems. This concerns her but she said: 'Let's say that you are totally self-serving and that the things you love to do are to eat great food, drink good wines, have a beautiful place to live for very little money, have lots of domestic help, never have to wash a dish or do whatever, then Phnom Penh offers of all this, and more.

'It offers easy and cheap access to surrounding countries, too. And if you want to lead a life that many would see as very spoilt and privileged and you didn't care about the fact that it was on the back of a lot of people who are very poor—then this is not a bad place to do that.'

Garry and Rita live in the Westerners' part of Phnom Penh, BKK1. It's full of restaurants and bars and it is very comfortable. They rent a large two-storey house. It is spacious and luxurious. You can live well in Phnom Penh.

> Cambodia is not just 'old Asia'. It also has a new and exciting aspect to it. Phnom Penh is changing fast and for the spoilt Westerner the comforts of life are appearing fast.

Rita is shocked by the fast pace of change in the city. 'Relative to when we came here four and a half years ago, I cannot tell you the amount of world-class restaurants and little back-street bars that have opened. Twenty places where you could walk in and feel like you're in Double Bay, Sydney, Melbourne or even in Paris, New York, London . . .'

Garry and Rita always felt that Phnom Penh was the right place for them, and now they are certain of it—their son, John, has since followed them to Cambodia with his partner and now they live there, too.

Cost of Living

Sydney vs Phnom Penh [% lower than Sydney]

Housing

Rent–3 bed'm apartment city centre*
$4,276 $1,484   65%

Rent–3 bed'm apartment outside city centre*
$2,815 $661   77%

Buy–apartment per sqm city centre
$9,795 $865   91%

Food

Bread
$3.47 $1.22   65%

Eggs
$4.13 $1.56   62%

Chicken breasts
$10.78 $6.41   41%

Tomatoes
$5.17 $1.44   72%

Restaurants

Mid range meal for 2
$80 $16.23   80%

Inexpensive
$15 $4.33   71%

Beer

Domestic
$4.80 $1.08   78%

Taxi

Per km
$3 $1.08   64%

One hour standby
$54.16 $4.33   92%

Electricity

Electricity, heating, water, garbage*
$238.97 $76.77   68%

Communications

Internet*
$61.66 $73.03   18%

Mobile phone (per min prepaid)
$1.02 $0.08   92%

* per month

Source: numbeo.com

Cambodia   119

The young couple has a great apartment—two bedrooms, two bathrooms, front and back courtyards, air-conditioning, and all for A$300 a month. You can't do that in Sydney.

'We were earning really good money in Sydney but absolutely struggling with no quality of life,' said John. 'Here, we earn a quarter of the money—but last year we could afford to travel to Germany, Portugal and Greece. We are leading a life we couldn't possibly afford in Sydney and yet we are earning local salaries here.'

This shows you how far your dollar goes in Cambodia. The cost of living is low, very low.

Cost of living

The magic of Cambodia struck Joanna as soon as she visited Phnom Penh more than twenty years ago. 'I fell in love with the place straightaway,' she said, 'and I'm still trying to work out why. I'd go out to visit a village and see that there is a cycle of growing rice, and it meant something to me. Maybe it is the connection with the cycle of life and nature. And the people are so delightful.'

Joanna rents a two-bedroom apartment that is above a cafe. It is in the centre of town, right opposite the palace wall and on a tree-lined street. She leases it from the owner of the cafe below, who is British. She pays a little over A$1000 a month, which is about average for the area. 'Prices vary but in the centre, where I am and which is very popular, it is a bit more expensive. I like this street so much; right next to the palace wall, it is a mixture of Cambodians and foreigners.'

Joanna believes that the cost of rent is 'up there'. 'Some things cost more,' she said. 'Petrol is expensive. I run a car for security. I bought my car for A$5000 ten years ago and it is still worth A$3000–4000. So it has kept its value.'

However, she quickly added that other costs of living are super low: 'Vegetables are really cheap. I go to a little shop on this street and buy three days worth of vegetables for A$3, or even less at the market. Fruit is a bit more expensive, but it is abundant. Three days worth of fruit might cost about A$5.'

Her electricity bill is very low, Joanna said. She runs all the usual appliances like a fridge, instant hot water service, lighting and fans, plus constant air-conditioning in the bedroom in the hot months, and it costs her between A$45 and A$95 a month.

'Mobile phones are very cheap, as are landlines,' Joanna said. 'On my landline it is a couple of dollars for a half-hour call to Australia. And there's also Skype.' The internet costs Joanna about A$10 a month.

Joanna estimates that, for her, the overall cost of living in Cambodia is about a quarter of the cost of living in Australia. She added that she can also have part-time house help for less than A$100 a month.

'And if I'm going out on Saturday night, I can have my hair washed and blow-dried, plus a manicure and pedicure, all for A$12.'

The cost of living in Phnom Penh is, in fact, around half of what it costs in Sydney. Grocery prices are around 30 per cent lower, restaurant prices are more than 70 per cent cheaper, rent is almost 75 per cent less in Phnom Penh, and a beer is 80 per cent cheaper.

Alan Parkhurst told us: 'Beer is not much more than A$1 a bottle—I can buy spirits and beer here cheaper than I can buy duty-free anywhere in the world. There are no taxes on alcohol.'

Ted agreed: 'Booze is ridiculously cheap, cigarettes are cheap.'

Alan believes that a single person can easily live on A$1000 a month. For Joanna, it's more like $2000 a month, while Ted said that a couple would want A$3000 a month to live comfortably. Despite personal variations, it's clear that living in Cambodia is well within the reach of Australians, even retirees who are watching their budget.

Property

Despite the increased influx of Westerners, rent in Cambodia is still very cheap compared to Australia.

The NGO area of BKK1, where Garry and Rita live, is upmarket— with tree-lined streets, larger homes, serviced apartments, a myriad of restaurants and bars. Rent ranges from about A$2000 to A$3000 a month for a pleasant house with gardens.

Alan pays A$600 a month for an apartment. At his previous place, the top half of an old house in the centre of town, which Alan described as beautiful, he paid A$450 a month. But, he pointed out, even that was expensive. 'A lot of the staff at the *Phnom Penh Post* would be paying A$200 to A$250 a month for a furnished and air-conditioned apartment,' said Alan.

Alan would buy a property in Phnom Penh if he had the money: 'Owning a property in Cambodia, though, would be a long-term investment. Tourism is going to explode and the political situation will steadily settle down.

'What I see in Cambodia now is what I saw in Thailand 35 years ago. The place is just starting to open up and take off. If people want to visit the real Southeast Asia, it is here in the countryside of Cambodia. People are living like they did 2000 years ago. Not much has changed; they're still using buffalos in farming, for example. You don't see that in Thailand anymore, but you see it here.'

Still, property prices remain most affordable for many foreigners: a pleasant two-bedroom, two-bathroom apartment in central Phnom Penh costs between A$50 000 and A$300 000. Outside of the city, it is significantly cheaper.

Alan told us: 'I have an American friend—a professional tennis coach—he bought a block of land and built a house on a hillside in Kep with ocean views. The land, the house, everything, cost him US$25 000.

'It's not a flash big house, but basic Khmer style with two bedrooms on stilts. It has power and water tanks. It is about ten minutes drive to the beach. Quite a few people also live on the beach down that way.'

Kep was Cambodia's top seaside destination until it was eclipsed in the 1960s by Sihanoukville. But today it is enjoying a renaissance, especially among Cambodians. This is partly because Sihanoukville is full of girlie bars and attracts sexpats.

Foreigners can own freehold property in Cambodian buildings above the ground floor. This works well for apartments, or even older buildings with several levels, like the top floor of a shophouse.

The intention of the law is that foreigners cannot own land or houses, only apartments. But we are in Asia, and the intention of the law is often circumvented.

Be clear, we never recommend circumventing the law. It can cause extreme difficulties over time. We are of the view that you should keep it simple. If you want to buy something, buy an apartment above the ground floor—and seek expert legal advice about the purchase. (See Appendix for more details on property.)

> 'What I see in Cambodia now is what I saw in Thailand 35 years ago. The place is just starting to open up and take off. If people want to visit the real south east Asia, it is here in the countryside of Cambodia. People are living like they did 2000 years ago.'

Medical services

Medical services are an issue in Cambodia. The health system is very third-world. Like in Vietnam and Indonesia, serious illness often means that you have to travel to Singapore, Malaysia, Thailand or back to Australia.

And, of course, if you are too sick to travel and you do not have medical evacuation cover, you could be in a lot of trouble.

This is a very real issue for the older retired person or anyone on a budget.

Cambodia is not a medical desert, though. Private Western clinics, like International SOS, a medical and travel security services company with clinics in 70 countries, do exist but they are expensive. There are some other cheaper Western-quality health services as well, like the French Cambodia clinic.

Again, the sensible path is to ensure that you have health insurance and, if you can afford it, medical evacuation insurance as well.

Remember, Australians who live outside of Australia for more than five years will lose Medicare cover. So private health insurance for Australia or your country of choice for medical attention is critical.

Joanna has no health insurance—at 70 years of age, it would be hard to get anyway—but she still regards herself as an Australian resident. She owns a house in Victoria in which her family reside. As such, she regards herself as being covered by Medicare in Australia.

Even so, she became ill recently and did not have time to get to Australia.

'I was very sick in August,' Joanna said. 'I had a bacterial infection in my leg. It was cellulitis. That can be dangerous. I had fever and chills and I was nauseous.

'My daughter made an appointment for me with an Australian doctor in Phnom Penh and he diagnosed it straightaway. He drew a circle on my leg around the infection site, but while he and my daughter were discussing which hospital to go to, the infection spread outside the circle.

'I was admitted into the French Cambodia clinic—it wasn't hard to get into the hospital—and stayed for ten days on an antibiotic drip. I had three doctors there—two French and one French Cambodian. It didn't cost much but if I had gone to the SOS clinic it would have cost a lot.'

Joanna recovered and she was more than happy with the quality of care she received.

Janet and Rick recognise that the medical situation is a real issue in Cambodia, but they, too, have no private health cover.

Janet said: 'We had health insurance when we first came here with a Hong Kong insurance group, but we decided it wasn't worth it. They were too unreliable. A friend of ours died while the doctors argued with the insurers about whether she was really sick enough to evacuate. We had actually dropped it before this sad incident with our friend because it was getting too expensive.'

Janet recently had to have heart surgery, so she returned to Sydney for it. She was lucky; the surgery was necessary but not an emergency. Even though she still has Medicare cover, she wanted it done quickly. 'We paid for it upfront as overseas patients and it cost A$45 000. The way we looked at it, A$45 000 is ten years of health insurance.'

An important tip for those living overseas but who still have a residential address in Australia is to ensure you can prove your residency—such as with an Australian driver's licence, council rates, electricity bills and so on. And make sure that you tick the 'resident returning' section of your inward immigration form when you land in Australia.

Garry and Rita have medical evacuation insurance and US$1 million cover in hospital, but only in Southeast Asia. This costs them a total of A$1400 a year for both of them. Though Garry, who is 58, warned: 'The minute you hit 60 it rockets.'

But what it means is that they can be medivaced out to Bangkok and receive excellent medical services there.

Alan said that most people will go to Bangkok or Vietnam for medical care. 'But it is getting a lot better here. A couple of big Thai hospitals have been built and they are quite good. And SOS is here.'

Cambodia's flagship international hospital is Calmette Hospital, a government-run medical centre located on Monivong Boulevard in Phnom Penh. It is funded by the Cambodian and French governments. It is a fee-for-service hospital and is targeted at both locals and expatriates that need affordable, high quality medical care. This 250-bed hospital offers a wide range of medical services, from surgical and obstetrics, to radiology and microbiology.

In Siem Reap near the famous ruins of Ankor Wat, the Royal Angkor International Hospital provides a high standard of health and medical care. It is owned and operated by Thailand's Bangkok Hospital Group. Patients, however, need to pay in cash or with private medical insurance.

James has also been living in Cambodia for over a decade. He has deep interests in Khmer culture and architecture, he has worked at the Museum, he has taught English and he is actively contributing to the country.

'I simply can't consider returning to Australia,' he said. 'I am over 65 now. So what would I be doing in Australia?'

James would be looking at a bleak and short future in an aged-care facility, and that's not for him. He will stay in Cambodia, where he intends to have carers look after him in his home until, hopefully, the very last days. He can afford to do that here, with home help readily available and cheap. He also emphasised that the general attitude towards the elderly in Cambodia is respectful.

Visas

Visas are no barrier to living in Cambodia. The situation could change, however, if only because of the rapid political and economic developments underway in the country.

Most visitors to Cambodia will obtain a 30-day tourist visa for a cost of US$20 (A$22). These can be obtained on arrival at Phnom Penh and Siem Reap airports and at land borders. One passport-sized photo is required. Make sure you have several photographs anyway and that you have foreign currency, preferably US dollars.

With the tourist visa you are allowed to extend your stay once, for an extra 30 days at a cost of around US$45 (A$48).

If you intend staying longer, though, it is best to apply for an 'ordinary visa', which is often referred to as a 'business visa'. Like a tourist visa, this ordinary visa is valid for 30 days but at a cost of US$25 (A$27). The 'ordinary visa', though, can be extended indefinitely. It also can be acquired on arrival.

You can extend your stay from within the country, so there's no need to leave. You have the option to extend for one, three, six or twelve months. The one- and three-month options will only get a single entry visa, which means that if you leave the country, you'll need to get a new visa when you return.

> Visas are no barrier to living in Cambodia. The situation could change, however, if only because of the rapid political and economic changes underway in the country.

It is much more convenient to get either a six-month or twelve-month extension, as they will both give you multiple entries. This means you can leave and return as often as you want to, on the same visa. The fee for a year-long multiple entry extension is US$280 (A$300). Both types of extensions take a day or two to process and are best handled through agents.

Alan said: 'I just pay an agent US$300 (A$322) a year and I get a new visa. You can do it through any travel agent here. I know people who have been here for years and have never left the country. Cambodia is the easiest place in Southeast Asia to stay long-term.'

CAMBODIA TIPS AND TRAPS

1. Cambodia provides an adventure, not just a retirement. Beware, it is fascinating but edgy.
2. It is infamous for the Khmer Rouge and the horrors they perpetrated. This scares a lot of people, especially retirees. It shouldn't. This is history.
3. Cambodia is the Southeast Asia of the 1970s. But this also means a rawness and poverty and dangers of theft. There is still a dark side, including prostitution, people trafficking and drug running. Carry cash and a credit card in your pocket rather than a wallet or a purse. And in a tuk-tuk, keep belongings well within the vehicle and secure.
4. It has a lot more to offer than girlie bars—if you don't like these places, simply stay away from them.
5. Medical and health facilities are of relatively poor standards, especially when compared to those in Malaysia and Thailand. Have insurance and medical evacuation cover if you can afford it.
6. English is widely spoken in Cambodia. But you should still learn the Khmer language if you're living there.
7. Cambodia is fabulously inexpensive.
8. Foreigners can only buy apartments above the ground floor. Rent, however, is extremely cheap and there is a range of comfortable options available, from traditional Khmer-style houses, to French colonial townhouses and modern serviced apartments.

CHAPTER 6

Europe

Now is one of the best times for Australians to pack up and move to Europe. The great attraction is real estate. In France, Spain, Greece and Portugal the real estate markets have collapsed. And combined with the current strength of the Australian dollar, this means that it has become affordable to live what is the European dream of many.

At the moment, you can buy the classic chateau in France for A$750 000 or the ubiquitous and gorgeous stone country cottage for less than A$120 000. Although, when the house is old, constructed in stone, classically provincial and 'full of character', it's likely to need some serious renovations.

But that is what many people dream about doing.

In Spain, apartments and luxury homes are up for grabs—cheap. Prices have fallen by almost half in many areas. You can buy a four-bedroom apartment in a hilltop town in southern Spain, with expansive rural views, overlooking the Atlantic Ocean, and beaches ten minutes away for about A$400 000. Or you can buy a two-bedroom apartment in downtown Barcelona for around A$150 000.

And, of course, there is the whole European lifestyle thing: the food and wine, the people, the culture, the proximity to so many wonderful countries, the landscape, including great skiing, and even the politics.

And for many Eurocentric Australians a very attractive aspect of moving to Europe is the fact that you are at the epicentre of European life, not down-under at its far fringes.

But the fact is, Europe is not as cheap as Asia. If you want a luxurious lifestyle in Europe, you will pay for it. Perhaps not as much as you would in Australia, but certainly more than in Asia. And, unlike most countries in Asia, Australia is not a mere six to eight hours away on a direct flight.

For some retirees though, Europe is worth the effort and the extra expense. This is especially so for those Australians who still strongly feel their distant European origins.

Will and Lisa, who decided to leave Australia for Barcelona said, 'We are Europeans, simple as that'.

Of course, those Australians living in Vietnam, Cambodia, Thailand or Bali would say 'so what?' They would argue that an Australian retiree or escapee, even with European ethnicity, would not feel any less comfortable in Chiang Mai than in Provence. Try and tell that to a Europhile.

For many Australians living in Europe is about living a life-long dream—spending a year or two in Provence, five years in Paris or even packing up and taking off forever to Barcelona.

Spain

It was the extended travel after finishing their careers and then living for nine months in Sri Lanka that triggered the urge for Will and Lisa to move away from Australia permanently.

'We came back here and thought 'Fuck, it's boring'.

Sixty-five-year-old Will and 61-year-old Lisa, who still feel European despite being third generation Australians, said: 'We have decided to move to Barcelona and not to Asia because in Asia you are always the foreigner.'

Lisa speaks French, her grandmother was French and her first husband French—though she prefers to live in Barcelona.

One reason is language. 'I have spent a lot of time in France. I have lived in Paris and it is like that book *Almost French*. You are never going to be French. Even though I am part-French, I am not when I go there. I babble away and my French friends will correct my grammar. "Do you mind, I am telling a story," I say. Whereas in Barcelona, I speak very bad Spanish, I yap away and they are so welcoming—"Oh okay, good, good." It doesn't matter.'

It was a year or so of travelling after finishing their careers that triggered the urge for Will and Lisa to move away from Australia permanently.

They had travelled widely in Europe and then spent nine months in Sri Lanka.

Will said: 'We went back (to Australia) and thought, "Fuck, it's boring." And that is a really shocking thing to say. We lived in a perfect little townhouse, overhanging the ocean at Tamarama in Sydney, and we were bored shitless. No adventures.'

Will and Lisa had effectively retired. But they spent the nine months in Sri Lanka in 2011, running a hotel for a friend, and discovered they liked the hospitality game and were very good at it. That was when they realised that perhaps the hotel industry offered them an adventure in their so-called retirement years. The question was: where?

The couple had always liked Barcelona but it became a contender after some very good friends bought and renovated an apartment near the Gaudi church. It has soaringly high ceilings, three bedrooms and had been untouched for 70 years. Their friends paid A$180 000 and spent A$120 000 doing it up, with the intention of renting it out.

For Lisa and Will, the light bulb went on. 'We thought, "Hang on, we know how to run a hotel. We could easily manage a rental apartment." And we were watching with interest the seismic shift in accommodation. It is all done online now,' Lisa said. 'We worked out that we could have a five-bedroom apartment, rent out the rooms, and live off the income. You don't need licences for that; you just take out an insurance policy and do it.'

It was the perfect solution to their sunset-years dilemma.

'There are 7 million tourists to Barcelona every year,' Will said. 'Barcelona is a port. It was always the place that everyone came to—a melting pot, a place of industry and business. The city and its people are open. And they are wealthy compared to the rest of Spain.'

The huge amount of tourism and the fact that property is cheap in Barcelona means that expats like Will and Lisa can generate an excellent income from rental holiday accommodation. And they get their slice of adventure as well.

Chelsea's rebirth

For many, Europe is the dream destination for an adventure or an escape. But Chelsea and Michael moved to Spain for very different reasons.

It was the death of Chelsea's Spanish-Australian father, when she was in her early 20s, that focused her on Spain.

Chelsea explains: 'My father came from Galicia in the northern part of Spain. My parents separated when I was four and he never taught me the language so I didn't know anything about his culture, country, family, anything. When I was twenty he was killed in a work accident in Sydney. I was his only child. He had promised me all my life that one day he would take me to Spain—so I decided that I would take him.'

Chelsea took her father's body back to his homeland.

When she arrived in Galicia, an area in the far north-west of Spain just above Portugal, Chelsea had an epiphany. 'I saw why I looked the way I did. I saw my blood everywhere. I felt it. I was really overwhelmed. I was freaked out in one sense that I had lost my dad, but on the other hand I got this family. I couldn't speak Spanish, neither could my extended family there speak English, but we just connected.

'And that started my obsession with Spain.'

Chelsea went back to Spain four years later and returned every two years. Usually she just went to Galicia and visited the family. Back home in Sydney, she tried to learn Spanish: 'Learning a language is really hard. I can speak it now—I am quite fluid but I am not fluent.'

Then, when she was 28 and in Europe for a month-long holiday with a girlfriend, they stopped in at Spain and that is when she decided: 'Right, I want to live in Spain. I am just going to do it.'

In Australia, Chelsea had a great job in media. She met her partner, Michael, a web design whiz, through work. Michael also played a part in the move. He needed international experience to sharpen his design skills so he was keen to take the leap, too. These days, he is freelancing from Spain and his business, which caters mainly to international clients, is strong.

Chelsea and Michael initially moved to Barcelona. 'It is like the gateway to Europe,' Chelsea said. 'You are in Spain but you're not. For us, it was a softer way to get in and get settled, and there were more work opportunities.'

However, things went a bit pear-shaped for a while, primarily because Michael was offered a dream job in Stockholm and Chelsea hated the place. They were there for three years before Chelsea 'spat the dummy'. They decided to return to Australia.

Chelsea and Michael had already shipped their possessions back, but en-route they visited southern Spain for a short holiday. A thoughtful friend had offered them his holiday house in Vejer de la Frontera, in the province of Andalucia in south-west Spain, not far from Cadiz, Jerez and Seville. They arrived in July 2012 and had planned to spend two months there.

'We haven't left,' Chelsea said.

Instead, Chelsea and Michael sold their apartment in Newtown in Sydney and bought a wonderful apartment on Vejer's old city walls.

The town is quite breathtaking. All the buildings are white washed. It sits on a low hilltop with views over the Straits of Gibraltar. It is surrounded by vineyards and orange groves and has several ancient churches and convents. Fighting-bulls are bred in the area and flamenco is celebrated.

There are many restaurants and bars, but they are all nearly impossible to find as you walk through the curving maze of cobble-stoned streets. Cars are not encouraged; it is a town for walking. The architecture of many of its houses reflects the period of Moorish rule, which lasted from 711 until the town was captured by Saint Ferdinand of Castile in 1248. It's full of history.

The area is the heartland of sherry and at its centre is the town of Jerez (which literally translates as 'sherry'). Chelsea has become heavily involved in the local sherry-producing industry and was paramount in establishing World Sherry Day. Her passion is to promote, what she believes, has been a poorly marketed but high quality wine.

As Chelsea said, 'Everything about here is all around sherry—flamenco, tapas. Did you know that tapas was created because of sherry? Tapa is a lid. Bread was placed on top of the glass to keep flies out of the sherry. So they started inventing lots of different tapas by placing tasty bits on the bread. It has been lost. There are tapas bars everywhere but they are not serving sherry.'

And the sherry is excellent. We had several glasses as we chatted—and left there glowing. Sherry is cheap. We drank a glass of 12-year-old sherry. The bottle cost only 10 euros.

'It is weird. I am living in a tiny country town but it is not boring compared to Sydney,' said Chelsea.

She added, though, that it is the community, the people and the laid-back lifestyle that are the great attractions.

And it is alternative and refreshing. 'No one asks you what you do. No one cares how much money you have got. It is such a sense of acceptance. I am not a country town person but what happened here is that I made friends really quickly in both the expat community and the Spanish community. The Galinda family has adopted us—the family I always wanted to have. The beach is 10 minutes away. It is cheap to live. The people are good people—we just got accepted. The people want to know your story, want to help you.'

> Vejer de la Frontera is quite breathtaking. All the buildings are white washed. It sits on a low hilltop with views over the Straits of Gibraltar.
>
> It is surrounded by vineyards and orange groves and has several ancient churches and convents. Fighting-bulls are bred in the area and flamenco is celebrated.

After interviewing Chelsea and Michael, we walked into an old hall in Vejer, bought a glass of wine and some tapas and watched an extraordinary performance of flamenco—gratis.

Clearly, Michael and Chelsea, both in their 30s, are escapees and adventurers rather than retirees. They have found a new and exciting life.

Another escapee is Mark. He, like Will and Lisa from Tamarama, fell in love with Barcelona. But that was not his only reason for leaving Australia at a relatively young age.

Mark was searching for himself in a similar way to Chelsea.

'I left because I had never considered myself necessarily tied to being in Australia,' he said. 'I think that might primarily be because my mother is German, my father is Austrian, I was born in Belgium. They were migrants from the UK after being concentration camp refugees.

'So I never felt that Australia was some place that I felt absolutely glued to and I had always thought about leaving after I finished university in the early 1980s.'

Mark worked in London and Barcelona, then he returned to Australia for a few years, but once again felt the pull of Europe. 'Politically and culturally I wanted to be there. I was increasingly unhappy with being back in Australia, I felt as if I was slipping back into being culturally isolated from the rest of the planet.'

'It's a slow drift that happens over a period of time,' said Mark. 'You don't actually realise that you are being disconnected with the world regardless of the internet et cetera.'

And that feeling of cultural and political isolation has deepened for Mark because he senses that Australia itself has drifted further and further away from Europe.

He is now a political refugee as much as he is a cultural refugee.

'My perspective now on Australia is that we have become culturally and morally much more North American than British even. We are becoming much more conservative, generally speaking, both culturally and morally, as a country. And inward looking.'

The arrival of the Abbott government only solidified Mark's position.

As Mark puts it, 'Watching the Australian elections (in 2013) from afar was really, for us, like watching a re-run of "children overboard" ten years ago. It is the same story, the same running-out the lowest common denominator factors, and incredibly depressing in terms

Cost of *Living*

Sydney vs Barcelona [% lower than Sydney]

Housing

Rent—3 bed'm apartment city centre*
$4,276
$1,598 — 63%

Rent—3 bed'm apartment outside city centre*
$2,815
$1,215 — 57%

Buy—apartment per sqm city centre
$9,795
$5,915 — 40%

Food

Bread
$3.47
$1.61 — 54%

Eggs
$4.13
$2.48 — 40%

Chicken breasts
$10.78
$8.7 — 20%

Tomatoes
$5.17
$1.94 — 63%

Restaurants

Mid range meal for 2
$80
$59.57 — 26%

Inexpensive
$15
$14.89 — 1%

Beer

Domestic
$4.80
$1.14 — 76%

Taxi

Per km
$3
$1.49 — 50%

One hour standby
$54.16
$29.78 — 45%

Electricity

Electricity, heating, water, garbage*
$238.97
$201.35 — 16%

Communications

Internet*
$61.66
$51.59 — 16%

Mobile phone (per min prepaid)
$1.02
$0.26 — 75%

* per month

Source: numbeo.com

of the lack of big ideas, lack of creativity and lack of engagement with the region.'

He was also fed up with the 'nanny state' attitudes of the Australian government and the litigious nature of the society. 'I find it frustrating when I go back to visit Australia. Obviously living in Spain, as a southern European country, there aren't many rules. They expect the pavement to be cracked and they don't pay any attention to it. And it is actually nice because they still have massive festivals here that involve huge amounts of fireworks and fire.'

Mark went back to Barcelona because 'I knew the place already, I loved the place.' He has since set up a successful public relations business and travels the world for work. His partner, Sophie, works in the food industry and is involved with gastronomy classes, tours, books. Their lives are entrenched here. And they made the best of the real estate slump. They only recently bought an apartment in Barcelona. Their timing couldn't have been better.

'We were going to buy something here five years ago and thank god we didn't because we probably would have paid 30 to 50 per cent more for the apartment we just bought,' Mark said.

'A lot of people, especially foreigners, are buying here now. In the centre of town in Barcelona you can get an apartment for A\$224 000. This would be absolutely unthinkable in London. You would be 20 kilometres out of town.

'Outside Barcelona, along the coast, property is even cheaper.'

Mark has no intention of returning to Australia. He still loves it but feels that he is more European than Australian, especially in Australia's current political environment.

'There are things I miss about Australia. I dearly miss the space and the green in the cities. But I don't miss the rest of it. People come over here now to visit—Barcelona has almost replaced Paris for Australian tourists.'

He also pointed out that his work is European-focused so Australia's distance would be a problem. 'I spend 60 to 70 per cent of the year travelling for work; that would be just impossible from Australia.'

Mark said that the cost of living has noticeably fallen since the financial crisis hit in 2008. 'You can see it in the bars and restaurants here. You can now buy a fresh orange juice, a croissant and a cafe latte for A$2.70. A daily menu—three courses with wine—costs A$15. There are a lot of deals here. People are being very careful about what they charge in restaurants.'

The costs of living in Spain are considerably lower than in Australia. In Barcelona, for example, consumer prices are 30 per cent lower than in Sydney, rent is almost 60 per cent lower, restaurants 14 per cent cheaper and groceries 40 per cent cheaper.

For Mark, though, the reasonable cost of living is not the critical issue. It is the free-flowing social values of the Spanish that he loves along with the language, work, politics and people.

He prefers to live in Spain, rather than other parts of Europe, because he finds the Spanish more inclusive, more tolerant with language, and quite welcoming.

'I loved the Spanish from the minute I met them and I still love them. They can frustrate the hell out of me as well. But the Spanish are incredibly loyal people. Sometimes I have gone years without seeing people and they still maintain friendships. They are incredibly spontaneous, too.

'Culturally one of the most attractive things about Spain is that the time spent with friends is valued every bit as much as work, if not more. Lunch time, everything is closed. The only things you can do in Spain at lunch time is eat and drink and sleep. You can't work. Nothing is open. You can't send a letter. Everything is closed. And that two- or three-hour part of the day when the family or friends or work colleagues get together in a restaurant and have a three-course meal and a glass of wine is absolutely precious.

'It is something that doesn't happen in many parts of the world and it is an incredibly healthy thing. It says a lot about a society and how they value communications with friends. Not just value work as the be all and end all.

'To emphasise that point, Sophie told me that up until recently— and she's been here a good eight years—none of my friends had asked her what she did for a living. People take you on your merits here. The status-work thing—the Spanish don't really care for it very much. And it is just amazing what that means. If someone knows you, they don't care how much you earn. I find that incredibly healthy and something that is disappearing in a lot of societies.'

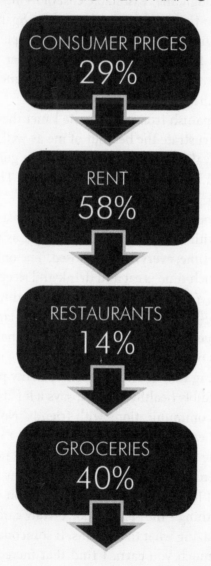

Cost *of* Living
INDICES
BARCELONA LOWER THAN SYDNEY

CONSUMER PRICES
29%

RENT
58%

RESTAURANTS
14%

GROCERIES
40%

Source: numbeo.com

France

Many people dream of living in France. The English love the south of France for the climate, the wine and the food.

Australians are a bit different. The climate is not the attraction. Sure, the climate in the south of France is pleasant—except for winter, unless you ski.

The great attraction for Australians is the food, the wine, the culture, the language, the architecture, the sophistication.

And many yearn to move closer to their cultural heartland; to put an end to the tyranny of distance many Australians still feel.

The move back to Europe and the UK for the Euro-antipodean provides the chance of rediscovering ethnic and cultural brothers and sisters; to find cultural and historic roots.

Many people also find France, whether provincial France or Paris or Marseilles or the Riviera, enticingly romantic. It is on many peoples' bucket list to have an exotic French adventure.

Gordon and Penny live part-time in southern France, just out of Avignon, in a wonderful village that is centred on the wine industry. The rest of the year they live in Newport, on Sydney's northern beaches.

Gordon always wanted a place in Europe. 'When I was 20, I was working in the UK. I always said, "Wouldn't it be good if we owned a pub here (in the UK) and spent six months of the year in France?" So I always had something in mind.'

After visiting France many times over the past 20 years, he and his partner Penny decided, on a whim, to buy a place. That was 15 years ago.

'It was Gordon's whim,' says Penny. 'My idea was "Why would you do something so crazy?" I think holiday houses in Australia are silly. Why would you buy a place 22 hours away? We don't even speak the language.'

Gordon pointed out, 'It was a bit of an adventure—the proverbial Peter Mayle job.' (Peter Mayle wrote the international best seller, *A Year in Provence*.)

But Gordon and Penny still love Sydney and the beach and they do not like Provence in winter. They sure like it in summer though and like many others, celebrate another life in France.

The French Alps—tower of dreams

Ex-Coolangatta couple Chris and Suzanne now live in the most extraordinary home. Its name is *La Tour du Treuil*—The Tower of the Trellis—and it dates back to 1170. La Tour, as they call it, was a treasury house as well as a tax office, thanks to its location right on the crossroads of three main trade routes in the Alps.

Almost all the wooden structure of the roof and ceilings presently in existence dates as far back as 1355, while the six-foot thick walls built of marble with traces of quartz have been standing since they were put there in 1170.

Chris and Suzanne acquired La Tour in late 2010 and are in the process of making it accessible to the public, for the first time in decades, as exclusive boutique accommodation. It was all unplanned.

'We came for a holiday—took a year out—and we didn't know what that would create or bring,' Suzanne said.

Initially, they settled for a year in the lakeside town of Annecy in the French Alps.

'One day in April a few years ago, Chris was cycling in a place called Tone. Around Annecy there are these huge mountains that glow in the sun—it was just a perfect day. I was driving a car to pick him up. It was then that he decided he didn't want to live in Australia anymore. He wanted to live here.'

Chris added: 'It was just the richness of it, I think. At that stage we had exposure to French life as outsiders. We had made many new friends—mostly English. Annecy has a lot of expats. But when we made that decision, life really turned and it started serving up all sorts of things. Like this; La Tour is in the middle of nowhere and this area is incredibly special.

'I like the culture, I like the diversity of it and I love the seasons which we don't tend to get in Queensland. I had lived in Brisbane since I was twelve—born in Sydney—then Coolangatta before we came here.'

Suzanne is a real *carpe diem* sort of girl. She argues that we must live our lives to the full and not be scared of the future. She was rocked by a recent event: 'There is another Australian woman around here—she was married to a heart surgeon and they had just retired and bought a house here. They were here a week and he died. Don't wait until you retire, live for today.'

'People, from what I have witnessed, need to have ducks in a row. If the ducks aren't in a row they can't do something. Whereas, if you wait for all your ducks to be in a row—you know: "I have got my pension, I have my super, I have sold my house, my daughter got married, my second daughter has a boyfriend, or the grandchildren are in school"—then the ducks are in a row and "Oh by the way, I have got breast cancer".'

She added, 'People get really frightened about making a move into the world of uncertainty—not knowing what it will look like.'

Nor did Suzanne and Chris have any clear plan. They were retired but now are set to do something else.

The move refocussed them on the big issues. It took them away from the mundane and the small things of life that they tended to focus on in Australia.

'In our own country or even here, people don't embrace the simplicity of life. But when we move away we tend to. Life becomes clearer. You tend to do what you want to do,' she said.

'When we move or when we run away or when we make dramatic change, we look to create. It is the routine that binds you (like the Sunday family lunch or the drink in the local bar at 6 p.m. each night). I think it can be detrimental to people's personal well-being because it becomes obligatory and they lose that flame. You know that flame: when someone talks to you about what they are passionate about and their whole face just shifts? They are uplifted.'

Once Suzanne and Chris complete the conversion of La Tour into a six-star boutique hotel, they look set to join the hospitality industry. Retirement for them was discovery. They have found a new life, a new country, a new culture, a new language and a new career. They are re-enthused. They talk like 40-year-olds. They have that passion that Suzanne was seeking.

> 'People, from what I have witnessed, need to have ducks in a row. If the ducks aren't in a row they can't do something. Whereas, if you wait for all your ducks to be in a row…then suddenly "Oh by the way, I have got breast cancer."'

Provence, wine and Rambo

The story of Gordon and Penny is not so different. Although, they do live two lives—a French life and an Australian life—and they love the contrast.

It was Penny who found the house—just out of Avignon in the south of France, in the centre of a wonderful village in a wine-producing heartland. For someone who thought holiday houses were a waste of time, it was certainly an interesting choice . . . a ruin.

The stone terrace house was pretty much a shell. Someone had previously decided to renovate, but all they did was demolish. There were no floors at all and parts of the roof had collapsed.

Penny did the house hunting with her sister, who could speak French.

As Penny tells the story, 'We were looking around and had some bizarre experiences. We had an appointment with an agent and she said, "Are you going to the wine festival in the next village? You buy a glass and they fill it up all weekend for you."

'And we said, "That is just what we need." So we ditched the real estate agent and came here. We pulled in, there was a parking space, we got out, they offered us a glass, we walked everywhere and they kept topping it up.' (Years ago, the wine used to come out of the town fountain during the festival.)

Penny said she and her sister, glasses in hand, wandered through the town and wound around a corner and 'there was an agent with the door open—he had a photo of exactly what we wanted—a little house on the prairie with the vineyards and everything.'

He showed them a couple of houses in town as well. The choice ended up being between the town terrace wreck or the French country house.

They went for the wreck. One reason was that it is easy to get to via train from Paris to Avignon and then either taxi or bus to their village.

Then the renovation began.

Penny, often with the help of her sister, spent about three months each year for two years, living in the village and handling the reconstruction. That's how she learnt a lot of her French. With language, you learn fast when you have to.

But there are always those cultural-linguistic hiccups. Penny's sister's name is Cheryl and she refers to her as 'Cher'. 'This means "love" in French,' Penny explained. 'So the villagers initially thought we were lesbians.'

And once they started working on the house the locals referred to them as 'Rambo One and Rambo Two.'

Now, the restored three-level house is superb, with three bedrooms, three bathrooms, and a large kitchen/living area that opens onto a rooftop terrace. One bedroom was so perfect for guests that, after three years of living there, Penny decided to run it as a bed-and-breakfast guesthouse.

'We have had the best time,' she said. 'We have met the best people. And the ones who are a little strange provide fantastic conversation. We have had probably about three really strange people stay here.'

Gordon added, 'Most guests have been fantastic and, if you get Australians, they are on the adventure of a lifetime. Good senses of humour, easy maintenance, they look after themselves, but they are always bad for our livers. You get people who don't really drink back home who then turn into lushes for a week on holiday—that sort of thing.'

So again, life has taken a very rich and interesting turn for Penny and Gordon at 60. No RSLs in Warriewood for them.

The process of buying a property in France is vastly different to the process of buying property in Australia. A French real estate agent at one stage tried to sell Gordon and Penny a property that had a long-term tenant. However, tenants in France have significant rights and purchasing a property that is rented can be a nightmare.

Also in France, rather than using a solicitor or conveyancer, you use a notaire. The notaire can, and often does, act for both buying and selling parties. This seems odd to an Australian. The transaction costs are high. The notaire receives about 7 per cent of the property purchase price. This includes government stamp duty.

Like many people living in France, though, Penny and Gordon are financially comfortable; they are able to travel annually to France from Australia and spend between three and eight months a year there. They have no plans to live in France full-time.

'Australia is just fantastic—a magnificent country,' Gordon said. 'We live in Newport in Sydney. We love the beach, and we do not like Provence in winter.'

Paris—cheaper than Sydney?

Fiona came to Paris seven years ago in her 50s. It was her dream and as she got older she realised that her dream was drifting away from her. She needed to grasp life afresh.

Who would have thought—the cost of living in Paris is actually cheaper than Sydney, Melbourne, Perth or Brisbane?

Certainly, the strength of the Australian dollar can account for some of this. Rent is another factor: it is surprisingly affordable. And it also helps that when you live in Paris, you live in a neighbourhood and you know where the best places to shop are.

Fiona is an Australian writer in her 60s who moved to Paris about seven years ago. She finds life much cheaper in her Parisian neighbourhood of Le Marais than it was when she lived in Elizabeth Bay in Sydney.

She lives in a typically Parisian one-bedroom apartment. It's spacious with lots of light, and faces into a large internal garden. The building dates back to around the 1860s and is near Place des Vosges in the very convenient 4th arrondissement. For this Fiona pays A$1950 a month (1300 euros).

The apartment would now be worth about A$750 000. It was bought for A$200 000 eight years ago. But Fiona is not interested in buying. Renting is so reasonable and the law really favours the tenant. After all, if she wanted to, she could rent her dream two-bedroom, 90-square metre, parquet-floored apartment on the Seine for A$3700 a month.

Fiona said that the cost of living is 'tons less' in Paris than in Elizabeth Bay. She explained: 'If you come to Paris as a tourist, you are likely to think that it is expensive. But when you live anywhere for a while, you learn where to go—like the markets on Thursday to Sunday here which have every possible form of fresh food, as well a flowers.

'I certainly can't compare the precociousness of Australian restaurants. I could take us for a two-course set lunch here for A$20, and there's 40 restaurants within walking distance.

'You are coming to the most visited city in the world, but you are really living in this beautiful village. You throw away all those material possessions like a car. You join the city and you cycle on your bike and you take the metro. If I was to cross Paris, coming home from dinner, it would cost 10 euros in a taxi. It is not expensive. There are now English language taxi services and phone companies.

'Phones and other communication costs are so cheap', Fiona said. 'My mobile calls any mobile in France for free. All my landline calls are free—international calls as well. And it costs A$50 a month for the landline and internet service. My mobile is another A$25 a month. All up A$75 a month for communications. And I am running a business.'

> 'I certainly can't compare the precociousness of Australian restaurants. I could take us for a two-course set lunch here for 14 euro (about A$20) to 40 restaurants within walking distance.'

Fiona has been travelling to Paris since her twenties—both for her work as a fashion writer and just because she's always loved the city.

She said she was influenced by her mother and her upbringing in rural Australia.

Moving to Paris was her dream and as she got older she realised that her dream was drifting away from her. She needed to grasp life afresh.

'I rented out my flat in Elizabeth Bay and I came to this apartment which I knew about through a friend. I had a few friends in Paris, I was familiar with the city, I had worked in and out of here all my life, had some French—about the same now! I never said to anyone "I am leaving Australia". I didn't know—could I survive, could I earn the money? Luckily, my then-editor was incredibly supportive and said the paper would take three stories a week. That sustained me for five years. But I knew that journalism had the "arse out of its pants".'

It was a process of discovery for Fiona.

'The first six months, first year, second year—it was working fine. I had an income. I could do it. I then made a decision to sell my apartment because I found Australian tenants just too difficult. It was an ongoing headache renting out an apartment in Sydney.

'I had a lot of treasured possessions. But the apartment I live in now would be 20 per cent of the size of my Sydney apartment. What I decided to do was to "sell or take", not to store. So I had a pretty emotional clear-out. But I kept what really mattered to me. I know people who open up storage units after five years and find rusting fridges. What a waste of money. So I was just ruthless. Possessions aren't everything.

'I brought furniture and personal things that reflected where I have travelled and lived all over the world. And those heavy books.'

Even though Fiona was already very familiar with France, it has taken a few years for her to understand the nuances of Parisian 'village life'. 'I learnt here that all the locals patronise the local businesses. They use the hairdressers, the beauty salon and go out to lunch on Saturday locally. They earn their money in this arrondissement and they spend it in this arrondissement.'

You even get this sense of local village life from the Government run schools in the neighbourhood. 'I have three schools in this street including the best in Paris—a primary school. If I walk out my door at 8.30 a.m. there will be 15 or so bicycles ridden by men with the school kids on the back and they are going to the most elite school in Paris. It is so sweet. Outside the school, they post up the menu every day of what the children will be served for lunch—always three courses, sometimes four, including cheese. This is so the parent, who delivers the child there, will know not to serve the same thing at night. If your child doesn't eat his spinach at lunch, you will get a note at the end of the month saying 'You must ensure he eats greens because he didn't like spinach.

'People don't go to private schools in France because French state education is so great.'

Bonjour Paris—que?

A move to a foreign country can be confronting. It was for Fiona.

'The first time I arrived, I came to live in a flat that a friend of mine (Thomas) from England, a wine writer, shared with my now-landlady, Lucy. They had had an apartment together for 25 years. He would stay there when he came from London to France to write about wine. He was here less and less once he got older so he said, "Fiona take my room for as long as it takes."

But the wine writer had forgotten to tell his old flatmate, Lucy, about the new tenant.

'My plane arrived from Australia at 6 a.m. I was at her door at 8. She had no idea that I was coming . . . I had quite an amount of bags you know. She was elegant. She was nice. She was confused. She is English but has lived here for 30 years. In her gracious way she said, "Well if that is what Thomas has agreed, we might as well have a coffee."

'She wasn't even dressed.

'I was pretty jet lagged. I thought, "Oh well maybe she is upset. Perhaps I will call Thomas." But I didn't have to call Thomas. We went to the cafe. By then it was 10 a.m. on a Saturday morning.

'She ordered "un café, un verre". Un verre, which normally just means a glass, in this instance meant a glass of white wine. I didn't know what un verre meant; that you didn't say un vin blanc. But it was her regular cafe.

'I thought, "Fucking hell, the French drink wine at 10 o'clock on a Saturday morning, this is a worry." And Lucy was one of the most important headhunters in her field in Europe at the time.

'We were poles apart. She was chic, drinking her coffee and a glass of wine. I was the Australian straight off the plane, jet lagged with red eyes drinking café crème. But somehow, because we had a lot of people in common through Thomas (the wine writer), it was very nice and away it went.

'She became a close friend and shared so much with me—true inside gossip.

'She bought this apartment [the one Fiona now lives in] and after about six months I moved into it.'

And like so many people that take the great leap and move into a new life in their mature years, Fiona suddenly grabbed hold of her youth again.

'I feel younger here,' she said. 'In France, everything in the pharmacy to do with sex and staying younger and thinner is cheaper. So much cheaper. I go to a gym. It is incredible: the women at 65 have sinewy bodies. They never gain weight.

'I am not spooked about going to the hairdresser. In Sydney, it would be "How much is it going to cost?" Here it is under A$150 for a cut, colour and blow dry and it is the best.

'The French are very impetuous, so you can just walk in off the street with no appointment. A$35 for a blow dry.

'There is everything you need to feel better about yourself—and it is on tap.'

Marseilles

The dream to move to Marseilles . . . it's a good one. And shared by many who have fallen in love—often at first visit—with this southern port city on the Mediterranean.

Marseilles is working class with grunt, crime and character. It is France's second largest city despite its small population of less than a million. It's also France's major port on the Mediterranean and the gateway to Provence.

Two large forts that flank the entrance to the Old Port—Fort Saint-Nicolas on the south side and Fort Saint-Jean on the north—are testament to the fact that the port of Marseilles functioned as the main trade port to the French empire.

Four islands lie out in the Bay of Marseille. On the smallest of these, the island of d'If, is Château d'If, once a fortress and later a prison, made famous by the Dumas novel *The Count of Monte Cristo*.

Marseilles comes to life in summer. The Old Port is the centre of activity. Locals and tourists promenade along the pedestrian boulevards fringed with restaurants and bars near the Old Port and the Hotel de Ville.

Australians Paul and Marie have lived in Marseilles for more than ten years. Marie said: 'It is one of those places that you either love or you hate—and I love Marseilles. I really like the way its people are so in your face. The people are loud. They are a bit noisy. Whereas if you are living in a rural area of France, it is very calm.'

However, their move to Marseilles—and indeed out of Australia—wasn't about living the south-of-France dream. Paul and Marie came to France partly to rediscover cultural roots, and partly because they could no longer face the political situation in Australia.

Paul had lived in Australia for 30 years, but he wasn't raised there. He was schooled in England. His Australian father worked for the United Nations and every three years the family moved countries. His mother was French. He went to university in France.

When his father retired he said to Paul, 'Do you want a free ticket to Australia?'

Paul was initially affronted and said to his father, 'Australia? I don't want to go there. They're racist.' He explained that he held this view because the Australian government was a good friend of apartheid South Africa. But it was quite an expensive ticket, and curiosity got the better of him so Paul decided he'd go and take a look.

'But when I got here, Gough Whitlam came to power. It was so exciting. I only planned to stay six months. I stayed eleven years without even moving.'

In that time he met Marie and together they regularly travelled back and forth to France, and in the mid 1980s they lived in northern France while Paul renovated a family house there. But it was so cold in winter they decided that if they were to ever live in France, it would have to be in the south.

They returned for another year in 2001 so their daughter, who was eight and at the French school in Sydney, could 'know the country that is part of her cultural background'.

Paul and Marie had decided the only way their daughter was going to be firmly anchored in the French language and culture was if she went to school there for at least a year. 'So she had one year of primary school in France,' Paul said. 'Previous to that, she wasn't

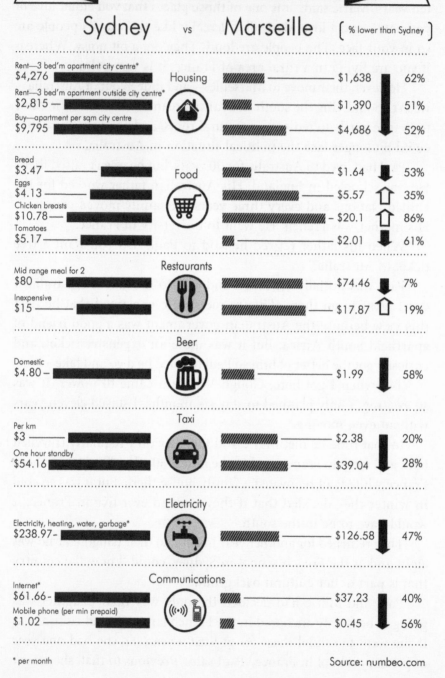

Cost of Living

Sydney vs Marseille [% lower than Sydney]

Housing

	Sydney	Marseille		%
Rent—3 bed'm apartment city centre*	$4,276	$1,638	↓	62%
Rent—3 bed'm apartment outside city centre*	$2,815	$1,390		51%
Buy—apartment per sqm city centre	$9,795	$4,686	↓	52%

Food

	Sydney	Marseille		%
Bread	$3.47	$1.64	↓	53%
Eggs	$4.13	$5.57	⇧	35%
Chicken breasts	$10.78	$20.1	⇧	86%
Tomatoes	$5.17	$2.01	↓	61%

Restaurants

	Sydney	Marseille		%
Mid range meal for 2	$80	$74.46	↓	7%
Inexpensive	$15	$17.87	⇧	19%

Beer

	Sydney	Marseille		%
Domestic	$4.80	$1.99	↓	58%

Taxi

	Sydney	Marseille		%
Per km	$3	$2.38		20%
One hour standby	$54.16	$39.04	↓	28%

Electricity

	Sydney	Marseille		%
Electricity, heating, water, garbage*	$238.97	$126.58	↓	47%

Communications

	Sydney	Marseille		%
Internet*	$61.66	$37.23		40%
Mobile phone (per min prepaid)	$1.02	$0.45	↓	56%

* per month

Source: numbeo.com

convinced that anyone else in the world, except for her parents and their nutty friends, spoke French.'

They again returned to Australia in 2002 but by now Paul was finding the political situation unbearable. 'The war drums were beating with George Bush and John Howard and I thought, "I can't believe all this crap going on. I can't stand it. I can see where it is going." Marie and I were not happy in Sydney, so we thought, "This is it, we'll pack up and leave, settle back in France."'

Their daughter is twenty now and is studying international relations, German and Spanish at Sydney University. She plans to do her masters at McGill University in Canada. She has become a citizen of the world, just like Paul.

Marie is now working as a real estate agent in the city, while Paul is a builder. He also consults to English speakers, be they from the UK or Australia, who are seeking to purchase a property in France. His primary advice to everyone is to rent for several months before buying.

Even so, it is a good time to buy real estate if you know your way around Marseilles. Marie said: 'it is a buyers market here. 2007 was the peak. Today if you were selling a property you would have to accept 20 per cent less.'

Paul warned though that 'acting too quickly with real estate can be very dangerous. People sometimes fall in love with a property and their due diligence evaporates.'

'People say "Oh if this place goes I will never find anything like it". This is not really the case. The more you know about the market the better you will be able to make a correct judgement in the longer term. Mostly you hear, "Thank god I didn't get that, it was overpriced, needed a lot more work."

'Try and inform yourself as best you can,' said Paul.

He added, 'People do really strange things—putting your heart where your head should be—especially if you are moving somewhere to follow a dream. You know, they come in all bright eyed having decided they don't want to live in Australia any more. They want to live a French life. They get a bit carried away—a travel drunkenness takes over.'

Marie said, 'The difference with buying real estate here is that in Sydney you have Domain.com. You know if something is sold

INDICES

MARSEILLE LOWER THAN SYDNEY

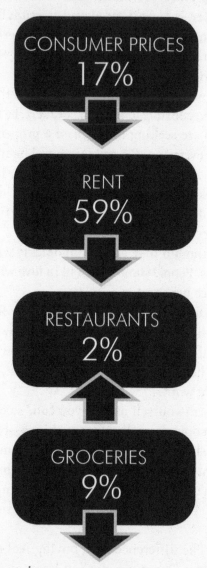

CONSUMER PRICES
17%

RENT
59%

RESTAURANTS
2%

GROCERIES
9%

Source: numbeo.com

at auction, the next week you can find out what it was sold for and that gives you the market price. What happens here is that the only people who can get the information are the buyer, the seller and the notaire because they don't have conveyancing companies here. The notaire is the only one who can tell you what the average selling price for a region is, and you have to pay for that information.

'There is a general lack of price transparency,' said Marie.

But returns from property ownership in Marseilles are attractive.

'As an investor you hope to get 6 to 6.5 per cent gross. It is nothing for investors in Marseille to own 150 properties,' said Marie.

'There are also issues if the property is rented. When an owner wants a tenant to move out it has to be before winter. Once it is officially winter you have to wait until March (to move tenants out),' Marie told us.

In Marseilles a standard lease is for three years for an unfurnished property. A three year lease requires the tenant to give three months notice and the owner has to give six months. A property that is rented for twelve months has to be furnished, although this could just be table and chairs, a fridge and a stove.

Marie also said it is a good idea if each party has a different notaire. It is difficult to represent two persons' interests.

The cost of living in Marseilles is, like Paris, surprisingly afford-able—in some cases much cheaper than Australia. Consumer prices are 30 per cent lower in Marseilles than in Sydney, rent is more than 50 per cent lower, and groceries 9 per cent lower. However, restaurants are about the same price or a little more expensive.

But in terms of cheap real estate, it is a great time to move to Europe.

And anyway, the food is great, the culture rich and the challenge to learn another language probably enough to keep dementia at bay.

Visas—an issue

A long-term stay visa, or at least the difficulty of getting one, is the primary problem confronted by anyone who wants to pack up and take off to Europe.

The Schengen Convention limits non-EU or non-UK citizens to just three months stay in any one six-month period in the Schengen area. Twenty-two EU states are part of the Schengen area. No visa is required for a three-month stay.

But if you want to stay for more than 90 days then a visa is required and this presents a problem (see Appendix for more on this). Applications for this visa must be made to the Schengen member country directly. The rules and requirements are determined by each individual EU country and can vary between countries. All is not lost though. Long-term visas are available, but it takes time, effort and it is never a sure thing that you will get one.

Fiona, who has lived in Paris for seven years, has never had a problem with visa renewal because, she said, 'France loves to welcome anyone who is creative. They have special rules for writers, artists and the like. It is time-consuming to apply and then to renew every year. But once you know the drill, it is fine.'

Similarly, Penny who lives in Provence was issued with a long-stay visa and a residence permit, or *carte de séjour*, over ten years ago when the rules were less strict. This gave her a visa for a one year stay which she renewed annually at the local prefecture. But while renewing this year she was surprised when they presented her with a ten-year visa. She was not told the reason for this but presumes it is because she has lived there for a decade. Needless to say, she is delighted.

The biggest problem Penny had encountered with the yearly visa renewal was providing proof of income. She needed a friendly bank manager to sign a letter every year confirming that she would receive an income equivalent to at least A\$1500 (1000 euro) a month. Of course, bank managers change periodically and some are less cooperative than others. Penny had to change her Australian bank at one stage just to ensure she could get the right documents for visa renewal.

It certainly helps if you have dual citizenship—Australian and EU. Mark in Barcelona already had an EU passport and therefore he had no problem with the visa issue. Similarly for Chelsea living in Vejer de la Frontera; she has Spanish citizenship. However, it took several months for Chelsea's Australian husband Michael to obtain his residency.

Carmen and John found themselves in a similar situation to Chelsea and Michael, and their story is a valuable lesson. Carmen is Spanish and had lived in Australia for twenty years but kept her Spanish citizenship. Her husband John has an Australian passport.

'We initially were misinformed by Spanish authorities in Australia,' John said. 'Their reaction was, "Well, you're married to a Spanish national so there will be no problems getting a visa to live there. Just apply once you arrive in Spain." So, naively, we did that. But bureaucracy was invented in Spain, I think, if not France.'

John began the process in Spain in the normal way—he started looking things up on the internet, found the appropriate office to apply for his visa, and off he went.

'But things were not that simple,' John said. 'First of all, they said things like, "You've come to the wrong office" or "We do not understand what you are trying to do." It all had to be communicated in Spanish, of course.

'The real challenge was getting the right information. We filled out forms we thought were correct on the internet, but they weren't. In essence, internet information on visas is not updated well.

'In the end I had to do what most immigrants do—I found an immigration agent. It cost less than A$700 for the whole thing.'

And there was still a lot of paperwork involved.

'To prove that I could support myself and had an income, I had to show bank statements, superannuation statements and so on,' John said. 'This was a real chore because the documents are in the wrong language and the authorities do not understand them. Plus the bank statements had to be signed by a bank manager, they had to be translated, and they had to include an official conversion of the bank balances to euro.

'But the agent was good. He knew when to push back. He knew how to argue with the authorities. It is a very arbitrary process. It depends on the person you confront in the bureaucracy.'

If John had his time over, he would have used a domestic Australian immigration agent. 'And I now know that there are agents in Australia who specialise in getting people Spanish visas.'

John has a retired Australian friend, with no EU links, who

handled her application from Australia and, although it took six months, she succeeded in obtaining a long-stay visa.

'She had to demonstrate that she had health insurance—I did as well—and she had to show she had a regular income. That wasn't so hard as she had super savings. She did that through the Spanish authorities in Australia—the consulate in Sydney. In fact, if you do not speak Spanish, it is much easier to apply in your home country.'

This is very sound advice from John and would apply to any country, but especially non-English-speaking ones: sort out your visa in Australia before you pack up and take off.

The shift to Europe—a personal journey

There are no great cost advantages in packing up and taking off to western Europe. The attraction is clearly cultural, social and political.

Fiona's new life in Paris is all about the lifestyle, the food, the fashion and the art. And she is living what has always been her dream.

Gordon and Penny love the complete lifestyle change offered by the wine producing town near Avignon. But they are in Europe for only part of the year. They do not want to leave Australia.

Suzanne and Chris are enjoying renovating their twelfth-century tower and the cycling, walking, skiing and village life that goes along with it. They have sold up, packed up and taken off and right now have no intention of returning.

France and Spain offer great food and wine, cheap real estate, at present, and a European lifestyle. For many a Europhile-antipodean it is like returning to the womb. Chelsea discovered this when she moved to Vejer de la Frontera in southern Spain as did Paul when he moved to Marseilles.

And there are the political refugees as well. Mark in Barcelona is one of these, although he lives in Europe now for other reasons as well. Similarly, Fiona, while loving the lifestyle in Paris, is pleased to get away from what she sees as the shallow politics of Australia.

Long stay visas are a roadblock to those wanting to move to Europe, or at least those countries in the Schengen area. It is not impossible though. Long-stay visas can be obtained, although with some difficulty.

Europe tips and traps

1. Real estate prices in many parts of Europe are low at present. It seems like good value for money. But beware—buying property in countries like France and Spain is a very different process to purchasing property in Australia. Transaction costs in France are about 7 per cent of purchase price. Always get competent legal and structural/building advice.
2. Rent before you buy.
3. Learn the language. If you don't, you will live in a bubble. Remember that in some places, like France, even though you may speak the language well, it is likely you will always be seen as a foreigner. Acceptance can be difficult.
4. Southern European countries, like Spain and Greece, are less of a 'nanny state' than Australia. This creates freedom, but dangers as well—ensure you know and respect the laws of the land, even if they might be poorly policed.
5. Europe is currently cheaper than Australia—but be very cautious about this. A fall in the Australian dollar against the euro can make life a lot more expensive in Europe.
6. Be aware of France's tax regime—wealth tax, inheritance tax and property taxes.
7. Long-term stay visas for Europe are tricky. It is best to apply for these from your country of origin. At least then, language does not present a barrier.

CHAPTER 7

Superannuation

The great news about Australian superannuation is that the pension you draw from it can be received in Bali or Thailand or Malaysia, just as it can be received in Australia.

But as we all know, superannuation and pension benefits are never simple, especially if you do something different, like live in another country, even if it's just for a while. So you do have to be careful, and pre-plan your move.

In this chapter, we set out some of the basic superannuation issues that you might face as a retiree living overseas.

One of the jewels of the Australian tax system is that a pension from your superannuation fund is tax-free once you reach the age of 60. If you are in that age category, the chances are that you will be relying partly on this to fund your new lifestyle.

And this is where you may need some very serious pre-planning before you leave Australian shores. The last thing you need is for the Australian Tax Office (ATO) to decide that your superannuation is no longer eligible for those generous tax concessions. It could blow your budget apart.

Superannuation law can be a minefield but the real danger zone, for our purposes, is restricted to those with a self-managed superannuation fund (SMSF).

> The last thing you need is for the Australian Tax Office
> to decide that your super is no longer eligible for those
> generous tax concessions.

If your Australian superannuation is with an industry fund, a public service fund or one of the big retail fund managers then you don't have much to worry about at all on the Australian taxation front. So let us deal with those first.

Any individual who holds his or her superannuation savings in an industry or retail fund will be able to move overseas without facing any new rules on eligibility. The superannuation benefits held in one of these funds will continue to receive concessional tax treatment.

In addition, the rules that govern access to superannuation benefits (these are called the preservation rules) apply indiscriminately to Australian citizens wherever they may live—in Australia or overseas. Moving offshore will not bring any extra headaches with the ATO or the superannuation regulators.

Where the headaches might arise, however, is with the tax office in your new country of residence. It all depends on the laws of the country you choose to live in and whether that country has a double tax treaty with Australia.

A double tax treaty effectively assigns taxing rights to one country or the other. If residing in a country without an agreement, your Australian-based income may be taxed under both Australia's and the other country's taxation regime. That is precisely what you want to avoid.

Most of the countries covered in this book—Indonesia, Thailand, Malaysia, Vietnam, Spain and France—have a double tax treaty with Australia.

If you plan to move to a country not on this list, it is easy to check whether there is a double tax treaty in force. The Australian Tax Office link for a list of tax treaty countries is: www.ato.gov.au/General/International-tax-agreements/In-detail/Tax-treaties/Countries-that-have-a-tax-treaty-with-Australia/

Cambodia, for example, does not have a double tax treaty with

Australia. Theoretically, any resident of Cambodia is subject to Cambodian income tax on their world wide income. The definition of resident is broad and includes anyone who spends more than 182 days (or roughly six months) in the country in any one tax year.

Theory differs from practice, however, and we did not meet any Australians in Cambodia who were taxed on their offshore income. Still, it is important to do your homework and seek professional advice if moving to a country without a double tax treaty with Australia.

There are a lot more details on residency for tax purposes in the chapter on taxation. This section deals only with the impact on superannuation benefits.

So let's get to the hard part.

Self-managed super funds

There is one key phrase to remember in respect of your self-managed super fund and that is: 'complying super fund'. Tattoo it on your fore-head—metaphorically speaking—because the taxation consequences of a non-complying super fund are horrendous.

A self-managed super fund becomes a non-complying fund if it loses its Australian nature—that is, if it is no longer considered to be an Australian superannuation fund by the Australian Taxation Office.

> Tattoo 'complying super fund' on your forehead—metaphorically speaking—because the taxation consequences of a non-complying super fund are horrendous.

You do not want that to happen. Let us give you a taste of the consequences. Should your self-managed super fund become non-complying at any point, the ATO can send you a tax bill that is equivalent to almost half the total assets in your fund. Say you have $1 million in your fund, then that amount will be taxed at the highest marginal tax rate in the year that the fund becomes non-complying—that is near $500 000. And that is not all. The ATO will also tax any earnings of the fund at the highest marginal tax rate for every year that the fund is non-complying.

And if the fund does regain its residency status and becomes an Australian superannuation fund once more, then there is another one-off penalty. This time, just to welcome you home, an amount (asset values less contributions) will be included in the fund's assessable income in the year the fund regains its Australian residency status. This amount will be taxed at 15 per cent if the fund regains its complying status or 45 per cent if the fund remains non-complying for other reasons.

Bottom line? Your superannuation fund needs to be a complying fund if you are to avoid onerous penalties. To achieve this, the fund needs to be considered an Australian superannuation fund for tax purposes.

So, what is an 'Australian' superannuation fund and how do you maintain this status?

It can be done. It just requires careful planning. A good accountant will be able to organise the appropriate changes to ensure that you stay within the law. What follows is an explanation, as simple as we can make it, of the legal requirements so that you can be prepared when you discuss matters with your accountant.

There are three tests for an Australian super fund. Each and every test must be satisfied in each tax year. And each and every test must be satisfied at the same time. It is not good enough to satisfy test one in February and test two in March, for example. All three tests must be satisfied on the same date.

The tests are:

1. The fund was established in Australia *or* any asset of the fund is situated in Australia;
2. The *central management and control* of the fund is *ordinarily* situated in Australia;
3. The fund has *no active* members or, if it does have active members, then at least 50 per cent of:
   (a) the total market value of the fund's assets attributable to superannuation interests is held by active members; or
   (b) the sum of the amounts that would be payable to active members if they ceased to be members is attributable to

superannuation interests held by active members who are Australian tax residents.

That sounds complicated, and we will deal with it in more detail below, but it applies if you are still contributing to your super fund or an employer is contributing on your behalf *or* there are other members of the fund still in Australia and still making super contributions.

Let us take these tests one by one.

Test one: an Australian fund

The first test—that either the superannuation fund was established in Australia or any asset of the fund is situated in Australia. This is the easiest test of all. Most funds for our purposes would have been established in Australia. But if not, it is still easy to meet the test—any asset of the fund must be in Australia and this can be just a simple bank deposit. If any shares in Australian companies are held by the fund, this would also qualify, as would Australian-based property.

Test two: central management and control

The second test is the hard one. The crucial words are 'central management and control'. Many people make the mistake of interpreting this to mean the administration of the fund—filing returns, keeping the books, keeping an eye on rollover dates for bank deposits, buying and selling shares. If administration of the fund was enough to satisfy the central management and control test, then it would be a simple matter of appointing an Australian-based accounting firm or super fund management company to handle your self-managed super fund for an annual fee. But this is not what the tax office has in mind—it is very specific about exactly what central management and control means.

Central management and control, according to the ATO, describes the strategic and high-level decision-making processes and activities of a fund. This includes formulating or varying the investment strategy for a fund, reviewing performance of a fund's investments and determining how the assets of a fund should be used to pay benefits to members. Administrative and general day-to-day activities do not constitute central management and control.

The issue is, who has the central management and control function? This is usually the individual trustees of the fund or the directors of the corporate trustee. Once again, it is easy to fall into a trap here. It seems easy enough, if you are moving overseas, to appoint someone else as trustee of the fund—a relative or close friend or even an accountant. But this is not enough. If you still make the final decision on investments of the fund and payments from the fund, then it is you who exercises central management and control. And if you are living overseas, then the chances are that your fund is non-complying. The onus of proof is on you. This means that you have to prove to the ATO that central management and control is ordinarily exercised in Australia—it is not a matter of whether you are caught out or not. The tax office has to be convinced.

So what can you do to satisfy the ATO? There are a few options.

The simplest option is to change the nature of your fund. How do you this?

A fund has the option to relinquish, or give up, its status as a self-managed super fund and arrange for an Australian resident commercial organisation to act as a professional trustee (for example, Australian Executor Trustees Limited). When this occurs the fund becomes a small fund regulated by APRA (Australian Prudential Regulatory Authority). It is no longer a self-managed super fund. This solves the residency problem. Your fund remains an Australian super fund regardless of which country you are living in at the time. It can be an expensive option, however, and it will result in a loss of investment flexibility.

A second option is to genuinely give up central management and control of the fund by either resigning as a trustee and appointing a trusted adviser or relative, who is a resident of Australia, to make the high-level strategic decisions for your super fund. Alternatively, you could grant an enduring power of attorney to this trusted adviser or relative. This can be risky and it is an option that few of us would consider. But it is an option. And if you choose this option, make sure the necessary arrangements are in place before you leave Australia. Also, ensure that the person you have granted authority to genuinely exercises central management and control, is a resident of Australia and does not ask for your approval on investment decisions.

A third option is to investigate whether you fall under the tax office exemption for 'temporary' non-residents. If your departure from Australia is considered to be temporary, then the tax office will consider that central management and control of the fund is still ordinarily exercised in Australia—even during your absence. The definition of 'temporary' is important. The tax office has said that an absence of up to two years will be considered temporary if there is evidence of an intention to return to Australia. In deciding whether you have a genuine intention to return, the tax office will take into account contracts of employment, whether you have kept a house in Australia, whether you have retained private health insurance in Australia, details of any previous absences from the country, and details regarding changes to personal bank accounts, credit cards, private health insurance and club memberships. And an absence of more than two years can still be considered 'temporary' as long as the tax office is satisfied as to your intention to return at a specific time.

For someone who has decided to relocate overseas during their retirement, it could prove almost impossible to convince the tax office that he or she fits into the temporary category for exemption.

There is one last option that can make it possible to ensure that your self-managed super fund retains its Australian status. And this is probably the most attractive option of all.

The tax office has determined that where there is an equal number of trustees or directors of a corporate trustee located in Australia and overseas, who all actively participate in the central management and control from these locations, the central management and control of a fund will ordinarily be in Australia. With the ability for a fund to have up to four members, a couple moving overseas could elect for two new members/trustees (for example, children or relatives) to join the fund. For this solution to be effective, the new trustees must equally participate in the central management and control of the fund.

Test three: active members

Now we come to test three—assuming you have satisfied the first two tests of central management and control of the fund ordinarily exercised in Australia *and* the fund has either been set up in Australia or holds assets in Australia. The third test is the active member test.

This test will not be a problem if you don't want to make any further contributions to your super fund. If you have retired, your contributions have probably stopped in any case. But you must also take into account whether you ever want to roll over superannuation balances from another fund into your self-managed fund, or whether you want to contribute from your personal savings under the $150 000 a year rule for non-concessional contributions.

The most important fact to keep in mind is that once you are considered a non-resident for Australian tax purposes, you cannot make contributions to your self-managed super fund unless more than 50 per cent of the assets of the fund are attributable to active resident members. For example, if you have four members of your fund, two of whom are still resident in Australia and still making contributions to the fund, then you have to ensure that their interests (i.e. the proportion of the fund they are entitled to) account for more than 50 per cent of the fund's assets at all times.

This assessment should be undertaken carefully and a buffer allowed to ensure there is no inadvertent breach.

If your self-managed super fund has only non-resident members—say, you and your partner—then you cannot make any contributions to the fund while you are a non-resident if you are to satisfy the active member rule.

SUPERANNUATION TIPS AND TRAPS

1. Tax-free pensions from your Australian superannuation fund are available for the over 60s both in Australia and overseas. But there are conditions attached.
2. If your superannuation is with a big industry fund or one of the big Australian retail funds, you won't have any problems maintaining the Australian tax-free status.
3. Self-managed super funds (SMSF) are a different story. Pensions will be tax-free in Australia as long as the self-managed fund is considered to be a 'complying fund'.

4. You may need to restructure your self-managed super fund to ensure tax-free status. This can be done but you will need to seek professional advice. And you must do this before you relocate overseas.
5. Check that your pension income is tax-free in your new country of residence. If there is a double tax treaty in place with Australia, you should be fine. But it pays to check thoroughly with the relevant consulate in Australia.

CHAPTER 8

Pensions

Australian age pensions can be paid overseas indefinitely. More than 60 000 Australian pensioners are living permanently overseas and still receive the age pension every fortnight. That is the good news—really good news.

The bad news is that there are quite strict conditions on Australian pensions paid overseas. It is critical that you are aware of these conditions and how they apply to your personal circumstances *before* you leave the country permanently—or even semi-permanently.

If you are already eligible for the age pension

If you qualify for a pension already—that is, you have met the required assets test, income test and residency test under Australia's Social Security Act—you should have few problems in transporting that pension or part-pension overseas.

It is important, however, that you apply for, and receive, your first pension payment while you are still a resident in Australia and before you make any move to relocate. This is the first and most critical rule. If you meet that condition, you are almost there.

But don't get too confident. There are some extra conditions to meet to achieve what the government calls 'full pension portability'.

For a start, you are going to have to learn and understand a few new terms.

> It is important that you apply for, and receive, your
> first pension payment while you are still a resident in
> Australia and before you make any move to relocate.

Australian Working Life Residency, or AWLR

The first of these terms is Australian Working Life Residency (AWLR). If you don't meet the AWLR requirement in full, you may receive only a proportion of your pension.

Put simply, whenever a person receiving an age pension is outside of Australia for more than 26 weeks, or just over six months, their pension payment becomes subject to the AWLR. The amount of pension they receive then depends on the length of their residency within Australia between the ages of sixteen and pension age, which is 65 for most people. It is not necessary to have worked or been employed for that time, simply living in Australia is enough.

From 1 January 2014, the AWLR requirement is 35 years. If you do the arithmetic, this means that if you have spent more than thirteen years living outside Australia between the ages of 16 and 65, it is important to have a close look at the AWLR requirements.

There are some important exemptions to this rule. For example, if you spent time in a country that has an International Social Security Agreement with Australia, then the years spent in that country can be included alongside your years spent in Australia to calculate your AWLR. Note that no countries in Asia have such an agreement with Australia, but many countries including the United States and Spain do have such an agreement. There is a full list of these countries on the Department of Human Services website. (The link to the relevant page is: www.humanservices.gov.au/customer/enablers/centrelink/international-social-security-agreements/countries-that-have-agreements-with-australia.)

If you do not meet the 35-year AWLR rule, your pension will be reduced. For example, if you spent only twenty years in Australia (and a qualifying country, as above) between the ages of sixteen and 65, you will receive 241/420 of the pension you were entitled to when you were residing permanently in Australia. (The calculation is done in months. In this example, the denominator 420 represents 35 multiplied by 12. The numerator of 241 represents 20 multiplied by 12 plus 1.) Don't ask why they calculate it this way—they just do.

Pension supplements

The age pension payment is made up of two parts—the pension itself and supplements. The pension part is fully portable subject to the AWLR rule. The supplements are not portable and most cease to be paid once you have been out of Australia for more than six weeks—it used to be thirteen weeks but it has recently been tightened up.

The pension supplement typically covers telephone, mobility and utilities, and can be worth up to $160 a quarter or $640 a year.

The other card that will be cancelled after six weeks out of the country is the Commonwealth Seniors Health Card. A reclaim for the health card can be made over the phone as long as it is made within thirteen weeks of the cancellation. But a full online or paper reclaim is required after you have spent 26 weeks overseas.

If you are under 65

If you are under 65 when you decide to live overseas, then eligibility for the age pension becomes a very serious issue and one that must be carefully investigated before you make your final decision.

Take the example of Judy and Bill. They decided to move to Thailand when they were both 62 with the intention of eventually applying for the age pension when they reached 65. They were confident that they would qualify under the asset and income tests set by the government. Plus, they had older friends who were living in Thailand and receiving fortnightly pension payments from Australia with no problems at all.

But Judy and Bill were not aware that they also had to meet a strict residency test. The bottom line was that if they wanted to receive the age pension they had to return to Australia and resume residence. They had to convince the Department of Human Services that they had returned to Australia permanently. And that's not all. Once granted the age pension, they could not leave the country for the next two years or they would risk losing their pension. It is pretty onerous.

Theoretically, Judy and Bill could have a two-year sojourn back in Australia, start receiving their pension shortly after they returned to the country and then, two years down the track, return to Thailand with full portability of their pension payments. But that is not the spirit of the law. If the government believes that is your intention then under the Social Security Act you are not considered a resident and therefore should not be granted a pension at all.

It is a pretty tough rule.

Qualifying for an age pension: residency requirements

These are the nuts and bolts that you need to know about getting an Australian age pension.

To qualify, an individual must have reached pension age, be an Australian resident (that is, living in Australia on a permanent basis), be in Australia on the day their claim is lodged, and be an Australian resident for a total of at least ten years, with at least five of these years in one continuous period.

There are other sections that apply to refugees, and widows who were born outside Australia and were previously married to an Australian citizen. But, for our purposes, the first requirement is—an Australian resident who has been resident in Australia for a total of at least ten years and who is resident in Australia on the day the claim is lodged.

Now, if you were Judy or Bill, you might argue that you were born in Australia, spent most of your life here and were 'resident' in Australia on the day that you lodged the claim. Unfortunately, the legislation is a bit stricter than that. The Department of Human Services takes into account a number of factors to determine whether you really qualify as a resident on the day the claim is lodged.

The Social Security Act is quite clear on the circumstances that the department will take into account in determining residency.

These are listed in the legislation as follows:

'In deciding for the purposes of this [Social Security] Act whether or not a person is residing in Australia, regard must be had to:
1. The nature of the accommodation used by the person in Australia;
2. The nature and extent of the family relationships the person has in Australia;
3. The nature and extent of the person's employment, business or financial ties with Australia;
4. The nature and extent of the person's assets located in Australia;
5. The frequency and duration of the person's travel outside Australia; and
6. Any other matter relevant to determining whether the person intends to remain permanently in Australia.

It states that all of these matters have to be taken into account—not just one or two matters.

Failing the assets test

Let's assume that everything has fallen into place for you—that you are eligible for the age pension, you have successfully applied for it while still a resident of Australia, and you meet the requirements of AWLR having spent at least 35 years in Australia between the ages of sixteen and 65. That's great—but there are still a few traps to consider.

For example, the assets test. In Australia, your principal place of residence, your home, is exempt from the assets test. Once you move overseas, however, that home may no longer be your principal place of residence for pension purposes. Be very careful on this issue. It is easy to confuse the Australian Tax Office's definition of a principal place of residence for capital gains tax purposes with the definition for pension purposes.

As you will see in the Taxation chapter, you can rent out your home for up to six years and it could still be considered a principal place of residence in determining whether or not you need to pay capital gains tax on sale. But that is not the case with pension eligibility. Under the Social Security Act your principal place of residence is where you actually live. It is only exempt from the assets test if you are living in it.

There is some room for interpretation and appeal. For example, there are special provisions if the pensioner moves into an aged care facility. And there is a degree of flexibility if the pensioner is overseas on a lengthy holiday.

If you sell your home before you relocate overseas, the proceeds of the sale will be taken into account in determining whether you pass the assets test.

If you rent it out, the income you receive in rent will be taken into account in determining whether you pass the income test, plus the value of the home will be considered in determining whether you pass the assets test. And it doesn't work to claim that you have sold your house in Australia but you have used the money to buy your new home, your new principal place of residence, overseas. The department will not accept that—only a principal place of residence within Australia, and one that you actually live in, is exempt from the assets test.

> In Australia, your principal place of residence, your home, is exempt from the assets test. Once you move overseas however, that home may no longer be your principal place of residence for pension purposes.

Keeping up with changes to the law

It is also important to keep abreast of any changes in pension eligibility. Retrospective legislation is very rare in Australia, so the chances are that if you have qualified for the age pension and for pension portability then your situation will be permanent. You should be safe—unless you return to live in Australia for a few months. If you do this, you may become subject to any changes in the law while you have been away. This has happened twice recently with two separate changes in legislation.

The first change was to the AWLR. Prior to 1 January 2014, pensioners moving overseas were required to have an Australian Working Life Residence of just 25 years between the ages of 16 and 65. From 2014 this requirement was raised to 35 years. Any pensioners who were already overseas on the date of the change were still subject to the 25-year rule. But if they return to Australia and reside here for several months, the proportionality rule changes to a 35-year AWLR requirement if they move overseas again.

There has been a similar situation with disability support payments. This is not really relevant for the purposes of this book but, just briefly, there is a new law that disability payments will be stopped for those pensioners who move overseas except under very strict conditions. The new law does not apply to those who already reside permanently overseas—they will still receive their disability support payments even if they don't meet the new tougher rules. But if they return to live in Australia for a while, they will be subject to the terms of the new law when they go overseas again.

The bottom line is, be prepared and remain informed. Research pension eligibility very closely before you finalise your move overseas. And keep an eye on any changes while you are away.

PENSIONS TIPS AND TRAPS

1. Australian aged pensions can be paid overseas indefinitely but you must be a permanent resident of Australia at the time that you first apply for the age pension.
2. Pension supplements will not be paid overseas in most cases.
3. The Commonwealth Seniors Health Card will be cancelled after you have spent more than six weeks out of Australia.
4. If you have lived outside of Australia for more than thirteen years between the ages of sixteen and 65, you may receive only a proportion of the age pension if you relocate overseas.

5. If you have been living overseas immediately prior to applying for the aged pension, you may be required to live in Australia for the next two years to confirm your eligibility.
6. Sale of your family home when you move overseas, or rental income from the family home while you are away, could affect your eligibility for the age pension under the income and/or assets test.

CHAPTER 9

Taxation

The title of this book—*Sell Up, Pack Up and Take Off*—has a carefree note to it. But when it comes to taxation, please beware. Your move is anything but carefree. It requires very careful planning. You will need professional advice, but it helps to be aware of the rules first. And this is where we can help.

Everyone's tax situation is different—depending on income, age, the nature of investments, whether you keep a home in Australia or not, the geographic spread of your assets and so on. The list is almost endless. But there are some rules that apply to everyone, and you need to be right on top of them if you are going to avoid a nasty surprise down the road.

We will go into greater detail later in the chapter. But first, this is a taste of what is to come.

The most critical aspect to consider for your taxation status is whether you will be a resident or non-resident for tax purposes once you move overseas. You cannot choose to be one or the other. It is a matter of fact and a matter of law. It depends on your individual circumstances. Unfortunately, there are no hard and fast rules, just guidelines. At the end of the day, the Australian Tax Office (ATO) will decide. But you can organise your affairs to influence the ATO's ultimate judgement on your residency status.

There are advantages and disadvantages in both categories—resident and non-resident.

> At the end of the day, the Australian Tax Office will decide. But you can organise your affairs to influence the ATO's ultimate judgement on your residency status.

For example, as a non-resident, only your Australian-sourced income will be subject to Australian tax. This includes your pension, rental income on any real estate assets in Australia, and income from any businesses you may have in Australia. Income on bank deposits and dividends from Australian shares will not be added to your taxable income but will instead be subject to a withholding tax of 10 to 15 per cent. (If the dividends are fully franked, withholding tax will not apply.) Capital gains tax provisions will continue to apply on any real estate assets you own in Australia, but they will not apply to other investments for the period that you are considered to be non-resident. (This is a tricky one and requires close attention. More details below.) However, you will lose the tax-free threshold as a non-resident and hence pay tax from the very first dollar you earn in Australia. As the tax-free threshold now stands at $18 200, this can be a real consideration. Finally, if you are a non-resident for tax purposes, the chances are that you will no longer be eligible for Medicare benefits when you visit Australia.

On the other hand, if you are considered to be a resident of Australia for tax purposes, your worldwide income will be subject to Australian tax. However, you are more likely to be able to obtain Medicare benefits on visits back to Australia and you will maintain the tax-free threshold for any income earned in Australia. There can be real benefits to remaining a resident for tax purposes while overseas.

Now let us get down to tin tacks. The first and most important issue to understand is the definition of 'resident' for tax purposes.

Are you a resident?

There are four tests that the Australian Tax Office applies to decide whether or not you are a resident:

1. The first is residence according to ordinary concepts.
2. The second test is domicile and permanent place of abode.
3. The third is the 183-day rule.
4. The fourth is the Commonwealth superannuation fund test.

In the past, the number of days spent in a particular country was a key issue in determining residency for tax purposes. The 183-day rule (just over six months) was important. This is no longer the case. You can now stay in a country for more than six months in any tax year and still be considered a non-resident or, conversely, you can spend zero days in Australia in any one tax year and still be considered a resident for tax purposes.

The Commonwealth superannuation fund test only applies to government employees, diplomats and the like.

For the purposes of the readers of this book, the two important tests are the first two—residence according to ordinary concepts, and the domicile and permanent place of abode test.

The first test that the Commissioner of Taxation will apply is whether you reside in Australia under the ordinary definition of 'reside'. For those who sell up, pack up and take off, the answer to that question is 'No'.

The next step is to look at the extended definition of resident. If the taxpayer's domicile is considered to be in Australia, then he or she will be a resident for tax purposes unless the Commissioner is satisfied that the 'permanent place of abode' is outside Australia.

Let us look at this more closely. What does 'domicile' mean? And what does 'permanent place of abode' mean?

The primary common law rule is that a person acquires a domicile of origin at birth. That domicile will be the country of his or her father's permanent home. A person will retain that domicile of origin unless he or she acquires a domicile of choice in another country.

It is quite difficult to establish that you have discarded your domicile of origin and acquired a new domicile of choice.

The common law test of domicile of choice is in section 10 of the Domicile Act: 'The intention that a person must have in order to acquire a domicile of choice in a country is the intention to make his home indefinitely in that country.'

How do you prove that? For example, it is not good enough to have a working visa for that country, you would need to have a migration visa.

So let us assume that, for most readers, their domicile would remain Australia. In those circumstances, the tax office will consider you to be a resident of Australia unless you can prove that you have established a permanent place of abode elsewhere.

There are no hard and fast rules on the definition of 'permanent place of abode'. But there have been plenty of cases decided in the courts and that gives us some handy guidelines.

The word 'permanent' in this context does not mean 'everlasting' or 'forever' but is used in the sense of being contrasted with temporary or transitory.

Factors that have been considered relevant in the courts and appeals tribunals include the following:

1. Length of stay in an overseas country—both intended and actual. For example, you may intend to stay overseas for ten years or more but actually return after one year due to illness. In this case, the intention would be important. Your home overseas may well be considered a permanent place of abode for the period of your absence from Australia.

2. Whether the taxpayer intended to stay in the overseas country only temporarily and then move to another country or to return to Australia at some definite point in time. For example, in the first case, if you are travelling the world. And in the second case, if you intend to return at the end of a defined employment contract.

3. Whether you have established a home (a house or other shelter that is a fixed residence) outside Australia.

4. Whether a residence or place of abode exists in Australia or has been abandoned because of the overseas absence.

5. The duration and continuity of the taxpayer's presence in the overseas country.

6. The durability of association that the person has with a particular place in Australia. For example, maintaining bank accounts; informing government departments such as the Department of Social Services that you are leaving permanently; the place of education of the taxpayer's children; family ties, etc.

No single factor will be decisive.

The Australian Tax Office has also given some indication of its attitude in its own rulings. It has said that, as a broad rule of thumb, a period of about two years would be considered as a substantial period for the purpose of a taxpayer's stay in another country. And a stay of less than two years would be considered transitory.

It is important to note that an intention to return to Australia to live in the foreseeable future does not prevent the taxpayer in the meantime from setting up a permanent place of abode elsewhere.

The Federal Court has found that the taxpayer's intention regarding the length of his or her stay overseas was just one factor to be taken into account. More importance was attached to the nature and quality of use that a taxpayer makes of a particular place of abode overseas.

> A period of about two years would be considered as a substantial period for the purpose of a taxpayer's stay in another country. And a stay of less than two years would be considered transitory.

There is an important level of emphasis placed on the permanence of the abode. This does not mean that you have to purchase a house or apartment overseas to convince the tax office that you are a non-resident. But it has to be convinced that your place of abode outside Australia is where you actually 'live'. If it is weekly or monthly holiday-style accommodation, or a barracks, or single men's quarters, or a mining camp, for example, then the tax office will not consider this to be a 'permanent place of abode'.

Another quirk of the law to take into account is travel while overseas. If you are travelling from one country to another (travelling the world if you like, instead of settling in one country) then you are not considered to have a permanent place of abode overseas. There have been cases where a taxpayer has spent, say, three years in London and then one year travelling throughout Europe before returning to Australia. The taxpayer was considered to be a non-resident for Australian tax purposes for the first three years, but a resident for the last year while they were travelling.

Decision time: choosing your resident status

The key decision you should make before you sell up, pack up and take off, is whether it is more beneficial for you to be considered a resident or non-resident of Australia for tax purposes.

Let us look at a couple of hypothetical cases.

Peggy and Ken are retired and have decided to live in Phuket— perhaps for the rest of their lives, perhaps just for a few years. They may return to live in Melbourne at some point. They have kept their family home in Melbourne and rent a comfortable townhouse in Phuket. They anticipate that any major health issues will be handled in Australia. They have kept their private health insurance cover and want to hang on to their Medicare cards. Most of their assets are in their Australian superannuation fund. They hold some Australian-listed shares, about $100 000 worth, in their own names. And they have $60 000 in bank deposits in Australia. They live on the income from their superannuation (a tax-free pension because they are both over 60), plus the rental income on their family home, and a small amount of dividends and interest.

> The key decision you should make before you sell up, pack up and take off is whether it is more beneficial for you to be considered a resident or non-resident of Australia for tax purposes.

Peggy and Ken's accountant has advised them to try and maintain Australian residency for tax purposes because:

1. They have no overseas income so it does not worry them that the Australian government wants to tax them on their worldwide income.
2. Their pensions from their superannuation savings are tax-free.
3. Their taxable income amounts to $23 000 a year each. (They rent their house for $900 a week but after repairs, maintenance and management fees, they net $700 a week or around $35 000 a year. Dividends amount to $8000 a year and interest on deposits $3000.)

Peggy and Ken don't have a tax problem. The tax-free threshold plus the low income and senior's tax rebate (if they are eligible) would mean that their likely tax bill is based on net income of around $3000 a year each; and there are real benefits in maintaining health cover in Australia.

Rhonda and Bill are in a very different situation. Bill likes to trade the share market and he has a substantial sum already invested in the Australian market. They also have $500 000 in cash deposits in their own names and intend to invest this in the stock market over the next couple of years. Like Peggy and Ken, they have kept the family home in Australia but their son and his family live in it rent-free. They also have an investment property that is heavily mortgaged, and negatively geared.

Rhonda and Bill's accountant has suggested that they try to become non-residents for Australian tax purposes because:

1. They can take advantage of the tax provision that allows capital gains on shares to be tax-free for the period that they remain non-residents.
2. Their income from dividends on shares and interest on bank deposits will not be subject to Australian income tax at high marginal rates during their absence but instead be liable to withholding tax at the lower rates of 10 to 15 per cent a year.
3. Their investment property is negatively geared (that is, no taxable income). But they will be able to accumulate tax credits (on their annual losses) for the period they are non-residents and then use those credits to reduce their income tax bills when they return to Australia.

4. The tax advantages that Rhonda and Bill achieve from their non-resident status more than offset the cost of generous private health insurance cover in their new country of choice.

Once you have made the decision on residency

So now you've decided whether it's best for you to be a resident or non-resident for tax purposes. Let's look at some of the documents you need to prepare to prove your status.

Being an Australian resident for tax purposes

It is important that your affairs are well-organised before you leave Australia if you want to retain your Australian residency status.

Get the documentation together that will help you prove residency, just in case the tax office should ever ask for it. A quick checklist would include:

1. Proof that you have kept a family home in Australia, even though you may rent it out during your absence. If you have sold your home, documentation showing that you have household goods in storage or a plan to purchase a new home on your return may assist.
2. A list of family ties that you have in Australia—children, close relatives.
3. Copies of documents showing that you have kept bank accounts, investments, private health insurance cover (even if suspended during your absence).
4. Proof that you are renting your overseas home or, if purchased, you bought it with the intention of resale at a later point in time.
5. Whatever proof you can muster, even if it's just a statement of intention, that your absence from Australia should be considered temporary because you have a firm intention to return to live in Australia in the foreseeable future.

It is also a good idea to be alert to any questions on residency on any government forms you may be required to complete. For example, the immigration forms you routinely fill out when you leave or re-enter Australia. Tick the box for 'resident departing temporarily' or 'resident returning', whichever is applicable. On your tax returns, answer 'yes' to the question on whether you are an Australian resident. If your pension is being paid overseas, inform the relevant government departments that your intention is to return to Australia at some point in the foreseeable future.

Keep on top of your income tax obligations. File your tax returns on time every year and pay any tax by the due date.

And remember, your liability to tax is an annual event so the question of where a taxpayer resides must be determined annually. So keep your checklist of documents up to date.

Being a non-resident of Australia for tax purposes

It is much trickier to prove that you are a non-resident of Australia for tax purposes than it is to retain your residency. A cynical person could suggest that this is because it benefits the tax office to keep you as a resident for tax purposes—the ATO can tax your worldwide income, ensure that your dividend and interest income will be taxable at your top marginal rate rather than at the lower withholding tax rates, and, as a bonus, it can also tax the capital gains realised on any of your Australian investments.

So it is wise to get the documentation together that will help you prove that you are a non-resident, just in case the tax office should ever ask for it. A quick checklist would include:

1. Proof that you have sold your family home or, if that is not the case, that you have rented it out on a long-term lease. (A two-year lease with an option to renew would be far better than a six-month lease, for example.)
2. Proof that you have established a permanent place of abode in an overseas country. This would include evidence of: the lease or purchase of a home or apartment; club memberships; bank accounts in that country; the purchase of a car and/or a driver's licence in your new country; a long-term or retirement visa; passport stamps showing the length of time you are spending in your adopted homeland.
3. It would help if you had surrendered your Medicare card and cancelled your Australian private health insurance.

4. Proof that your family ties with Australia do not include, for example, children at school within Australia.
5. Proof that you have informed relevant government departments that you are leaving Australia permanently.

Not all of these items on the checklist will apply to you—and some of them may be unpalatable. The list is simply an indication of elements that may be helpful in proving your status as a non-resident.

Once you, and your accountant, are satisfied that you will qualify for the status of non-resident for tax purposes, there are a number of further steps that you should take before you leave the country, including:

1. Informing your bank and other financial institutions where you may have funds on deposit that you are now a non-resident and the 10 per cent withholding tax should be deducted at source from your interest receipts.
2. If you have shares in Australian companies, informing your stockbroker (or alternatively inform the companies directly) that you are now a non-resident and that the 15 per cent withholding tax should be deducted at source from the unfranked portion of your dividends.
3. Determining the capital gains tax status of all your share investments and any other investments other than real estate. This is important—read on.

Capital gains tax events for non-residents

When you cease being an Australian resident, you trigger what is known as a 'capital gains tax event'.

This means that all assets that you own (apart from real estate) are assessed for capital gains tax on the date you become a non-resident, even though you haven't sold them.

> When you cease being an Australian resident, you trigger what is known as a 'capital gains tax event'.

You can, however, opt out of this position. You can choose that the assets are considered to be taxable Australian property until the earlier of:

- their sale, or
- the date that you again become a resident for tax purposes.

The general rule is that you must make a choice to defer your capital gains liability by the day you lodge the tax return for the year in which you become a non-resident. That first tax return in the year you become a non-resident is really important.

Even though you are a non-resident for tax purposes, you will still need to lodge an Australian tax return every year if you have any rental income in Australia, sell any assets that may attract capital gains, or have any Australian employment income or business income. Australian pensions and annuities must also be included in your tax return. You will not pay the Medicare levy and you will not be entitled to Medicare health benefits.

If you buy shares in Australian public companies while a non-resident, those shares will be free of capital gains tax for the period that you are overseas. When you return to Australia, the shares will become subject to capital gains tax on sale, but only on the gains made in excess of market value from the date at which you returned and took up Australian residency once again. Dividends on those shares are subject to withholding tax at the rate of 15 per cent for as long as you are a non-resident.

> If you buy shares in Australian public companies while a non-resident, those shares will be free of capital gains tax for the period that you are overseas.

The family home or principal place of residence in Australia

One of the gems of the Australian tax system is the capital gains tax exemption on your principal place of residence. A big question for those who choose to live overseas is what happens to the tax status of the family home if you decide to rent it out while you are away.

The good news is that you can choose to have a dwelling (house or apartment) as your main residence for capital gains tax purposes even if you don't live in it. There is one fundamental rule—you can only treat one residence as your main residence for capital gains tax purposes at any one time.

If you don't rent out the dwelling, you can treat it as your main residence (for capital gains tax) for an unlimited period after you stop living in it.

If you do rent out the dwelling, you can choose to treat it as your main residence for capital gains tax for up to six years after you cease living in it. If you rent it out for more than six years, when you sell it you must pay capital gains tax on the gain from the date it was first used to produce income to the sale date.

If you wanted to extend this six-year period, you could rent it out for the first six years after you cease living in it and then leave it vacant until you sell it (unless of course you have returned to live in it by that time).

TAXATION TIPS AND TRAPS

1. Get your tax planning in order before you leave the country.
2. A key factor to consider is whether you are to become a resident or non-resident for Australian tax purposes.
3. Residents for Australian tax purposes are taxed on their worldwide income but they are more likely to qualify for Medicare on visits home and they benefit from most superannuation concessions as well as the tax-free threshold.
4. Non-residents for tax purposes only pay tax on their Australian income and have valuable tax advantages on their share investments and funds on deposit in Australia. But they lose the tax-free threshold, and will not qualify for Medicare benefits.
5. Make sure all your documentation is in order to prove your status as either a resident or non-resident.
6. Pay particular attention to the tax return for the year of your departure to ensure that you do not trigger a 'capital gains tax event'.

7. The capital gains tax exemption for your family home (principal place of residence) can be retained for up to six years if you rent out your house while you are away or indefinitely if you don't rent it out.

CHAPTER 10

Health insurance

Choosing your health insurance cover is one of the most important decisions you face when you decide to relocate overseas. And this choice presents a real dilemma.

There are two extremes when it comes to health cover. Full international health cover is very expensive. Lack of health cover can be catastrophic.

Luckily, there are middle paths that can be taken. But as a general rule—if you can afford full health cover, take it. It is worth it for peace of mind. You are moving overseas to enjoy life, not to worry about 'what if'.

The people we spoke to in the research for this book had very firm, and very different, views on health insurance. They ranged from a blanket—'I can't afford it, so I don't worry about it.' To the more hopeful—'I will just go back to Australia if I get really sick or need an operation.'

There was the downright negative—'It is not worth having it. My friend died while the insurer argued with the doctor about whether she needed to be medically evacuated.'

And the cynical—'They never pay up. You can be sure of one thing if you are over 60—anything that goes wrong with you will be considered a pre-existing condition.'

At least half the people interviewed had no health insurance at all. Of the remainder, a few had international health insurance policies but most relied on travel insurance policies for peace of mind.

Let us look at the options, which can essentially be divided into three broad categories. In order of expense, they are:

1. An international health insurance policy
2. A travel insurance policy
3. No insurance, usually with the intention of returning to Australia and relying on Medicare and, in some cases, Australian private health insurance cover.

We will start with the no cost option—no insurance.

No insurance

This is, of course, the riskiest option. When you choose this option you are, perhaps unconsciously, making a number of assumptions, such as:

1. You have enough funds to cover occasional visits to the local doctor for temporary illnesses.
2. If you suffer in the future from a chronic illness, you will return to Australia and be treated under Medicare and/or your Australian private insurance.
3. If you have a serious accident while overseas, you can afford care in local hospitals, and the local hospitals are capable of providing adequate care. Alternatively, you have enough savings to cover the cost of an emergency medical evacuation. As an example, an emergency medivac from Indonesia to Australia can cost upwards of A$40 000.

If you are prepared to accept these assumptions, then you need to be aware of a few facts.

The first relates to Medicare. There is no guarantee that your medical and hospital treatment will be covered by Medicare during return visits to Australia. This comes as a great surprise to many people, but Medicare has quite firm rules on non-residents.

Medicare, Australia's healthcare system, is principally designed to serve Australians living in Australia. Theoretically, you are not entitled to Medicare benefits if you are not a resident of Australia. This is true even though you may still be lodging tax returns in Australia and are still paying the Medicare levy.

> There is no guarantee that your medical and hospital treatment will be covered by Medicare during return visits to Australia.

In practical terms, the Medicare system is a little more flexible. It recognises that some residents may be 'temporarily' out of Australia. As a rule of thumb, if you are leaving the country for less than two years, you will be considered to be 'temporarily' absent and still entitled to Medicare benefits when on short visits home. You are not entitled to Medicare benefits overseas, although there are a handful of countries where Australia has a reciprocal healthcare arrangement for travellers. (These include the United Kingdom, Finland, Ireland, Italy, Malta, the Netherlands, New Zealand, Norway and Sweden.)

The 'two-year rule' is informal but it will work as long as you insist that your absence from Australia is temporary.

The ironclad rule is the 'five-year rule'. Once you have been living outside Australia for five years, you are no longer entitled to Medicare during your visits home. When you return to Australia permanently after a five-year absence, you have to convince Medicare that you are in Australia to stay before they will reinstate your Medicare card. The best proof you can offer is shipping documents to show that you have transported household goods and furniture back to Australia. An employment contract is also strong proof. But failing either of those documents, you must present evidence of a lease on a dwelling, or if you own your house, evidence of electricity and telephone bills in your name at your current address in Australia.

Private health insurance is more flexible. You can suspend your private health insurance membership for two years. This suspension is renewable for up to six years by most reputable insurers. After six years you must resume payment of premiums or lose your cover. The beauty of suspension is that you will be covered on your return (once you have informed the health fund that you are back in the country and you resume premiums) and there are no waiting periods for the resumption of benefits and, crucially, any new illness you have contracted during the period of suspension will not be considered a pre-existing illness for the purposes of your insurance.

> You can suspend your private health insurance membership for two years. This suspension is renewable for up to six years.

So, it is possible to take the risky route on health cover for up to five years. But it can devastate your savings if you have a medical emergency and need to be medically evacuated to another country. And if you contract a chronic disease, such as cancer, you will be forced to return to Australia. Chemotherapy and radiotherapy don't come cheap, even in the lowest cost-of-living countries in Asia.

Travel insurance policies

Travel insurance policies can be as cheap as $700 a year if you include an excess of at least $100 on every claim. This means that you pay the first $100 of every eligible bill and the insurance company picks up the rest. Any claim for pre-existing medical conditions is excluded from the standard policy, although it is possible to negotiate with the insurer to include certain pre-existing conditions for an additional fee. (More of that later.)

Most travel insurance policies make it clear that the medical cover is only for 'unexpected sudden illnesses or serious conditions'. Remember, travel insurance includes everything from lost baggage, to stolen property and flight interruptions. The emergency medical coverage is only one part of the policy. But the great attraction of travel insurance policies for expatriate Australians in Asia is that they generally include medical evacuation costs. This cover looks generous. Standard policies boast that they will cover medical, dental and evacuation costs of up to $300 000. Surely that would cover the most dire emergency, right? Well, it may. But make sure you read the fine print in the policy documents. The product disclosure statement is the document that must be gone through with a fine-tooth comb.

Following are the traps to keep an eye on:

1. Most policies won't cover applicants over 70 years of age unless they submit to a medical appraisal test first. This can range from answering a set of questions online, right through to a full physical examination signed by a medical practitioner.

2. Travel insurance is usually for a maximum of twelve months and renewable for a further twelve months. Big reputable insurers for example, will not renew policies after 24 months. And there is a trap in the renewal provisions. If you contracted an illness during the first twelve months of the policy, it is considered to be a pre-existing medical condition and therefore excluded, in many cases, from the coverage in the second year. This varies from usual private health insurance where only pre-existing medical conditions at the time you first take out the policy fall under the exclusions.

3. It is worth having a close look at the definition of 'pre-existing medical conditions'. Some policies will have a list of conditions that are automatically pre-approved, including asthma, high cholesterol, high blood pressure, etc. The kicker is that you must declare these conditions when you apply for the policy. If you don't, they could be excluded from cover.

When an insurer excludes a pre-existing medical condition, they will also exclude any consequences of the condition. The policy often states 'direct or indirect consequences'. The interpretation can be very broad.

For example, if your travel insurance policy excluded high blood pressure as a pre-existing condition, it would not only exclude the associated medication but also any selected subsequent conditions such as a heart attack or angina.

This is one definition of a pre-existing medical condition from Health Care International: 'An illness, injury or related medical condition which within the last five years you have experienced symptoms, received treatment, medication, advice or investigation.' That's a pretty broad definition, which shows how careful you need to be with choosing your insurance.

Medical evacuation

This is the big ticket item that many expatriates fear most. For some, it is one of the two main reasons that they take out travel insurance, together with on-ground hospital treatment in the event of a medical emergency.

Once again, it is important to scrutinise the fine print in the product disclosure statement.

Most policies will only cover medical evacuation costs if the insurance company's doctor agrees with the treating doctor that you need to be moved *and* if the insurance company organises the transportation.

It is often stated that travel must be at the same fare class as originally selected by you. So, if you have booked an economy return flight, the insurance company will fly you back economy *unless* the insurer's doctor agrees otherwise on the basis of a written recommendation by your attending physician.

Some policies also state that the insurer will not cover the cost of a full return ticket to Australia if you have not already booked and paid for it before the company brings you home. In other words, you must have a return ticket already and if you don't then the ordinary cost of a flight back to Australia will be deducted from your claim.

You can see that there is plenty of room for 'argy bargy' between the insurance company and the treating doctor before a medical evacuation takes place.

International health insurance

This is the gold-plated option for health cover. It doesn't come cheap. It can cost more than $15 000 a year per person or as little as $2000, depending on the level of cover chosen, the size of the excess, and the level of co-payment.

The two key pieces of advice for anyone seeking to purchase international health cover are—shop around, and read the fine print of the product disclosure statements.

The big Australian health insurers each offer international products. You may feel more comfortable dealing with an insurer who has been efficient—and paid up—in the past. But remember that there is a big international market out there for expatriate health insurance and it is very competitive. So do shop around. There are internet sites such as Medibroker that provide broking services and comparisons of dozens of different health insurers. There are big UK-based companies like Health Care International and BUPA who provide a comprehensive range of health insurance packages.

Choosing the cheapest option may not be the best idea. You need an insurer with a good reputation and one that is recognised by the major hospitals and quality medical practitioners in your country of residence. Check out the hospital that you are most likely to use and ask them which insurers they accept.

Most health insurers provide a basic plan plus a number of add-on options to choose from. Or they may provide different levels of cover—for example, standard, executive and concierge.

Within each plan there are further options—for example, the level of excess you are prepared to pay yourself for each claim, and then the level of co-payment beyond the excess. For example, you may choose to pay the first $100 of each claim and 20 per cent of the amount in excess of $100, in order to reduce your premiums.

Some plans will not cover you at all for chronic illnesses, such as cancer. Others provide 100 per cent coverage for cancer treatment even in their standard plans. You can also add cover for pre-existing conditions. Check carefully the definition of pre-existing condition and scrutinise the policy for renewals. Will the insurer consider your pre-existing conditions to be only those that existed when you first took out the policy, or is there a new test every time you renew? Does the policy cover you for treatment in your 'home country'—for example, back in Australia? Are terrorism-related injuries covered? Does the policy allow you to renew over the age of 70? Do premiums go up every year with age?

Some plans will not cover you at all for chronic illnesses, such as cancer. Others provide 100 per cent coverage for cancer treatment even in their standard plans.

Age is a big factor in deciding premiums. This may be an obvious statement but premiums can double depending on whether you are aged 60 to 64, or 65 to 70.

Your health is a key factor in ensuring that you enjoy your new life in your country of choice. Buy the best insurance cover you can afford, shop around before you purchase, consider using a broker to search out the policy that suits you best, and, above all, make sure you read the fine print in the product disclosure statement.

HEALTH INSURANCE TIPS AND TRAPS

1. If you can afford full international health cover, take it. It is worth it for peace of mind.
2. The cost of an emergency medical evacuation from Asia can be upwards of A$40 000.
3. Travel insurance policies can be used as a stop-gap for health cover but they are principally intended for emergencies. Read the fine print.
4. Tell the truth to your insurer about any pre-existing illnesses. Failure to do this can lead to a denial of claims.
5. International health insurance can be expensive, but there are a number of different levels of cover, from catastrophe insurance to a gold-standard policy, and prices vary widely.
6. Shop around. International health insurance is a very competitive market.
7. Check if your proposed insurance company is recognised by major health care providers in your new country of residence.
8. Medicare is principally a health system for Australians who live in Australia.

9. Non-residents are theoretically not entitled to Medicare on visits home to Australia but there is some flexibility for temporary absences, usually of up to two years.

10. Once you have lived outside Australia for more than five years, there is no flexibility—you are not entitled to Medicare on visits home.

Thoughts in the bath

Retirement, or any period in your life that leads you to sit in the bath for a while longer than normal and take a good hard look at yourself and your life, should be seen as a great opportunity.

Life is big and it offers all sorts of adventures. And life is also short. Those adventures should be willingly grasped—while they are still available.

It is often fear of the unknown and fear of change that stops us from leading a more interesting and adventure-filled life.

It is clear that we all have a host of lifestyle alternatives. It is also clear that it is entirely up to us to choose which path to follow.

We all need to take control of our lives rather than the reverse. That is, allowing others to control our destiny. Or simply resigning to apathy and inertia and the flow of events so that we just plod along until we die.

The need to take a strong grip on your life is especially so at 50-plus. It is high time to take charge. And when work ends, and a new freedom arrives, then no time is better than this to take charge; no time is better to get bold and pack up and take off.

Of course, this is not for all. If you are financially comfortable and you are already living your dream life, then do not *take off*. Rather, *stay put*.

But, if you feel a little restless, if you feel that a lot of life has just drifted by, then it is high time to take control and put an end to this. If you feel the past 40 years have been a little too monotonous. If you feel that Australia is too expensive. If you feel that a much better quality of life can be enjoyed in a cheaper country, then you need to seriously reassess your future and lifestyle.

This book has hopefully elevated levels of confidence so that you can become proactive and fully take control of the rest of your life. This book has shown you that many others have done this, so why can't you? And hopefully, it has provided a decision-making framework that you can follow to optimise, to fully enjoy, the rest of your life.

After all, there is a bucket load of questions that you need to address.

How happy are you really? Do you think a change in lifestyle would enhance and enrich your existence? What should you be considering? What sort of financial advantages or disadvantages are there in a shift to another country? And what country should you choose? What are the best strategies to follow so that you can realise dreams, or at least safely test some ideas? Should you 'sell up, pack up and take off' forever or just have a sabbatical from your normal Aussie life—a year or so? Should you live some of the year—say, three months—in another country rather than permanently in that country? And critically, as time goes by, and inevitably you become increasingly frail and need more care, where do you want to end up—at home with a carer or in a nursing home?

The people we met moved for a variety of different reasons and chose their new country on a range of different criteria. Some were haphazard in their decision-making, some thorough and analytical.

Josh and Kendal's new life in Malaysia was triggered by a heartfelt conversation and couple of bottles of red wine shared with a friend who was moving there. Although too young to retire, they were simply bored with their lifestyle and needed a new challenge.

The shift worked for them, although they are struggling to find employment that pays well. After all, they did move to a much cheaper country and that often also means lower paid work. Even so, they have enriched their lives. Their strategy, though, was high risk: they literally did 'sell up, pack up and take off' and had very little idea of where they were going to live and what they were going to do when they got to Penang.

Bob and Marion were much more thorough. Bob set out the criteria that enabled him to isolate the perfect country for them to move to. He looked at the health system, the tax structure, crime rates and other safety issues, the legal system, costs of living, and the cultural back-story of the country. He chose Malaysia and, more specifically, Penang.

Despite Bob's analytical approach, he really wanted to just get out of Australia anyway. After living in a number of countries, Bob said, 'I didn't want to go back to Australia for two reasons. I remember years ago a 300-pound, diabetic, one-legged, gun-toting, short-back-and-sides private detective said to me, "If you want to catch a shark, don't fish in the gutter".

'I always wanted to get out of Australia and play in a bigger pond. I spent decades getting out of Australia and I just didn't want to go back to the place. The second issue was the dog. We initially rescued him in Australia from death-row at the pound.' And, Bob said, they could simply not put him through all the quarantine issues that are required for a re-entry to Australia.

Others are living overseas for cultural or political reasons, to address issues of trauma, to relive their youth, or to tick off long-held desires from their bucket list.

Interestingly, all of them were absolutely convinced that the decision to have a fresh adventure and change their lives was the right one.

But nothing is forever. Many of those who are now living what they see as 'the dream' in Phuket or Penang or Vejer de la Frontera or Phnom Penh or Paris, may well return to Australia. The dream may fade over time.

The important issue is that all those people were brave enough to launch into a new life; just to give it a go. None of them are going to die, wondering.

And so many of them felt younger, more alive, healthier and motivated by doing so.

A framework

1. The starting point for any strategy is to know yourself. This means that you should have a clear view of the sort of life you want to live. Do you want to live on the beach or in the mountains or in a big city? Do you want to live in a foreign country, and if so what sort of culture and country attracts you the most? Could you live away from your extended family? Would you be comfortable living in a new culture with a new language? Does your preferred country meet with a minimum set of criteria, providing you with a safe and healthy environment? And, when you get old and frail, where do you want to end your days—in aged-care accommodation or at home with a carer?

We have talked about the tree-change to Chiang Mai or Ipoh or Ubud or Provence, and the sea-change to Phuket or Penang or Vung Tau, or the city-change to Bangkok, Phnom Penh, Ho Chi Minh City or Paris.

We talked about the different lifestyles in each of those places and the vastly lower costs of living in them all.

On balance, the cost of living in Southeast Asia is more than 50 per cent less than what it is in Australia.

2. You need to understand the health and medical issues you will confront and whether or not you should have health insurance. Health services in Thailand and Malaysia are excellent. Not so for the rest of Southeast Asia.

Take a look at the chapter on Health Insurance. We strongly recommend taking out the best health cover you can afford. This is especially so for those over 60.

3. You need to understand the visa requirements of the country you are planning to visit or move to.

We talked about visa issues at length. Something like the Malaysia My Second Home (MM2H) visa is perfect for retirees.

There are, in fact, few visa restrictions in most other Southeast Asian countries, although some provide less security of tenure than others. Vietnam, for example, requires a renewal every three months. European countries are tougher on providing long-term visas, although they can be obtained if you are well-organised, patient and persistent.

4. You need to fully understand superannuation, pension and taxation issues confronted by people who are considering a move to another country. We provide a full chapter on each of these issues.

5. It is important to visualise where you would like to live as you become increasingly frail. There are effectively two choices—entering aged-care accommodation or staying in your own home with a carer. Few can afford a full-time carer in Australia, but that is not the case in Southeast Asian countries.

We talked about the very old and how they enjoyed their final days with a carer at their home in Phuket or Bangkok rather than in an antiseptic-smelling nursing home in suburban Australia. This is *The Best Exotic Marigold Hotel* concept.

As Dame Judi Dench, 77, the lead actress in that film, said of aging in Britain, 'We're not good at dealing with old age in this country. We shove people in a room and leave them sitting around a television.' The same applies to Australia.

Bill Nighy, 62, another star of the film, bemoaned how the elderly are 'warehoused and medicated, rather than nurtured and listened to'.

We spoke to Barry Petersen, an ex-Australian army officer, in Bangkok. He is now near 80 and is celebrating his decision to move to Thailand 20 years ago. As he becomes increasingly frail, he is cared for by his Thai work associates and an in-house full-time carer. But Barry is not lonely; he is content. He hopes to spend the rest of his days being cared for at home by his new 'family'.

Bill moved to Phuket at the age of 77, after his wife's death. He was lonely and unwell in Australia, having had a triple-bypass heart operation. His daughter, Sonja, lived in Phuket. The move to Thailand gave Bill a second life. He was reinvigorated. He was looked after in his home by a caring Thai lady for the last six years of his life. He died in 2013 and he died at home.

Neither Bill nor Barry could afford home care in Australia.

6. Knowing yourself also means that you know your financial position and how much your chosen lifestyle or country will cost. If you want to live on the beach at Byron Bay, then of course you will need to have net assets well north of $3 million to retire comfortably in that environment. A beachside apartment alone will cost you a million dollars. And then there is the breakfast at a cafe that will cost about $25 each, or a night out at a pleasant restaurant that will cost anywhere between $50 and $150 a head. Or you may choose to live in Phuket, Penang or Canggu in Bali at a fraction of this cost. Eat out for $15.

If you want to live part of your life in Australia, and part in a foreign country, then you will need to be reasonably well off, although not rolling in money. Remember Kevin and Jean in Hoi An. They dramatically cut their cost of living by living about eight months of the year in Vietnam and four months in Australia. Their decision to move to Vietnam was both a search for a cheaper lifestyle and an adventure. Their retirement is dynamic.

7. Your financial profile will also be critical to your decision to sell that house or not. If you have virtually nothing in your superannuation fund, but you are living in and own a house in Sydney worth $600 000 or more, then you may well have to sell that asset to live even modestly well in your retirement. It will not be enough, though, to live modestly well in expensive Australia.

If you rent out the Sydney house and move to a cheap country in Asia, you will be living mainly on that rent, as your pension will likely be reduced. Alternatively, if you stay in that house, you may receive the Australian age pension, but that means a very difficult cash-deprived life; a life that sees you financially handcuffed in Australia.

And if you sell that house and have nothing much else, then you would be well-advised to check out a life in a much cheaper country. Your funds will go at least three times further.

Elizabeth had no choice. The Storm Financial collapse devastated her financially. She lost her house along with her life's savings. She had to move to a cheaper country so that she could survive and maximise her enjoyment. She chose Ubud and did well.

It was also primarily financial considerations that drove Geoffrey and Michael to Ubud. They had lived a fairly opulent life while working in theatre, hotel management, the restaurant and catering game, and arts administration. But they had spent-up. They'd had a ball of a life. They had always rented their accommodation.

When they retired it meant that they were asset-poor. They could not live the life that they were accustomed to—nowhere near it. They faced the prospect of living out their retirement in a caravan park outside of Sydney or in country Victoria.

Instead, they sold everything and moved permanently to Ubud. For $60 000 they bought the lease on some land, built a traditional Javanese open-plan tropical house and in-ground pool in magnificently landscaped gardens. They now live a life of luxury on an Australian pension, albeit a War Veterans pension.

John and Sandra were well off and could have retired to anywhere in the world they wished. They wanted the personal freedom and the change of culture that Bali offered. They built a dream home looking over a river and rice paddies in Seminyak.

8. Critically, if you do sell a house and move to a foreign country, *rent before buying*. Better still, move to that country and rent before selling your Australian property.

If you are going to buy, ensure that you fully understand the property ownership structure of the chosen country. Get expert legal assistance. Trust nobody else.

9. Knowing yourself means that you must also know where you sit on the 'spectrum of escape'. Whether you want to move permanently out of Australia, or just for stints of, say, three months of each year. Or maybe you want to live outside of Australia full-time, but only for a sabbatical of perhaps a few years. You may want to have a year or two away to tick off that bucket-list dream of living in Ubud, Provence or Chiang Mai.

Gordon and Penny live in Provence for part of the year and the remainder in Australia on Sydney's northern beaches. They love France but hate the French winters. They are now realising their dream to own a wonderful terrace house in a wine-producing town in southern France. They had an incredibly rich experience buying and renovating the property. Penny learnt another language and another craft—she takes in paying guests every now and again. Sure, Penny and Gordon could afford to realise a dream. But this does not take away from the fact that they got off their haunches and turned that dream into a reality.

Rose and Sam moved to Ho Chi Minh City for a one-year sabbatical and lived like kings in a very expensive, fully serviced apartment. Their move had nothing to do with saving money, but everything to do with adding some adventure, interest and experience to their lives. They came back to plenty of assets in Australia, but Rose says that she would return to Ho Chi Minh City in a heartbeat.

A permanent move to Spain was an easy decision for Chelsea. Spain allowed her to discover herself and it allowed her to grieve after her father's death. Chelsea realised just how Spanish she really was and why she always felt a little out of kilter with Australian life. Her decision was emotionally and culturally driven.

Mark's decision to leave Australian permanently was also easy—it was cultural and political. His parents were European and moved to Australia after World War Two. He, like Chelsea, always felt that there was something missing. He loved the lifestyle in Australia but he hated the politics and there was a hollowness in his heart. When he moved to Barcelona he felt as if he was finally centred. He felt that he belonged there.

* * *

In coming decades, there is going to be millions of retirees all scratching for a living. The demographics of Western societies points to a tsunami of aging people. Health services will be stretched. Governments may be forced to cut health funding. Health care will become increasingly expensive. Pensions will be pared back as governments slash budgets. Housing will become less and less available for the aged.

In short, the world of retirement is going to be very competitive and a harder world to cope with.

Unfair? Yes.

The cost of living out those retirement years in financially stretched Western countries is going to skyrocket. Australians need to look at alternatives.

We have mapped out what we think is a viable alternative but, more than that, it is an option that can also be a youth elixir, providing change, adventure and a new life.

Go get some.

Sell up, pack up and take off.

Property

Property is discussed in each chapter, but the situation in Bali and Cambodia is more complex than most, so we've gone into a little more detail here.

Bali property

It is illegal for foreigners to own freehold property—land, houses, villas or apartments—in Bali. This is written into the constitution. However, foreigners can legally buy leasehold property. The leases can be for at least 25 years and perhaps as long as 100 years.

Some foreigners still insist on freehold ownership. We see this as presenting potentially serious problems. Nevertheless, it is quite common practice.

Foreign buyers can engineer freehold ownership in one of two ways:

1. USE AN INDONESIAN NOMINEE

The nominee will sign the following four documents:

i.   Loan agreement. This acknowledges that the foreigner has lent to the nominee the purchase price of the land.

ii.   Right of use agreement. This allows the foreigner to use the land.
iii. Statement letter. In this document the nominee acknowledges the foreigner's loan and intention to own the land.
iv.   Power of attorney. The nominee signs an irrevocable power of attorney giving the foreigner the complete authority to sell, mortgage, lease or otherwise deal in the land.

2. USE A COMPANY: A PMA

The most significant change in Indonesian investment law came in 1997 when the government introduced the *Penanaman Modal Asing* (PMA), or foreign investment company. This allows foreign investors to set up a company in Indonesia, without having to have Indonesian partners.

The PMA can be 100 per cent owned by the foreign investor. PMA companies are allowed to own the title of the property for a period of 25 years. Then they must apply for their company status to be renewed by the government.

To set up a PMA, you will be required to:

i.   Submit a detailed business plan.
ii.   Operate in a business environment that adds value to Indonesia in terms of foreign skills, employment and environmental benefit.
iii. Make an appropriate cash deposit in an Indonesian based bank. The amount varies and is calculated on the capital employed in the business.
iv.   Show that there is property investment as an asset of the company.

The process takes approximately three to four months and once it is completed, the company can apply for work permits for the foreign directors—three permits in the first year of operation. The cost of setting up the PMA is between 30 to 40 million Indonesian rupiah (A$2800 to A$3800).

FEES

1.   Notary: 1 per cent of the value of the transaction.
2.   Vendor tax and purchaser tax: Both the vendor and purchaser pay 5 per cent tax on the value of land and property sales.
3.   Mortgage certificate: 1 per cent of value of mortgage.

Remember, any effort to circumvent the law is a path fraught with potential future heartache for the foreign purchaser.

To conclude a freehold property purchase with a local nominee, a notary is generally used. The notary creates the multi-party, multi-document legal construct that puts the freehold title in the hands of an Indonesian nominee.

By the way, a 'notary' in Indonesia is a local legal expert registered as a legal expert by the Indonesian Government.

The Indonesian nominee's name is on the property title and it is he or she who *freeholds* the parcel, not the foreign purchaser fronting the money for the land.

The notary will also usually create an irrevocable power of attorney in which the nominee owner surrenders all rights to use, sell and lease the subject property to the foreign purchaser.

But is this legally enforceable? A foreigner may have to test this arrangement in court if in future he or she wishes to sell or transfer the ownership/title to another party. This transfer will be heavily dependent on the good grace and continued docility of the Indonesian nominee who will need to attend the notary and sign over the deed to the new owner or their nominee.

There is one legal view that such contracts are from the very beginning 'void ab initio' and therefore unenforceable in Indonesia. This is partly because the contract refers to a non-existent transfer of money between the parties during the so-called 'purchase' transaction.

Good legal advice is essential if you wish to buy freehold property.

Cambodian property

Foreigners can own property in Cambodian buildings above the ground floor. This works well for apartments or even older buildings with several levels, like the top floor of a shophouse.

The intention of the law is that foreigners cannot own land or houses, just above ground-floor apartments.

A number of real estate agents and lawyers talk about mechanisms that allow foreigners to fully control the purchase, sale and use of real property. They claim that there are five options for buying real property (other than above ground-floor apartments), which are as follows:

1. Forming a company with a Cambodian citizen

Form a limited company in partnership with a Cambodian citizen. Any real property purchased for investment is then registered in the name of the company. The company must have a minimum 51 per cent Cambodian shareholding. However, careful allocation of shares, and careful drafting of the rights attached to share certificates can ensure the foreigner's full control of the company and its assets. Additional mortgage, security and power of attorney documents can also be created to accompany ownership documentation.

Under this option, the foreigner is expected to pay 100 per cent of the purchase cost of real property plus any construction costs. If the real property is later sold, 100 per cent of the sale price goes directly to the foreigner. This includes any profit accrued as a result of the property increasing in value. This issue should be detailed carefully in any company and/or sales documentation.

2. Purchase plus long-term rental

This method allows foreign nationals to purchase real property and register the title deed in the name of a Cambodian citizen. The foreigner and the Cambodian then enter into a long-term rental agreement by which the Cambodian citizen leases the property back to the foreigner. Lease periods can last up to 99 years.

The problem many foreigners have with this option is the concept of renting back property that has already been purchased.

However, correct drafting of the terms of the property holding and lease arrangements make this a reasonably secure method of controlling real property in Cambodia. Under this method, the foreigner may sell the property at any time and keep 100 per cent of the revenue from the sale. The Cambodian citizen is not permitted to disagree with or obstruct the sale. The foreigner retains the original copy of the new title deed as a security precaution: sale of real property is impossible without the original copy of the title deed.

Though the foreigner can sell the property at any time, the Cambodian citizen's signature or thumbprint is generally required before any sale can take place. A good working relationship between both parties is therefore very important.

3. Registering real property with a Cambodian citizen

This method is very similar to option two, but requires 100 per cent trust in the Cambodian citizen.

Foreign nationals have rights, under the kingdom's statutes, to choose a Cambodian in whose name their title deed is registered. That is, a foreign national can purchase property and register the purchased property in the name of the Cambodian citizen.

Once the title deed is transferred to the Cambodian citizen, the foreigner retains possession of the new title deed. This is a security precaution that protects the foreigner's interests by preventing the Cambodian citizen from selling the land or property: sales are impossible without the title deed. Transferring the Cambodian's rights to the foreigner via a mortgage or lease agreement provides additional security for the foreigner's investment.

Copies of the title deed and any mortgage or lease agreements must be registered with the Department of Provincial Land Management, Urban Planning and Construction, as well as the appropriate district and central government departments that handle land registry. Most importantly, a copy of the land title and any mortgage or lease agreements must be lodged with the Cadastral Land Registry Office.

The Cambodian citizen in whose name the title is registered does not need to be resident in Cambodia. For example, the title can be registered with a Cambodian citizen living in the USA or Australia. The Cambodian citizen must be able to prove Cambodian nationality.

4. Marriage to a Cambodian national

Foreign buyers who are married to a Cambodian national can register real property using the name of their wife or husband on the title deed. It is also possible for a foreign national married to a Cambodian citizen and resident in the country for a long period to apply for Cambodian citizenship. In the event of citizenship being granted, Cambodian law holds that land can be registered in the names of both parties. Neither partner can subsequently sell the land or property without mutual agreement.

In the event of divorce or separation, division of the land or property is dependent on the conditions under which divorce or separation takes place, and the decision of any court ruling or arbitration relating to the divorce. It is often a source of conflict between the divorcees.

5. Acquisition of Honorary Cambodian Citizenship

A foreigner may be granted honorary Cambodian citizenship if he or she donates a significant sum of money to the Royal Government of Cambodia for the purposes of benefiting the people of Cambodia. Foreigners who have made a special impact or rendered exceptional help to the kingdom may also be granted this honour in recognition of their expertise or altruism.

One consequence of being granted honorary citizenship is that it becomes possible for a foreign national to acquire a 100 per cent right of ownership over real property purchased within the kingdom. This arrangement is recognised by the Ministry of Land Management, Urban Planning and Construction for the Kingdom of Cambodia, and by the Royal Government.

Honorary citizenship is recognised by the Royal Government of Cambodia as a legitimate means of purchasing real property within the kingdom but it does not affect the foreigner's original nationality or citizenship in any way.

Visas

Bali visa

Visas do not present a problem for those wishing to spend extended periods in Bali.

Australian tourists can obtain a tourist visa on arrival. That is, at the airport when you land in Bali or Jakarta. This is a 30-day single entry visa and costs US$25 (A$27).

There are several types of visas that cover a longer period of stay in Indonesia. These are business visas, employment visas and retirement visas. We will focus on the retirement visas for the purposes of this book.

Full details are listed below but there are a few general points to note for those who are close to retirement, or at retirement age, who do not wish to work in Indonesia. The retirement or renewable-stay visa is available to those over 55 years of age who can prove they have an income of at least US$18 000 (A$19 300) a year. Note that this is close to the annual amount of the Australian age pension at the time of writing. Applicants must also show proof of health insurance in either their own country or Indonesia. They must agree to employ an Indonesian maid, not to work or undertake business activities, and show proof of accommodation that is either rented for at least US$500

(A\$535) a month or purchased for at least US\$35 000 (A\$37 600). The visas are for one year but can be renewed in-country up to a maximum of five years. After five years, it is possible to apply for a permanent stay visa or KITAP (permanent stay permit).

Retirement visa
If you are 55 years of age or older, renewable stay permits (or retirement visas) of one year's duration are able to be obtained for Indonesia.

Requirements
This retirement visa requires:

1. the applicant to be 55 years of age or older
2. an application form to be completed in duplicate (this form is available from the Republic of Indonesia website www.embassy-ofindonesia.org)
3. the applicant's passport with at least 18 months before expiry and a minimum of three blank pages
a. All passport pages must be photocopied and submitted along with passport photographs—ten 4 cm × 6 cm photographs, four 3 cm × 4 cm photographs and four 2 cm × 3 cm photographs
b. An applicant whose spouse wishes to apply for a retirement visa must also supply a copy of the marriage licence
4. a flight itinerary
5. a curriculum vitae
6. a bank statement or pension fund showing monthly income of US\$1500 (A\$1600) or US\$18 000 (A\$19 300) a year
7. proof of health insurance in country of origin or Indonesia
8. a statement showing cost of accommodation
a. minimum purchase price of house or apartment of US\$35 000 (A\$37 600)
b. minimum rental cost of US\$500 (A\$535) a month for Jakarta, Bandung and Bali; US\$300 (A\$325) a month in other cities in Java, Batam and Medan; US\$200 (A\$215) a month in other cities
9. a statement proving there is or will be employment of an Indonesian maid
10. a statement agreeing not to engage in business activities or work.

The maximum stay on the retirement visa is one year and this can be renewed five times, meaning a maximum stay of five years.

You can enter the country on a 'visit on arrival' (VOA) visa and after a month apply for a longer term (limited stay) visa (KITAS—the Indonesian acronym for the longer stay visa).

The visa fee is A$165 at time of writing.

If you use an agent, which does in fact make life a lot easier, the fees range from 5 million rupiah (A$500) to 7 million rupiah (A$700).

PERMANENT STAY PERMIT

After extending the visa five times, foreign retirees can apply for a permanent stay permit or KITAP (Indonesian acronym for the permanent stay visa) through a Senior Foreign Tourist Bureau.

After obtaining a KITAP, citizenship or naturalisation can be sought in a process over a year but certain qualifications need to be met by the retiree.

Note that you need a KITAS or KITAP to be able to ship personal items to Indonesia. If shipping, it is best to use a door-to-door agent so that you avoid customs and port issues.

It is also easiest to use an Indonesian immigration agent to obtain a long-stay visa.

BUSINESS VISA

There are two types of business visas for people visiting Indonesia for normal business activities. They are:

1. a single entry 60-day visa
2. a multiple entry twelve-month visa.

The visa applicant's business counterpart or an agent in Indonesia should apply in Indonesia on behalf of the applicant for a letter of approval from the Immigration Department of Indonesia.

Once the applicant has this letter of approval, he or she can then apply for a business visa.

The following documents are required for a business visa:

1. a passport with a minimum validity of six months from the proposed date of entry into Indonesia

2. a fully completed visa application form
3. one passport-size colour photograph
4. evidence that the applicant has sufficient funds to cover the cost of applicant's intended stay in Indonesia (e.g. a bank statement).

For the relevant business, the following are also required:

1. two supporting letters, one each from the applicant's company and sponsor/counterpart in Indonesia, setting out the reason and duration of the proposed visit, and responsibility for incurred costs
2. copy of written approval from the Immigration Office in Jakarta, Indonesia, if the duration of business is to exceed 60 days.

EMPLOYMENT VISA

Employment visas are for foreign nationals who want to work in Indonesia.

An employment visa requires sponsorship by an Indonesian company.

For the required documents see the website www.visabali.com/employment-visas.php.

Thai visas

Retirement visas are readily available in Thailand and full details are below. But first, a few general points:

1. You must be over 50 years old and have proof from your bank that you either have a bank balance of at least 800 000 baht (about A$26 500) or a monthly income of at least 65 000 baht (about A$2200). It is also possible to meet the test with a combination of bank balance plus income in the event that your monthly income is less that 65 000 baht (A$2200).
2. You must also provide a police report from Australian police. (These can take a while but are easily obtained from your local police station.) In addition, you must have a medical check to prove that you do not have a 'prohibited disease'.
3. The retirement visa is for twelve months and can be extended in-country. It is a multiple entry visa but there is a requirement to report to immigration officials once every 90 days.

The visa application processing fee is A$225.

How to obtain a Retirement Visa (also known as an OA Visa) in Thailand

The requirements for a retirement visa in Thailand are as follows:

1. a passport with validity not less than eighteen months
2. a copy of the passport—each page must be copied and signed
3. four completed and signed visa application forms—Form A (available at www.thaiconsulatesydney.org) with one photo (3.5 cm × 4.5 cm) taken within the last six months without wearing glasses or headgear (photocopy not accepted) attached to each of the four application forms
4. a completed Personal Data Form (which can be downloaded from www.thaiconsulatesydney.org)
5. a copy of a bank statement showing a deposit of the amount equal to but no less than 800 000 baht (A$26 500), or an income statement (an original copy) with a monthly salary of no less than 65 000 baht (A$2200), or a deposit account plus monthly income totalling no less than 800 000 baht (A$26 500) a year.
6. An original copy of a letter from a bank or financial institution confirming sufficient funds, which needs to be stamped and signed by a bank officer
7. a police name check certificate issued no longer than three months prior to submitting the application
8. a medical certificate (www.thaiconsulate sydney.org) indicating that the applicant has no prohibitive diseases as indicated in the Ministerial Regulation No.14 (B.E. 2535) issued no longer than three months prior to submitting the application.

Note: If the applicant's spouse does not qualify for a retirement visa in Thailand, a marriage certificate will be required (the spouse will be considered for a non-immigrant visa category 'O').

Applicants may submit an application at the Royal Thai embassy or Royal Thai Consulate-General in their home or residence country or at the Office of the Immigration Bureau in Thailand located on Soi Suan Plu, South Sathorn Road, Sathorn District, Bangkok 10120.

Important visa notes

When you have prepared all the original documents as required above, you must then make three copies of each document. (Photos and signatures must not be photocopied.)

1. After you have made copies of all the documents, you must separate the documents into four sets. Within these sets, arrange the documents in the order given above. All together you will have one set of the original documents and three sets of copies.
2. After the four sets of documents have been prepared, you must take them to a public notary to bind and notarise each set of documents (the documents must only be binded by the public notary).

Bringing your household items to Thailand

You will be given six months from your entry to Thailand to bring in your household items from your country. If your permit grants you to stay for a year, these items will not be taxed. Otherwise, they will be taxed at a rate of 20 per cent for import duty and 7 per cent for value added tax.

However, the deadline can be flexible. If you expect your items to arrive past the six-month deadline, you may inform the customs department two months before the deadline to request an extension. This, though, is not applicable on shipments arriving in some ports, especially in Bangkok.

Obtaining a re-entry permit

Most people misunderstand the concepts of 'extension of stay' and 're-entry permit'. These are two distinct categories. You need both during your stay.

The extension of stay is simply the controlling date. Everything else is dependent on this. Everything is invalidated when your extension of stay expires. That is, the re-entry permit's validity is subject to the validity of your extension of stay. However, leaving Thailand without a re-entry permit automatically invalidates your extension of stay, so you need to know the following:

1. Extension of stay can be requested at the Office of Immigration Bureau (see details above).
2. At the end of the twelve months, if you wish to extend your stay you can submit a request for the extended period of stay at the Immigration Bureau along with evidence of money transfer, or a deposit account in Thailand, or an income statement proving that you have the amount of no less than 800 000 baht (A$26 500), or an income statement with a deposit account that adds up to no less than 800 000 baht a year.
3. If your spouse wishes to extend their stay as well, a marriage certificate has to be produced.

A one-year extension of stay shall be granted at the discretion of the immigration officer to the foreigner as long as he or she meets the above requirements.

REPORTING YOUR STAY EVERY 90 DAYS AND VISA EXPIRATION

You are required to report to the Immigration Police every 90 days if you are on a long-term extension of stay. Persons holding a multiple entry visa will simply depart Thailand and renew their extension of stay after each 90-day entry.

If you cannot obtain your extension inside Thailand, you will have to get a new non-immigrant visa from a Thai embassy or consulate abroad.

RESTRICTIONS ON RETIREMENT VISA

The retirement visa, once approved, allows you to stay in Thailand for one year. You are not allowed to have employment while on this type of visa.

Retirement visa holders are also restricted from owning houses or land in Thailand. However, all visitors to Thailand, including tourists with no long-term visa, are able to purchase condominiums, apartments and other residences that do not include the purchase of Thai national land.

Malaysia visa

Malaysia is the most retiree-friendly country in Asia. The Malaysia My Second Home (MM2H) program offers non-Malaysians a ten-year renewable multiple entry visa. This is very attractive to retirees. It gives certainty of tenure. It provides a streamlined application process. And it is tax friendly—all non-Malaysian income is tax-free for MM2H visa holders.

Just a few general pointers before we get into the details of the program. There are different rules for the under-50s and the over-50s. The income and asset test for applicants is relatively high. You will need proof of liquid assets (cash on deposit) of at least RM350 000 (A$120 000) and an income of at least RM10 000 (A$3400) a month if you are over 50. (It is slightly higher for the under-50s.) This benchmark will be lowered if you buy property in Malaysia. You will also need proof of health insurance coverage in Malaysia (although this can be waived if you can show that an insurance company has knocked back your application on the basis of age). A police report and a health check are also required.

So far, some 23 000 people have been approved, according to the Malaysian government.

The program is primarily attracting people who wish to retire in Malaysia or spend extended periods there.

The government website www.mm2h.gov.my/index.php/en/ provides all the required documents and application forms and outlines clearly the steps to be followed (www.mm2h.gov.my/index.php/en/apply-now/where-to-apply/steps-to-apply).

Applicants have the option of using an approved MM2H agent or submitting their application directly. Using an agent will make the process a lot easier and avoid the need to place a cash security bond (the agent will sponsor you). But this, of course, involves paying the agent their fee.

All agents have to be approved by the Ministry of Tourism. These can be identified by the initials (MM2H) in their company name. The Malaysian government sets the maximum fee of RM10 000 (A$3400) that an agent can charge an applicant.

The MM2H Application

Applications can be submitted while you are in Malaysia or can be submitted from overseas.

Once the committee reviews the documents (original submission) and approves the application, they will issue a letter of 'Conditional Approval'.

The applicant then has six months to complete the remaining conditions (obtain medical insurance, complete the medical examination and open the fixed deposit) and collect the visa.

Document requirements

The following documents are required to complete the application process, some at the time of original submission and others after receiving the letter of conditional approval:

1. Covering letter. This should state the names of all people who are applying with you, how you will support yourself in Malaysia and which financial criteria you wish to use (see below).
2. Three copies of IM.12 Social Visit Pass. (You can download this form and others from www.mm2h.com/mm2h-application-forms. php.)
3. One copy of the Application Form MM2H.
4. Four passport-sized photographs of the applicant; if accompanied by a spouse, you also need four photos of your spouse.
5. Certified true copies of all pages of passport/travel document of applicant (and spouse if relevant). All certified true copies of documents must be countersigned by an embassy, high commission, justice of the peace, commissioner of oaths, solicitor, lawyer or notary public.
6. Certified true copy of every page of previous passport if your current passport is less than one year old (only the page with personal particulars needs to be certified).
7. Certified true copy of marriage certificate if accompanied by spouse.
8. Certified true copy of children's birth certificate if accompanied by children.
9. A current resume outlining employment history of primary applicant.

10. Evidence of financial assets (see Financial Requirements below).
11. Evidence of regular monthly income.
12. Medical report of applicant: Form RB1. This can be a self-declaration initially but after the conditional approval letter is issued, it must be signed off by a doctor in Malaysia.
13. Letter of good conduct by a government agency where you currently live (if you have lived there several years) or your home country (usually the police department).
14. Authorisation letter from applicant to Malaysia My Second Home Centre which allows them to verify the financial documents with the relevant financial institutions.
15. Evidence of purchasing property in Malaysia over RM1 million (A$340 000) if requesting approval to make lower fixed deposit.

Once the application is approved, you will be issued a conditional approval letter. This can be presented to any bank in Malaysia to open an account.

Visa collection on conditional approval

After receiving the letter of conditional approval, the following documents must be submitted when collecting the visa:

1. evidence of placing the fixed deposit—if applying under this criteria
2. copy of Malaysian medical insurance
3. copy of medical report
4. a letter of good conduct from a government agency.

All applications for people who want to live in west (peninsular) Malaysia are submitted to the Second Home Centre in the Ministry of Tourism, which has information about the program.

Applications to live in Sabah or Sarawak have to be submitted to the respective state immigration offices. Agents can assist with application for peninsular Malaysia and Sabah.

If you wish to live in Sarawak, you will have to contact the authorities in that state as they do not permit agents to assist with submissions of applications.

Contact details

Malaysia My Second Home Centre
Ministry of Tourism Malaysia
Level 10, No.2 Menara 1
Jalan P5/6, Presint 5
62200 Putrajaya, Kuala Lumpur
Email: mm2h@motour.gov.my
Tel: 03 8891 7434
Fax: 03 8891 7100

Department of Immigration, Sabah
Tingkat 6, Bangunan Wisma Dang Bandang
Jalan Tuanku Abdul Rahman
88550, Kota Kinabalu
Sabah, Malaysia
Tel: +6088– 80700
Fax: +6088– 240005

Department of Immigration, Sarawak
Tingkat 1 & 2, Bangunan Sultan Iskandar
Jalan Simpang Tiga
93550, Kuching, Sarawak, Malaysia
Tel: +6082– 245661 / 240301 / 230317 / 230280 / 230314
Fax: +6088– 240390/ 428606

Approval

Currently, approval takes around 90 days for the documents to be processed and approved from the submission date.

Fees

A payment of RM90 per year (A$30) is charged for the issuance of a Social Visit Pass under the MM2H program. The visa fee is charged according to the existing rate applicable to each country. The fee for a ten-year visa is therefore RM900 (A$300); however, if the applicant's passport has less than ten years left, the visa will only be valid until the passport expiry date and the fee lower. Other visa charges may apply for certain nationalities but should not amount to more than RM600 (A$200) per person.

Visa renewal requirements

The applicant must be present in person at the Immigration Department of Malaysia and bring the following documents:

1. letter explaining why you wish to renew the visa
2. original and photocopy of passport (certified true copy of every page)
3. Form IMM.55 (one copy per person)
4. Form IMM.38 (one copy if applicable)
5. proof of current offshore income of RM10 000 (A$3400) or more per month
6. evidence your fixed deposit is still in place
7. original and copy of confirmation letter from the bank (if applicable)
8. original and copy of conditional approval letter
9. original and copy of health insurance
10. original medical report (RB2 Form, which is available at MM2H Immigration Unit)
11. payment of RM90 per year for the visa.

Application for an extension with new passport

The visa is only issued for the validity of your passport. If you did not get the full period of the visa in your passport, you need to return to the immigration office in person when you have a new passport to get the remainder of the visa stamped in your passport. The following documents are required for an extension:

1. letter of intention by the principal/sponsor
2. copy of approval letter
3. Form IM.12
4. Form IMM.55
5. the original and a copy of both your old and new passport for applicant and principal.

MM2H ELIGIBILITY AND REQUIREMENTS

The MM2H program is open to all countries that are recognised by Malaysia but the program has numerous requirements. These requirements are outlined below:

Financial requirements

Applicants are expected to be financially capable of supporting themselves on this program in Malaysia.

1. Upon application
   i. For applicants under 50 years of age:

      Applicants aged below 50 years are required to show proof of liquid assets worth a minimum of RM500 000 (A$167 000) and offshore income of RM10 000 (or A$3400) per month. Applicants must provide the latest three months certified copies of their bank statement showing each month's credit balance of RM500 000 (A$167 000) or more.

   ii. For applicants aged 50 and above:

      Applicants aged 50 and above need proof of RM350 000 (A$120 000) in liquid assets and offshore income of RM10 000 (A$3400) per month. Applicants must provide the latest three months statements showing each month's credit balance of RM350 000 (A$120 000) or more. For those who have retired, they can waive the deposit requirement if they can show proof of receiving pension from government-approved funds of RM10 000 (A$3400) per month.

      New applicants who have purchased properties worth at least RM1 million (A$340 000) qualify to place a lower fixed deposit amount upon approval.

2. Upon approval
   i. For applicants under 50 years of age:

      Open a fixed deposit account of RM300 000 (A$100 000). After a period of one year, the participant can withdraw up to RM150 000 (A$50 000) for approved expenses relating to house purchase, education for children in Malaysia and medical purposes.

      Must maintain a minimum balance of RM150 000 (A$50 000) from second year onwards and throughout stay in Malaysia under this program.

      Approved participants who have purchased and own property bought for RM1 million (A$340 000) and above in Malaysia may comply with the basic fixed deposit requirement of RM150 000 (A\$50 000) on condition that the property has been fully paid and ownership documents, such as grant and land title, have already been issued. This amount may not be withdrawn until the participant decides to terminate their participation in MM2H program.

ii. For applicants aged 50 and above:

Open a fixed deposit account of RM150 000 (A\$50 000). Note that applicants over 50 who can prove they receive a government pension in excess of RM10 000 (A\$3400) a month can request exemption from making the fixed deposit. All others have to make a fixed deposit.

After a period of one year, participants who fulfil the fixed deposit criterion can withdraw up to RM50 000 (A\$17 000) for approved expenses relating to house purchase, education for children in Malaysia and medical purposes.

A participant must maintain a minimum balance of RM100 000 (A\$34 000) from the second year onwards and throughout their stay in Malaysia under this program.

Approved participants who have purchased and owned property for RM1 million (A\$340 000) and above in Malaysia may comply with the basic fixed deposit requirement of RM100 000 (A\$34 000) on condition that the property has been fully paid and ownership documents, such as grant and land title, have already been issued. This amount may not be withdrawn until the participant decides to terminate their participation in MM2H program.

Medical report

All applicants and their dependents are required to submit a medical report from any private hospital or registered clinic in Malaysia.

Medical insurance

Approved participants and their dependants must possess valid medical insurance coverage that is applicable in Malaysia from any insurance company.

However, exemptions may be given for participants who face difficulty in obtaining medical insurance due to their age or medical condition.

Security bond: Direct applicant only

Applicants applying directly are required to fulfil the security bond condition. The rate per person changes by nationality. Australians pay RM1500 (about A$300).

Personal bond: Application via agent

Licensed companies are required to provide the personal bond for their clients who have been approved under the MM2H program.

Employment and business investment rules

MM2H visa holders aged 50 years old and over can work for up to twenty hours a week. This is applicable to visa holders who have specialised skills in certain approved sectors. We are advised the decision on whether to approve part-time work is based on the approving committee view on whether a Malaysian could do the job.

Visa holders are permitted to set up and invest in businesses in Malaysia. They will be subject to the same regulations as other foreign investors but will not be permitted to become actively involved in the day-to-day running of the business. If they wish to do this, they must switch their visa to a work permit.

Dependants

Applicants are allowed to bring along their dependants (children below 21 years of age, stepchildren, disabled children, and parents) under their MM2H visa. Older dependant children will have to get a separate visa. Dependants attending school in Malaysia are also required to apply for a student pass, which allows them to continue their education in schools or institutions of higher learning recognised by the government.

House purchase

Each participant is allowed to purchase an unlimited number of residences above the minimal applicable price set for foreigners buying property in the state where they make the purchase. In most cases the minimum price is RM1 million (A$340 000) although some states, like Penang, have lower minimums for MM2H visa holders. All purchases must be approved by the state authorities. Certain types of property cannot be purchased by foreigners, such as those on 'Malay Reserve' land.

Taxes

Successful applicants are subject to Malaysian taxes on income sourced from Malaysia but income from overseas is not taxable.

Security vetting

Approvals are given subject to security vetting clearance conducted by the Royal Malaysian Police. Applicants will also have to show a police clearance certificate (letter of good conduct) from their home country to prove they do not have a criminal record.

Restrictions

Successful applicants are not permitted to participate in activities that can be considered as sensitive to the local people like political or missionary activities.

Vietnam visa

In black and white terms, a retiree who plans to live in Vietnam does confront a visa problem.

Vietnam does not issue retirement visas. The government issues tourist visas and long-term stay visas. But these long-term stay visas are only issued to diplomats and officials or for business and employment.

Tourist visas are available for a one-month stay and can be single entry or multiple entry.

What retirees to Vietnam normally do is to extend these tourist visas. The initial visa is for 30 days. Then this visa is extended for an additional three months. This process, although not officially recognised, is then repeated every three months.

Long-term foreign visitors are constantly concerned, however, that one day their renewal request will be refused. This would then require them to leave the country and reapply for a fresh tourist visa.

In Australia, a tourist visa can be obtained by post through the Vietnamese government embassy. The application form can be downloaded from www.vietnamembassy.org.au.

Simply complete this application form and then send by registered mail to the embassy, along with:

1. a passport with at least six months validity and at least one blank page
2. one passport-sized photo affixed to the form
3. a return self-addressed prepaid envelope (express post or registered mail)
4. the visa fee, which must be paid in cash, money order or bank cheque, payable to 'The Embassy of Viet Nam'. Only Australian dollars are accepted. Visa fees vary and depend on the length of stay and visa type.

Contact the embassy for further information at: The Embassy of the Socialist Republic of Vietnam, 6 Timbarra Crescent, O'Malley, ACT 2606.

A business visa requires the sponsorship of a Vietnamese employer or business partner. This visa allows for multiple entries and a stay of up to one year. If you do not have a business partner, employer or other sponsor who can provide you with an entry clearance, you can also apply for a business visa for a stay of up to 90 days.

Immigration agents in Vietnam can be used and this does make the process much easier although more expensive. Extensions can be obtained via an agent within Vietnam.

Europe visa

Visas are a serious roadblock to Australians who want to live in Europe. This is because of the visa restrictions imposed on non-EU citizens by the Schengen Treaty.

Ironically, visiting short-term is simple. Australian (and New Zealand) passport holders planning a visit to any of the 27 member states of the EU do not require a visa if their stay is no longer than 90 days in a six-month period within the EU.

The Schengen Convention, now part of EU law, is an area without internal borders; an area within which citizens, many non-EU nationals, business people and tourists can freely circulate without being subjected to border checks.

Twenty-two EU states are part of the Schengen area and have a uniform visa policy.

In addition, four countries outside the EU—Iceland, Liechtenstein, Norway and Switzerland—adopt the same uniform visa policy as they are also part of the Schengen area.

Four EU member states—Bulgaria, Croatia, Cyprus, and Romania—are not yet part of the Schengen area, but nonetheless have a visa policy that is based on the Schengen *acquis* (a set of legal regulations forming the legal basis of the Schengen cooperation).

Two EU member states—Ireland and the UK—are not part of the Schengen area, instead operating a travel zone known as the Common Travel area. The two countries each operate separate visa policies that are different to those of the Schengen area.

The recent tightening of the law to limit stays of 90 days in any 180-day period for non-EU or non-UK passport holders poses a real issue for Australians who want to move to Europe for extended periods. What typically must occur is that Australians have to leave the Schengen zone—return to Australia or live in Turkey or another non-Schengen state or travel in the non-Schengen world—for an entire three-month period once their visa expires. No longer can Australians zip across a border for a renewal.

FRANCE: LONG-TERM VISAS

The French requirements for a long-stay visa (of 4–12 months) can be found on www.ambafrance-au.org/Long-Stay-Visitor-visa.

Those expats planning on living in France for more than a year must apply for a formal residence permit (*carte de séjour*) in addition to the long-stay visa. In order to obtain this card, it's necessary to have entered France on a long-stay visa (Category D).

Expats can apply for their residency permit at the Service des Étrangers section of their local authorities (*préfecture*). Foreigners have reported that the required documents for application will vary depending on the préfecture.

The general documents required for residence permit application are:

1. passport with long-stay visa
2. birth certificate (with French translation)
3. work contract details, if applicable

4. signed work contract, if applicable
5. proof of residence (official bill or lease)
6. proof of sufficient funds (bank statement)
7. a fee in the form of OFFI (Office Francais de l'Immigration st de l'Integration), at times still referred to as ANAEM (Agence Nationale d'Accueil des Étrangers et des Migrations), stamps (340 euro or A$510, but varies according to category)—stamps available at any tabac (corner store).

Once you have submitted all the appropriate documents, you will be given a receipt and a date for the required French medical check-up, which includes an x-ray. Once you have passed this, bring the successful confirmation back to the préfecture to complete the last step necessary for the application process.

From this point, you will be notified when your residency permit is ready to be retrieved. Some expats report receiving their permit within days and others have had to wait a number of nail-biting months. Don't be afraid to contact your local préfecture to check up on the status of the permit.

The residence permit is valid for one year, and the renewal process can be started two months prior to expiration.

Unfortunately, dealing with the process over and over again is a reality of life in France.

SPAIN: LONG-TERM AND RETIREMENT VISAS

Australian citizens wanting to work or reside in Spain must apply for the appropriate visa from the nearest Spanish embassy or consulate. You should apply for the relevant visa from *outside of Spain*; if you do not, you will be issued the standard 'Schengen visa' upon arrival which does not grant you the right to reside or work in Spain. Spanish immigration authorities will not generally grant a work or residence visa to Australian citizens who enter Spain on a Schengen visa.

If you have a work, residence or ancestry visa for any other European Union country, such as the United Kingdom, this visa is not transferable to Spain.

Any visa application for Spain must be presented in person and requires the following documents:

1. passport valid for a minimum of six months and three photocopies of the personal information and photo page
2. four recent passport-sized photos
3. original marriage certificate
4. original certificate of good conduct issued by the police department of the city or cities where the applicant has spent six months or more in the last five years, with a translation into Spanish
5. original medical certificate typed on doctor's stationery verifying that the applicant is free from the quarantine diseases (yellow fever, cholera and the plague); and must also certify that the applicant is free of drug addictions and mental illness, with a translation into Spanish
6. original policy documents of medical insurance that will cover you in Spain.

It is also necessary to submit two photocopies of all the documents.

Retirement visa for Spain

You can apply to live in Spain as a retiree, providing you don't intend to work. To apply for this visa, the following requirements must be submitted to the embassy in person (and by appointment):

1. passport valid for a minimum of six months, along with three photocopies of the personal information and photo page
2. money order for A$100 to cover processing charge
3. four recent passport-sized pictures
4. original marriage certificate, and a photocopy (if applicable)
5. certificate of good conduct issued by the police department of places where you have lived for six months or more during the past five years, along with a Spanish translation, and one photocopy
6. a medical certificate printed on a doctor's letterhead, verifying that you are free from yellow fever, cholera and the plague, and drug addiction and mental illness, along with a translation into Spanish, plus a photocopy
7. original certificate of a public or private institution, stating that you receive a pension, and specifying its monthly amount (the

cost is at the discretion of the consulate and depends on the cost of living where you plan to live), plus a photocopy

8. proof of any other source of income and/or properties in Spain, plus one photocopy of each document.

Processing your application may take up to six weeks.

Acknowledgements

We are very grateful to all those adventurous people who shared part of their lives with us and patiently answered our detailed questions. This allowed us to bring to you real life stories of what it's like to sell up, pack up and take off.

They were generous with their time and many invited us into their homes. Most were comfortable with the use of their actual names. Others, however, for reasons of privacy, preferred to use pseudonyms.

Thanks also to Patrick Gallagher, Louise Thurtell and Aziza Kuypers of Allen & Unwin who backed our belief that this is the way of the future for Australians who want more out of life and want their dollars to go further.

For more information on how to sell up, pack up and take off, go to:
www.planet-boomer.com

About the authors

After more than 20 years in financial journalism, Stephen Wyatt and Colleen Ryan now live near Byron Bay, where they have planted a rainforest, surf, write and run **www.planet-boomer.com**.

Married with two adult kids, they have packed up and taken off overseas to live several times—in Papua New Guinea, London, Washington DC and, most recently, in Shanghai, where they were the joint China correspondents for the *Australian Financial Review* from 2004 to 2010.

Both are economists with majors in accounting: Colleen worked as a tax accountant for an international accounting firm in her early career and was later editor of the *Australian Financial Review*; Stephen was a banker with Merrill Lynch for 15 years, before turning to journalism.

Stephen and Colleen believe their experiences living abroad have enriched both their own lives and those of their children. They are passionate about the benefits of selling up, packing up and taking off at various stages of life, especially retirement.

Notes

....
....
....
....
....
....
....
....
....
....
....
....
....
....
....
....
....
....
....

Notes

Notes